A Mere Kentucky of a Place

A Mere Kentucky of a Place

The Elkhorn Association and
the Commonwealth's First Baptists

Keith Harper

America's Baptists
Keith Harper, Series Editor

Knoxville / The University of Tennessee Press

The America's Baptists series will bring broader understanding of the places Baptists have occupied in American life. Many of these works will be historical monographs, but the series will embrace different types of primary and secondary works, including but not limited to annotated collections of diaries, letters, and personal reflections as well as biographies and essay collections.

Copyright © 2021 by The University of Tennessee Press / Knoxville. All Rights Reserved. Manufactured in the United States of America. First Edition.

Library of Congress Cataloging-in-Publication Data

Names: Harper, Keith, 1957- author.

Title: A mere Kentucky of a place : the Elkhorn Association and the commonwealth's first Baptists / Keith Harper.

Description: Knoxville : The University of Tennessee Press, [2021] | Series: America's Baptists | Includes bibliographical references and index. |

Summary: "This work provides analysis of leadership in the Elkhorn Association during the early national period. Often portrayed in the historiography as the vanguard of a new frontier democracy, this group, upon closer inspection, reveals itself to be far more complex. Harper argues that the Elkhorn Association ministers were neither fully fledged frontier egalitarians nor radical religionists, but formed their identities in the crucible of the early national period. They were challenged by competing impulses, including their religious convictions, the market economy, Jeffersonian Republicanism, and honor, with mixed results"— Provided by publisher.

Identifiers: LCCN 2021001173 (print) | LCCN 2021001174 (ebook) | ISBN 9781621906421 (hardcover) | ISBN 9781621906438 (kindle edition) | ISBN 9781621906667 (pdf)

Subjects: LCSH: Elkhorn Association of Baptists—History. | Christian leadership—Baptists—History. | Lexington Region (Ky.)—Church history.

Classification: LCC BX6359.794.K4 H37 2021 (print) | LCC BX6359.794.K4 (ebook) | DDC 286/.176947—dc23

LC record available at https://lccn.loc.gov/2021001173
LC ebook record available at https://lccn.loc.gov/2021001174

"To borrow Lewis Craig's phrase in comparing the kingdom of heaven he says it is a mere Kentucky of a place."

Samuel Meredith Jr. to John Breckenridge
March 2, 1791

For Johnnie

Tibi Magno Cum Amor

Contents

Acknowledgments

One of the more pleasant tasks of any author is thanking the people who helped them along the way. I have incurred many debts in preparing this book, and it is a joy to return credit where credit is due. I will start with Scot Danforth, director of the University of Tennessee Press. It is a long story—most of mine are—but when Scot said that he wanted to see the manuscript, I was happy to oblige. Thanks, Scot. I remain unconvinced that academic publication is the way to universal acclaim, but that is a conversation for a different day.

I have been working with the Elkhorn Association's early history off and on for quite a while. Some of this material appeared before in a slightly different form. Portions of chapter 3, "Good Old Virginia Doctrine: Ministers and Ministry," first appeared in the *American Baptist Quarterly* (Fall–Winter 2013), 395–413, under the title "Decently and in Order: The Philadelphia Association and the Search for a Usable Polity"; portions of chapter 4, "Revive Us Again," first appeared in *The Register of the Kentucky Historical Society* (Winter 2012), 3–32, under the title "'And All the Baptists in Kentucky Took the Name *United Baptists*': The Union of Kentucky's Separate and Regular Baptists"; portions of chapter 6, "A Story to Tell to the Nations," first appeared in *Ohio Valley History* (Fall 2009), 25–42, under the title "Downwind from the New England Rat: John Taylor, Organized Missions and the Regionalization of Religious Identity on the American Frontier." I want to thank these journals for permission to use this material for this book.

Writers rely on feedback from other readers. With that in mind, I have known Ed Crowther and Rich Holl longer than either would care to admit, and I have relied upon their historical eye and good judgment before. Both read multiple drafts of earlier manuscripts; both made helpful suggestions; both endured stories about the trials and travails of Elkhorn; both learned more about Kentucky Baptists than they ever imagined or desired. Somehow, we have remained friends through it all. It is amazing, and I am profoundly grateful.

I doubt that anyone knows more about Kentucky history than Jim Klotter and Tom Appleton. I am truly fortunate to claim both as my friends. Both made excellent suggestions for strengthening this work. I appreciate all they have done for me through the years, and I owe Jim more cookies than I can ever repay. I have also relied on several conversation partners through my time with Elkhorn, and I am especially grateful for Joanna Lile, Bill Leonard, Laura Levins, Betsy Flowers, Alex Kinchen, and my administrative assistant, Melody Bush. Here's to hot coffee, multiple drafts, and good times all around. Thank you, all!

Throughout this project I have worked with top-notch organizations like the Earhart Foundation, which provided financial support for this study. Likewise, facilities like the Kentucky Department of Library and Archives and the Kentucky Historical Society (KHS) were extremely helpful. I am especially indebted to Beth Van Allen and Lynne Hollingsworth, formerly of KHS. Beth supported this project from its earliest stages, and Lynne is one of the best archivists I have ever worked with. I was so impressed by her skill that I appointed myself president of her fan club. To date, neither of us has grown rich but we remain hopeful. Lynne also introduced me to Kandie Adkinson, and what a joyous day that turned out to be! In addition to some of the best brownies ever, Kandie gave me a crash course in early Kentucky land claims, and no one knows more about that subject than Kandie. My heartiest thanks to you all.

I teach Baptist history at Southeastern Baptist Theological Seminary in Wake Forest, North Carolina. Members of my administration have given me tremendous support throughout my career, especially Provost Bruce Ashford, Vice President for Graduate Studies Chuck Lawless, and Vice President for Institutional Effectiveness Keith Whitfield. We are privileged to have a fine library and outstanding staff. Director of Library Services Jason Fowler made sure that I had plenty of room to work, and Inter-Library Loan Assistants Heather Teater Kinnebrew, Scott Brazil, and my own wife, Johnnie Harper, went to extraordinary lengths to find obscure material for me. While Dustin Toone and Joshua Alley joined the project late, they provided helpful and timely contributions. Additionally, Adam Winters of the Southern Baptist Theological Seminary, Louisville, Kentucky, was very helpful in supplying material from Southern Seminary's fine collection. Thank you, all!

Much closer to home, I would be remiss if I failed to mention my gratitude for my family. Neither our son, David, nor our daughter-in-law, Alexa, is a historian, but they provided much needed diversions from this project, and I can never thank them enough. David has always been my "helper man" and he always will be. Alexa is a voracious reader, but she has not seen earlier drafts of this manuscript, so I am eager to hear what she thinks about it. Finally, I owe my deepest debt of gratitude to my wife, Johnnie. Through the years, she, too, has been regaled with seemingly endless stories and random facts about the Elkhorn Association and the churches therein. We both suspect that if we could be transported back in time, we would recognize the principal characters in this book. As a Lexington, Kentucky, girl, she was especially eager to see this story told, and I am equally eager to dedicate this book to her.

The Buzzel about Kentuck

In 1786 Rev. John Gano appeared to have everything going for him. Widely regarded as an excellent preacher and gifted with great common sense, he enjoyed the respect of his fellow ministers. He was a warm-hearted patriot and demonstrated his commitment to the American Revolution not only by serving as a chaplain in Gen. James Clinton's army, but also by recruiting others to the cause. Now, with the Revolution behind him, Gano could reflect on his life and ministry from his pastorate at First Baptist Church, New York. If America's late-eighteenth-century Baptists claimed a singular hero, it might well have been John Gano.[1]

Appearances, however, can be deceiving. Notwithstanding his professional fame, John Gano faced a personal crisis after the war. Like many other post-Revolution Americans, he found himself in considerable debt with few prospects for recovery. As he weighed his options, he met William Wood, a fellow Baptist and land speculator from Kentucky. Wood assured Gano that a man of his stature and ability would do well in the West. The potential to acquire land, the opportunity to make a fresh start, and engage in "useful ministry" convinced Gano that God was leading him to Kentucky. Of course, dangers and uncertainties would lay along the way. But given the seemingly limitless opportunities west of the mountains and the persistent "buzzel about Kentuck," Gano's prospects on the frontier appeared brighter than his prospects in New York. Thus, upon resigning his pastorate, he sold his goods, paid his debts, and trekked westward. On June 17, 1787, Gano and his family arrived at Limestone, Kentucky, where they joined other like-minded souls who had made the move before them.[2]

Baptists began settling Kentucky in significant numbers as early as 1781. Four years later a group of these pioneering preachers formed the Elkhorn Association, widely regarded as the oldest Baptist association west of the Appalachian Mountains.[3] They had heard glowing stories about vast tracks of rich land, lush hardwood forests, and a superabundance of game. For those familiar with biblical imagery, Kentucky sounded like a new Garden of Eden, a land of milk and honey, a Promised Land. Others certainly saw it that way. Upon seeing Kentucky for the first time, Daniel Boone's fellow-explorer Felix

Walker noted, "We felt ourselves passengers through a wilderness just arrived at Elysium, or at the garden where was no forbidden fruit."[4] Beauty, abundance, and the absence of "forbidden fruit" made Kentucky sound almost too good to be true, but best of all, the land was available for a price. From the Commonwealth's earliest days, there were fortunes to be made by land speculators who sold Eden by the acre.

Given the various state-level and specialized studies of Kentucky Baptists, one might ask if another work that focuses on the Elkhorn Association is even necessary.[5] The answer lies, at least in part, in the association's uniqueness. When compared with other Baptist associations, the Elkhorn Association generated a wealth of material, including church minutes, books, and pamphlets. Moreover, these documents indicate a number of important things about these ministers. Perhaps most telling, their writings suggest that they knew that formerly they had been social, cultural, and political "outsiders." Some had even been persecuted for their faith, but in their new frontier homes they were not content to remain on society's periphery. Rather, these pioneering Baptists were men on the make who defied common stereotypes and received wisdom regarding frontier preachers.[6] That is to say, the Baptists of the Elkhorn Association did not wait to be recognized as anyone's equal. Instead, they *self-consciously* fought to achieve economic wealth, status, and full social and cultural acceptability.

Consider, for instance, the issue of religious freedom. Most of Elkhorn's earliest ministers came from Virginia, where they had been a persecuted and largely marginalized minority. Kentucky offered the prospect of religious freedom even before the area petitioned for statehood.[7] Like other early settlers, Elkhorn's faithful trained their attention on obtaining land and securing their property rights. If half of the tales told about the land were true, they sought to seize every opportunity that Kentucky offered. They positioned themselves deliberately in what would come to be known as the "Bluegrass Region," the very heart of early Kentucky wealth and political power. Unlike in their former days in Virginia, however, these pioneering spirits intended to share power rather than challenge it. As for religious liberty, associational records reveal little about it. Rather than actively campaigning for religious liberty, Elkhorn's ministers acted almost as if it were a *fait accompli*.

Through their westward adventure, there existed a supposed "frontier democracy," a leveling effect that eradicated social stations and class differences. Yet, a careful reading of Elkhorn's *Minutes* and the various writings of their ministers paints a somewhat different picture. Certain ministers wielded more power and influence than others. Certain ministers commanded more respect from their peers than others. Certain ministers dominated associational affairs—or sought to do so. The Elkhorn Association represented a particular kind of community, and far from being the "rugged individualists" of frontier mythology, these Baptists conducted their business according to well-defined lines of deference within their associational bounds and beyond.[8]

If the Elkhorn Association's ministers are neither fully-fledged frontier egalitarians nor radical religionists, what—or, more precisely—*who* were they? Simply stated, they were a people in significant transition. Among the first generation to struggle with mapping the contours of religious liberty, they also tried to square the free exercise of their religious beliefs with unprecedented opportunity and cultural change. Assuming their place among Kentucky's elites forced Elkhorn's Baptists to juggle three sometimes complementary and sometimes antithetical impulses—their religious convictions, Jeffersonian Republicanism, and honor—with mixed results.

In religious matters there is no question that Elkhorn's Baptists preached an evangelical gospel. Defining evangelicalism with precision can be tricky, but historian David W. Bebbington argues that it possesses four distinct characteristics. First, evangelicalism relies on a high view of the Bible. That is, evangelicals tend to see the Bible as an authoritative guide in spiritual matters. Given their high view of scripture, evangelicals also maintain what Bebbington calls "crucicentrism," or the importance of Christ's death on the cross. Third, evangelicals believe that people are sinners and need to be reconciled to God through personal conversion. Finally, evangelicals express their faith through some kind of activism. Granted, Bebbington's definition is not without its critics. Nonetheless, his now-famous "quadrilateral" is a helpful, brief description of how Elkhorn's Baptists articulated their faith.[9] It should be noted that others, most notably Methodists and Presbyterians, likewise held a high view of the Bible, called sinners to repentance by way of Christ's cross, and looked for the kind of changed life in a professing Christian that demonstrated genuine conversion. Elkhorn's Baptists, however, did not consciously style themselves as "evangelical" in any modern sense of the word. In describing the Cane Ridge Revival, one writer claimed that while Presbyterians and Methodists "are in full communion with each other . . ." Baptists "preach with each other, but do not commune."[10] In a word, Kentucky's earliest Baptists were not frontier ecumenists intent on building religious bridges into their neighboring communities. Rather, they devoted themselves to seeking unity with other Baptists of like faith and order.

Preaching Christ in the western territory and maintaining certain Baptist theological tenets did not prove especially difficult for Elkhorn's Baptists. They faced a number of complicated issues, however, when they tried to apply their faith to their circumstances. After the Revolution, Americans throughout the new nation struggled to consolidate gains from the American Revolution in the New Republic Era. What did freedom really mean? Politically, Elkhorn's Baptists tended to express themselves as Jeffersonian Republicans. The literature on this subject is so extensive that one scholar claims that republicanism has its own career.[11] Broadly considered, republicanism emphasized the right of self-rule, civic mindedness, and virtue, qualities that resonated with Elkhorn ministers who strongly identified as Jeffersonians in all matters bearing on freedom and property. According to some, the post-Revolutionary Era represented a time of harmonious relations, with near equality between black and white Baptists. Others, however, maintain that under no circumstances can salvation be equated with political freedom or acceptance of African Americans as social equals. Moreover, whatever semblance of equality that may have existed had a short life. The majority of Baptists in the southern states either endorsed slavery or got shouted down when they voiced opposition. Western land offered opportunity and many even among the Baptists believed that one could scarcely capitalize on that opportunity without slave labor.[12] In fact, slavery quickly became a much more significant issue for pious Kentuckians than religious liberty.

Balancing religious conviction and political inclinations is difficult, especially in a context like frontier Kentucky. Here, strong notions about honor mediated between evangelicalism and Jeffersonian Republicanism. Honor is an ancient concept whereby a man established his position in society by quasi-formal, but clearly delineated, social structures. According to Bertram Wyatt-Brown, honor rests on three fundamental pillars. First, honor begins with a man's self-assessment or the inner belief that he is somehow "worthy." Next, a man must make clear that assessment in an open, public context. Finally, the public judges the man's claim.[13] In short, Wyatt-Brown contends, "Honor resides in the individual as his understanding of who he is and where he belongs in the ordered ranks of society."[14]

Elkhorn's ministers understood social position and status both within the association and the community. They recognized leaders in their midst and expected them to lead. Consequently, well-positioned men like James Garrard could speak to associational issues, and when the former militia colonel was elected Kentucky's second governor, Baptists had someone who could represent them to the rest of Kentucky and the nation. But as the Elkhorn Baptists quickly learned, balancing religious conviction and political inclination was one thing; consolidating and maintaining social and cultural gains was another matter.

This study thus examines the Elkhorn Association, focusing particularly on its ministers and their leadership. By focusing on these personalities, new perspectives emerge. As chapter 1 indicates, for example, Elkhorners saw themselves as patriots. They self-consciously styled themselves as Jeffersonians, and they prided themselves on being thoroughgoing republicans. Many of Elkhorn's founders were persecuted for their faith. This persecution is well documented, but there is more to their story than public humiliation and jail time. These Revolutionary Era Baptists were also eager to attain a social status they had not enjoyed in Virginia. Kentucky represented both wealth and the possibility for economic and social advancement as much, or more, than religious freedom broadly defined, and most of the preachers who came to Kentucky were interested in far more than simply fleeing religious persecution. These patriots had fought for their freedom and they intended to consolidate their social, economic, political, and religious gains in Kentucky. Transitioning from cultural outsiders to insiders was no easy feat.[15] Striking a balance between freedom, acquisitiveness, and being good "Christian" citizens may have proven even more difficult for Kentucky Baptists than their Virginia brethren.

Chapter 2 charts the difficulties of gaining a foothold in early Kentucky. Land acquisition and ownership raised serious issues, as any chronicler of early Kentucky quickly discovers. Land may have been available, but it was far from secure. Bad surveys, unscrupulous land agents, and a host of related problems created tensions for early would-be Kentuckians. Beyond these issues, the first settlers who pushed beyond the Appalachian Mountains faced an even larger question: would Kentuckians allow slavery in their Commonwealth or would they forbid it? Ultimately, the majority opted for slavery, but the issue continued to simmer in the background, with good men and women differing on the matter.

The debate surrounding slavery raised haunting issues among the members of Elkhorn's constituent churches, especially those who had imbibed the sort of Revolutionary rhetoric that had proclaimed "all men are created equal." But in human terms, who gained the most from the American Revolution and what had it really meant? Had the fight really been about freedom from tyranny for everyone regardless of color, or freedom to chase mammon, usually at the expense of people of color? Elkhorn's ministers soon fashioned a kind of honor culture that tried to balance the sort of material prosperity one could obtain by slave labor with equitable treatment of others. Their honor culture established clear lines of authority and interdependence that frequently countermanded democratic, equalitarian impulses.

Chapter 3 details the existence of a "ministry culture" among Elkhorn's leaders. As such, ministers responded to what they believed to be a divine calling on their lives. Other seasoned ministers affirmed this calling through examination and ordination. Superficially, associational life appeared to be democratic. Those attending church or association meetings referred to each other as "Brother" and so forth. One historian goes as far as arguing, "For people enmeshed in webs of deference, the affective bonds of evangelical churches were liberating indeed. Gone were ceremonies designed to confer honor and connote rank; in were rituals that celebrated Christian fellowship, without regard to age, sex, and sometimes even race."[16]

Unfortunately, it is easy to mistake a few democratic impulses as normative for all circumstances. Honorific ceremonies may have been gone, but deferential patterns persisted. For instance, Elkhorn's Baptists were scarcely democratic toward women, and they were even less democratic toward slaves. Indeed, the sources indicate clear deferential patterns and obvious "firsts among equals" whose voices usually carried considerable weight.[17] Elkhorn's "ministry culture" also demonstrated that these ministers were not the radical individualists of folklore. As Daniel Blake Smith aptly notes, "While emigration required a certain amount of courage and self-reliance, the West was not peopled by a collection of rugged individualists. Most settlers migrated in family groups, often prompted by family motives. Most settlers did not simply head west on a whim but coordinated with neighborhood kin and friends for practical as well as emotional reasons."[18] Once in Kentucky, Elkhorn's ministers never completely jettisoned deferential-style politics. Rather, they followed a communitarian impulse that shaped their collective decision making and expected a certain amount of deference both to the association's collective wisdom and its leaders. This kind of communitarian impulse filtered down into the churches and leaned more toward hierarchy than radical democracy, and it was present in the Elkhorn Association from the beginning.

Most of Kentucky's earliest Baptists had professed conversion in Virginia revivals of the 1760s. Consequently, one may conclude that revivals played a significant role in shaping early Commonwealth churches. Chapter 4 details how important revival was to Kentucky's Baptists. Elkhorn's faithful longed for revival in part because it meant church growth, but even more they assumed revival to be a spiritual barometer by which they gauged divine favor. Conversely, absence of it spelled divine displeasure or undisclosed sin. Elkhorn frequently found itself between extremes, either lamenting lethargy in its member churches or noting localized revival and praying for more on a larger scale. Of course, revival could also serve as a catalyst for change. When the great revivals of the early nineteenth century swept through Kentucky, the Elkhorn Association laid aside longstanding grievances against the neighboring South Kentucky Association and became United Baptists. It also forced both the Elkhorn and South Kentucky Associations to affirm their own doctrinal fidelity by confronting Unitarianism within their ranks. However, it is scarcely a coincidence that Elkhorn and South Kentucky forged their union *after* slavery had been firmly ensconced.

Revival-wrought unity proved short-lived. Chapter 5 explores associational turmoil between 1805 and 1810. In this short span, longtime friends parted company as Elkhorn found itself in a series of conflicts over slavery. Indeed, the Forks of the Elkhorn Church, one of the association's more prominent institutions, experienced the kind of dramatic upheaval that likely typified many Kentucky churches. Ultimately, the association divided three ways, as the Friends to Humanity and Licking Associations split from Elkhorn when they considered fellowship no longer possible.

Revival by itself would not heal Elkhorn's wounds or reunite offended brethren. With the loss of ministers and church members, Elkhorn needed a new rallying point, a re-centering of sorts, and they found what they needed in the modern mission movement. Missionary work on the international level provided a new consensus and, thus, a way forward. Chapter 6 stresses that organized mission work allowed Elkhorn to close the book on its schisms and open new doors of opportunity by casting a broad vision for Christian service. Missions dovetailed with their understanding of Jeffersonianism and in its early phases challenged neither slavery nor individual acquisitiveness. Even theological differences could be laid aside for the sake of global evangelization. In a word, the modern mission movement demanded organization on an unprecedented level, interstate communication, and entirely new ventures that allowed Baptists to take their final stride, albeit reluctantly in some cases, toward America's emerging social, cultural, and political mainstream.

And so it was that settlers came to Kentucky. Some were patriotic; some religious. All sought something other than what they already had. For most, that meant creating a new life of freedom but without a universally recognized definition of what freedom meant or what the War for Independence was all about, it remained to be seen how Revolutionary rhetoric would be reconciled with reality. The role that religion played in shaping the Early Republic remains open for inquiry. But in the late eighteenth century, a group of Baptist ministers and their closest associates settled in Kentucky's Bluegrass Region and created new lives for themselves. In so doing, their stories reveal much about how they viewed their world, their expectations, their challenges, and their responses. This is their story.[19]

A Mere Kentucky of a Place

1

A Vortex of Baptist Preachers

On a Sunday morning in September 1781, members of the Upper Spottsylvania Church (Baptist) gathered outside of Fredericksburg, Virginia, for a special service. In addition to observing the Lord's Day, this service marked one final opportunity to say goodbye to family and friends. Some two hundred church members, along with their children and slaves, were about to travel more than six hundred miles overland to "Kentucke." As pastor of the Upper Spottsylvania Church, Lewis Craig commanded center stage on this day. Craig and Captain William Ellis would lead the "Travelling Church" through the wilderness to what they hoped would be a land of freedom, opportunity, and prosperity.[1]

Such stories are easily romanticized, but these pioneering souls were not living a fairy tale. The trip was difficult. Fear, uncertainty, and numerous other challenges attended Craig's band and scores of others who sought a better life west of the Appalachian Mountains. One early chronicler recorded, "How many died on the way, how many were slain by savage foes and how many were injured for life by exposure no records remain to tell nor is there a list extant of the heroic men and women who survived the perils of the wilderness and planted the banner of their faith at Gilbert's Creek."[2]

Notwithstanding the difficulties of such a long trip, Craig and company finally reached their destination near present-day Lancaster, Kentucky, in November. Others soon followed. By the early nineteenth century, Virginia Baptist historian Robert Baylor Semple noted that so many of his brethren had moved west that Kentucky had become a "vortex of Baptist preachers."[3] Had he been on site Semple might have surmised that Kentucky's Bluegrass Region represented the center of that vortex.

But why would people risk their lives and the lives of their families by migrating west with no guarantee of success? According to one historian, Kentucky actually began as "an idea born out of need and hope," depending on one's perspective. For the needy, Kentucky represented a place where land was both fertile and available, unlike the more expensive, depleted lands of Virginia and the Carolinas. The hopeful saw Kentucky as a place where they might live quietly and, if favored with a bit of good fortune, where they might even leave an inheritance for their children. For those who aspired to greater things, Kentucky offered opportunities for fame and fortune. Most of all, it represented a better future, in various ways. In any event, coming to Kentucky required a self-conscious decision to face the risks associated with crossing the mountains. Settling in the place that would become known as the "Bluegrass Region" required yet another self-conscious decision. According to one writer, the Bluegrass Region "occupies the broad rolling area of east-central Kentucky, from the Ohio River south to encircling, hilly Knobs zone."[4] This part of Kentucky quickly became a center for wealth and political power. Frontier Kentucky may have been born from an idea, but it quickly became a reality that was "forged out of dreams and desperation."[5]

The early Baptists who made Kentucky their new home and formed the Elkhorn Association might have shouted a hearty "Amen!" to that assessment. Their story suggests that Kentucky offered them hope and fulfilled a need. Many of their number had been persecuted in Virginia for their religious beliefs, and those who had escaped imprisonment, fines, or other forms of personal endangerment knew others who had not been so fortunate. To many, they preached an unpopular message to a people who saw them as nuisances at best and threats to social and cultural order at worst. Most of Elkhorn's earliest ministers had converted to Christianity during the Great Awakening and their stories begin in Virginia. In moving west these pioneers risked much, but they believed Kentucky offered a fresh start that would furnish both financial and religious opportunities scarcely imaginable in Virginia.

Eighteenth-Century Revivalism

By the middle of the eighteenth century, American colonies began to experience a wave of religious revivals that lasted into the nineteenth century. Some ministers discouraged the emotionalism that so often accompanied the revivals. They especially disdained "revival exercises" in which converts wept, writhed, shouted, and otherwise tottered between despair and spiritual ecstasy. Not surprisingly, many Christians, especially the new converts, favored the revivals because they believed they had found God's mercy in the revival's message. Before long many of the new converts began wondering why their own ministers did not preach like the other ministers who encouraged the revivals.

Ultimately, churches divided along pro- and antirevival lines. The so-called New Lights favored the revivals; the Old Lights did not. Those who felt uncomfortable in Old Light congregations, especially Congregationalists and Presbyterians, separated themselves from their churches and formed New Light congregations. These new congregations encouraged revivalism—emotionalism and all.[6]

Some converts went one step further when they submitted to baptism by immersion and joined Baptist churches. The term "Separate Baptists" applied to zealous, revivalistic eighteenth-century Baptists, many of whom were former Congregationalists or Presbyterians. They identified themselves as "Separate" because they had separated themselves from what they deemed cold, nonrevivalistic churches. Those believers claimed the Bible as their only guide to faith and practice.[7]

Shubal Stearns numbered among those who identified with the Separate Baptists. A Connecticut native, Stearns converted under New Light preaching about 1745. He joined a Baptist congregation in 1751 and soon began preaching as a Separate Baptist. With his family, he relocated to Sandy Creek, North Carolina, in 1755. Within a few years the Sandy Creek Church had grown from an initial membership of sixteen to over six hundred. Under Stearns's leadership ministers left the Sandy Creek Church and established other Separate Baptist churches in Virginia, South Carolina, and Georgia, as well as North Carolina.[8]

As Separate Baptists spread throughout the South, they encountered scattered pockets of Regular Baptists, nearly all of whom maintained close ties to the Philadelphia Association. The Separate and Regular Baptists shared numerous characteristics and many doctrinal similarities, yet they eyed each other suspiciously. It is easy to exaggerate their differences, but generally speaking the Regulars insisted on grounding any fellowship between the two groups on the Philadelphia Confession of Faith, a slightly modified version of the Second London Confession (1689). For them, the confession served as a safeguard against doctrinal error, and they used it as a touchstone for maintaining theological integrity. The Separate Baptists saw no such advantage in a human-made creed and countered that strict subscription to any confession subordinated the Bible to the confession—a position they were unwilling to accept.[9] They chose to define themselves according to their church covenants. Other issues, frequently petty and inconsequential, also hindered fellowship between Regular and Separate Baptists. Early Baptist historians noted that Separate Baptists tended to look upon Regulars as "worldly," especially in their dress. Regulars responded in kind, observing that Separates preached with great zeal, but little else.[10]

John Leland had first-hand experience with the Awakening when it began in Virginia. An established leader among Virginia's Revolutionary Era Baptists and a warm-hearted Jeffersonian, Leland wrote prolifically on religious and political issues, and he served as the leading voice for Virginia Baptists and for many who moved to Kentucky. He recorded his insights into Virginia's revivals in a work titled *The Virginia Chronicle*. In his assessment, Baptists experienced dramatic growth from 1767 to 1774 and fell into two different groups. Baptists in Virginia's northern reaches tended to be Regular Baptists, with ministers who had relocated from "Pennsylvania and the Jerseys." The southern preachers tended to be Separate Baptists, due in large part to Shubal Stearns's influence. Leland described them as preaching like "the old Baptist John, 'Repent for the kingdom of heaven is at Hand,' and great numbers of people went out unto them and were baptized, confessing their sins."[11]

Leland did not know why Regulars and Separates kept each other at arm's length. Representatives from both groups met in 1767 but failed to reach satisfactory terms of union. Those present knew the particulars, "but those who lived at a distance were ignorant of the reason, and whenever they met, they loved each other as brethren, and much deplored that there should be any distinctions or shyness among them." Even so, Leland observed that the Separates grew much faster than the Regulars, and they did so with a flair. He summarized revival preaching by noting, "The people would cry out—fall down—for a time, lose the use of their limbs; which exercise made the by-standers marvel. Some thought they were deceitful, others thought they were bewitched, and many being convinced of all, would report, that God was with them of a truth."[12]

The revival claimed converts from all walks of life. For example, James Ireland reckoned himself to be one of mid-eighteenth-century Virginia's more infamous sinners. Nonetheless, upon his conversion he soon felt what he perceived to be a divine urging to preach the gospel. Ireland believed God was working among Virginia's Baptists. He knew of two distinctions between them, Separate and Regular. "Both parties were Calvinistic in their sentiments," he recalled, "and our little religious body were disposed to join with them, by submitting to the rules of their society. . . ."[13] Ultimately, Ireland aligned himself with the Separate Baptists because they were particularly zealous, "although the ministry of both names were warm and zealous men."[14]

James Ireland never moved to Kentucky, but William Hickman did, and he became a stalwart in the Elkhorn Association. He professed conversion under zealous revivalistic preaching on the eve of the American Revolution. Orphaned at a young age, Hickman grew into an imposing figure of a man. One writer claims that even in his seventies, Hickman stood "erect as palm tree, being at least six feet high, rather of a lean texture, his whole deportment solemn and grave."[15] He and his sister lived for a time with their grandmother who warned them sternly about hell. "Those things bore heavily on my mind," Hickman claimed, "and more so on the death of our parents; the thought of my father, fearing he was miserable, deprived me of many hours of sleep; my mother, I hoped, was in glory."[16] At fourteen, Hickman was "put out to a trade." He soon fell away from his grandmother's religious instruction, choosing to embrace various "evil habits." Over the next seven years he listened to the local parson "when he was sober enough to go through his discourse," but he all but abandoned prayer and Bible reading. He had heard of "Babtists," but they sounded peculiar and he wanted nothing to do with them.[17]

In 1770 Hickman heard that "new light" preachers were in his area. Curiosity drove him to hear John "Swearing Jack" Waller and James Childs, but he was not prepared for what he saw that night. "God's power attended the word," he recalled, "numbers falling, some convulsed, others crying out for mercy. . . ."[18] Baptisms followed the next day, and once again Hickman could not believe what he saw. Before long he and his family moved to another part of Virginia, where he soon lapsed back into his former bad habits. More preachers followed, and this time there was no escape. His wife came to Christ first, converting in the fall of 1772. Hickman followed in the spring of 1773. He began travelling with itinerant preachers, proclaiming the same message he once spurned. One biographer described Hickman as "a truly venerable and useful servant of Christ," while another remembered him as a zealous, capable minister who, as of the early 1820s, had probably baptized more people than anyone else in Kentucky.[19]

John Taylor's conversion experience resembled William Hickman's in several respects. Like Hickman, Taylor had heard that some Baptists preached enthusiastically, and curiosity led him to investigate for himself. Taylor claimed to be simultaneously drawn to and repulsed by what he experienced. He described Separate Baptists as "constituted on a Church Covenant," but hearing the terms of one such covenant convinced him that "no man on earth can comply with it." Yet, baptism captured his attention and left him in awe. Upon witnessing the rite, Taylor recalled that even though he "would not have become a Baptist for all the world," he considered himself "a serious observer of all that passed."[20] The more he listened the more he warmed to revivalistic preaching but no matter how agreeable the message, Taylor found himself lapsing into sinful ways. He struggled with issues ranging from unbelief to hard-heartedness until he finally professed his faith in Christ in 1772. Upon his baptism Taylor began an itinerant ministry, though he believed his conversion and call to ministry had come toward the end of a "harvest season" in his home region.[21]

Among Elkhorn's earliest preachers, John Taylor appears to have been an unlikely candidate for frontier life, much less ministry. Taylor described himself at age twenty as short, boyish, and timid "only a fit associate for mill or school-boys . . . my boy-hood was such, even in stature, that seemed to forbid my addressing grown people. In a strange place I was taken to be about sixteen years old—in one place, it was said my head came but a little over the pulpit."[22] Over time, Taylor proved to be a decent farmer, but he defied all frontier stereotypes by admitting that he was not a good hunter. Fortunately for Taylor, he did not have to hunt alone, and his fellows, "with the common generosity of hunters," shared their kill with him.[23] On another occasion, he recalled stalking a deer. "I could sometimes see him," Taylor said, "but I at length got a fire at him and accidentally shot him through the heart; this was a greater treat to my family, than the largest bullock I have ever killed since, for he was large and very fat."[24]

Virginia's ingathering of souls began to wane as the American Revolution neared, but there was more to the revivals than conversion. If historian Rhys Isaac is correct, revivalism played an instrumental role in "transforming" late-Colonial Virginia into Early National Virginia.[25] For some preachers the turmoil that led to the American Revolution ushered them into the political arena, especially in matters bearing on religious liberty. Notwithstanding any number of religious dissimilarities, the Revolution prompted many Virginia Baptists to become lifelong Jeffersonian Republicans. For instance, few could equal John Leland's ardent Jeffersonianism. On New Year's Day 1802, Thomas Jefferson received a wheel of cheese that measured just over 4 feet in diameter, 15 inches thick, and weighed 1,235 pounds. The cheese came from Cheshire, Massachusetts, farmers, and John Leland, who had moved there from Virginia in 1791, had paid for its shipment to Washington, DC. Allegedly, the cheese had been made from nine hundred "Republican cows" and bore the inscription, "The Greatest Cheese in America, for the Greatest Man in America."[26] Apart from Jefferson himself, no one exercised greater influence on the political thought of the Elkhorn Association's Baptists than John Leland.

From Pietists to Patriots

It is impossible to separate religion from the war for independence, but North American evangelicals, especially Baptists, did not single-handedly trigger the American Revolution.[27] As one historian argues, Baptists were "far too small and controversial a sect to precipitate war."[28] Rather, they became increasingly active participants in America's emerging political process. In 1776 the Commonwealth's dissenting sects, especially its Baptists, could not help but rejoice over Virginia's Declaration of Rights. In this document, Article 16 promised religious liberty to all. Sensing an opportunity, Baptists and others began flooding the Virginia legislature with petitions for redress of particular issues. A student of the era notes, "The first petition arrived just days after the Article 16 was completed, and it clearly sought to exploit the wartime context to advantage, promising Baptist loyalty to the patriot cause in exchange for further privileges and specifically requesting relief from parish taxation, the right to worship freely, and the right to 'be married, buried, and the like, without paying the clergy of other denominations.'"[29]

As eager as America's Baptists may have been to obtain their religious freedom, they were not unanimous in supporting the American Revolution. For example, David Thomas's sentiments may have changed over time, but he originally hoped a revolution would not be necessary. In 1774 Thomas wrote a lengthy treatise titled *The Virginian Baptist,* in which he answered a number of allegations usually leveled against Baptists. He categorically denied using church services and other gatherings as forums for sedition. "At these meetings," Thomas claimed, "we meddle not with any state affairs. No; we leave such things to the common wealth, to which they belong." Church meetings were not political gatherings unless, of course, congregants were praying for the "eternal and temporal welfare" of everyone in the colony. Thomas further claimed, "We form no intrigues. We lay no schemes to advance ourselves, nor make any attempts to alter the constitution of the kingdom to which men belong." Thomas gladly recognized "King George the third" and agreed "to pay him all due homage, and allegiance."[30]

In principle, Thomas believed that citizens were obliged to obey temporal powers provided that "they rule in righteousness." He also argued that Christians had a legal right to defend their country in the event of unlawful invasion.[31] Nonetheless, Thomas insisted that Baptists were far from being revolutionaries. Rather, they remained the Crown's loyal subjects. They freely paid their taxes and levies, cleared roads, and obeyed the King's law. He maintained that America's Baptists wanted religious freedom and desired no "further liberty, than peaceably to enjoy the fruit of our own industry; and to worship GOD in that manner which we verily believe is most acceptable in his sight, without molestation."[32]

Persecution unto Patriotism

Notwithstanding David Thomas's eloquence, other voices raised other concerns. For some, liberty "without molestation" would not come easily if it came at all, and they spoke from experience. Lewis Peyton Little tallied some seventy-nine Baptists who had been persecuted in the years leading up to the Revolution.[33] Among Virginia's persecuted preachers who had migrated to Kentucky in the 1780s, few could speak more forcefully on persecution than the Craig brothers, Lewis, Elijah, and Joseph. Their bold, confrontational preaching placed them at odds with Virginia's standing order, which limited religious exhortation to Anglican ministers, and they figure prominently in Little's *Imprisoned Preachers and Religious Liberty in Virginia.*[34]

His contemporaries recognized Lewis Craig as a fine pastor with a voice that stilled one's emotions. Born into a religiously minded Anglican household, Lewis grew into a man "of middle stature, rather stoop shouldered, his hair black, thick set, and somewhat curled, a pleasant countenance, freespoken, and his company very interesting, a great peacemaker among contending parties."[35] According to one writer, Lewis Craig became concerned about his soul upon hearing Samuel Harris's preaching. Before long, Craig began following Harris from one preaching engagement to another. He even exhorted listeners to repent even though he claimed he had no hope. Ultimately, Lewis Craig "rejoiced in Christ" in 1767, whereupon he was baptized and began to preach.[36] He was not a towering intellect claims one writer, "but being a sensible man, and having a very musical voice, with agreeable manners, and, especially going forth under the constraining influence of the love of Christ, he excited much interest among the people he addressed."[37]

It did not take long for Lewis Craig's preaching to attract attention. On one hand, many listened and some professed faith in Christ. On the other hand, Craig's preaching displeased many others. Ultimately, Craig and several others were arrested. As John Taylor recalled, Craig was brought before three Spottsylvania magistrates, who bound him along with several others. They were charged with disturbing the peace. "The prosecuting attorney," said Taylor, "represented them to be a great annoyance to the county by their zeal as preachers. 'May it please your worship,' said he, 'they cannot meet a man upon the road but they must ram a text of scripture down his throat.'"[38]

The court was willing to release the prisoners provided they agreed not to preach in the county for the next year. The ministers refused these terms and were promptly returned to jail, where they spent the next month before being released. Throughout their incarceration Craig and his fellows preached through their bars to anyone who would listen and proved almost as much of a nuisance from inside jail as they had been when they were free.[39]

That was not the last time Lewis Craig saw the inside of a jail cell. He was arrested again in 1771, this time in Caroline County. Upon seeing a number converted under his preaching, Craig once again faced incarceration. As one writer says, "A warrant was issued, and Mr. Craig was carried before a magistrate, to whom he gave bond not to preach in the county within a certain number of days, but feeling hampered by this measure, he thought it best to incur the penalty. . . ."[40] Authorities arrested Craig for preaching on Reuben Catlett's plantation and he served three months in jail. His stints behind bars both stiffened his own determination to continue preaching and emboldened others to do the same.[41]

In addition to facing opposition from local authorities, Lewis Craig also faced opposition from hostile neighbors. For instance, long before his own ministry so impressed William Hickman, the aforementioned John "Swearing Jack" Waller enjoyed heckling local Baptist ministers. As a young man Waller briefly trained for a career in law but his education was cut short when an uncle who was underwriting his education died unexpectedly. Still, according to one chronicler, Waller had always been more inclined to break the law than practice it. Upon his uncle's death, Waller pursued "every species of wickedness and profanity, and quickly acquired for himself the infamous appellation 'Swearing Jack Waller,' by which he was distinguished from others of the same name."[42] "Swearing Jack" also claimed the equally colorful alias, "the Devil's Adjutant," because of his alleged ability to muster a devilish cohort.[43]

On one occasion, Waller assembled a number of friends in order to put Lewis Craig "on trial." A well-known local minister, Craig thanked this group of hooligans for honoring him. "While I was wicked and injurious you took no notice of me," Craig observed, "but since I have altered my course of life, and endeavored to reform my neighbors, you concern yourselves much about me. I shall take the spoiling of my good joyfully."[44] Impressed by Craig's sincerity, Waller began attending preaching services, ultimately professed conversion, and became a Baptist preacher himself.[45]

Elijah Craig endured many of the same humiliations as his brother Lewis. Born in Orange County, Virginia about 1743, Elijah first became concerned about spiritual matters upon hearing David Thomas in 1764. He was converted about one year later under Samuel Harris's ministry. Much like his brother, Elijah immediately began to preach and exhort others to repentance. "His tobacco house," says Semple, "was their chapel. Being most of them laboring men, they used to labor all day, and hold meetings almost every night, at each other's houses, and on Sundays at the above mentioned tobacco house."[46] Physically, he was described as a man of "delicate habit, a thin visage, large eyes and mouth, of great readiness of speech, the sweet melody of his voice, both in preaching and singing bore all down before it."[47] Lewis may have been more popular but their contemporaries agreed that Elijah was a better preacher.[48]

As Elijah Craig became better known, he received more opportunities to preach. Such opportunities exposed him to persecution and arrest. In Culpeper County, Craig was jailed for a month but not before he appeared before a panel of three magistrates. Allegedly, a lawyer present encouraged the judges to release Craig and several other unnamed preachers, arguing that they would be less trouble if they were freed than they would be if they were kept in bonds. He compared Baptists to a bed of chamomile in that any attempt to eradicate it only caused it to spread. The argument painted a vivid mental image, but it failed to convince the judges. They sent Craig to jail for a month where he dined on rye bread and water.[49]

Then there was Joseph Craig, the third member of the Craig brotherly preaching triumvirate. Joseph may be described most kindly as mercurial. No one questioned his zeal but some probably questioned his sanity. Joseph was unpredictable, and his eccentricities frequently bubbled to the surface, even in his preaching. On one occasion as he was delivering a sermon outdoors, he stopped mid-discourse, looked up in a tree and said, "Brethren, there is a fork that would make a good pack saddle," and then immediately returned to his sermon.[50] Fearing that Joseph might do Christ's cause more harm than good, his brothers encouraged him to curtail his preaching. They reminded him that he had been "trying to preach" for twenty years, and they solemnly observed that he claimed only one convert to show for his trouble. Undaunted, Joseph responded, "Thank God. If Christ has saved one soul by me, in twenty years, I am ready to labor twenty more for the salvation of another."[51]

Apparently, Joseph Craig was never incarcerated for his preaching, but it was not for lack of effort. On one occasion authorities apprehended him along with several other preachers, but at some point, Joseph slipped away undetected. To his way of thinking, it was "no dishonour to cheat the devil."[52] On another occasion, he ran out the back door of the house where he was preaching before he could be apprehended. Authorities pursued him into a swamp with a pack of dogs and even shook him out of the tree where he was hiding. According to John Taylor: "After reasoning with him a while, he refused to go; but they forced him on a horse, and perhaps tied his hands. On the way he reasoned: Good men ought not to go to prison, and if you will put so good a man as Jo. Craig in prison, I will have no hand in it—and threw himself off the horse and would neither ride nor walk. Behaving perhaps as David did, before Achish, King of Gath."[53]

Joseph Craig could be equally unpredictable when he was surrounded by friends. Early in his ministry John Taylor remembered preaching at an associational meeting in Virginia. Upon finishing his sermon, he recalled being approached by "a very excentrick man Joseph Craig." As Taylor reached for Craig's hand to shake it, Craig proclaimed, "'Here is the Ass' colt on which my Master rode to Jerusalem,' laying hold of me, [he] called aloud to the people 'to come see the colt;' while a number of people pushed up to see some strange sight. And I do suppose truly, that neither Craig nor any of them, had ever seen so unlikely an appearance for a preacher." Flustered and embarrassed, Taylor added, "After this, Craig would introduce me to strangers as 'the Ass' colt without telling my name."[54]

Revolutionary Ties

Virginia's Baptists challenged authority across political and religious lines, notwithstanding occasional eccentricities. But if David Thomas appeared to be a reluctant revolutionary, there may have been good reason. As friction between the colonies and Great Britain increased, Baptists throughout the colonies faced a hard decision. In the event of war, who should they support? If they supported the colonial revolutionaries, they would in many cases be abetting the people who had oppressed them. On the other hand, they had no guarantee that the King would grant them special favor for their support. As William G. McLaughlin put it, "Here is the epitome of the Baptists' dilemma between patriotism and pietism. As pietists they were prepared to believe both sides were wrong, but as patriots they were inclined to support those who had oppressed them most. Yet, the quarrel with the Mother country was not of their making. As opponents of the Standing Order, as members of the poor, the outcast, the powerless, the Baptists had not shared in the making of colonial policy. To solve the dilemma the Baptists had to emerge from their pietistic shell and decide just how they would stand in the secular world."[55]

By 1775 some embraced religious liberty as a cause too sacred to leave to mere chance. They may have been late entering the debate, but generally Baptists became convinced that the King was a despot who intended to rob them of their freedom. Even more, they were willing to take up arms against Great Britain. With liberty in the balance, many Baptists rallied around the Declaration of Independence and the Revolution.[56]

Among Elkhorn's early stalwarts, John Gano modeled the "Patriot-preacher" perhaps better than anyone else. Reared in a Presbyterian home, Gano became a Baptist and received ordination in 1754. He quickly established himself as one of the Philadelphia Association's more capable ministers. In addition to several successful evangelistic forays into the southern colonies, Gano served as the first pastor of First Baptist Church, New York, from 1762 to 1787. He likewise fought for independence during the American Revolution, serving as a chaplain in Gen. James Clinton's 2nd New York regiment.[57]

Ambrose Dudley likewise distinguished himself during the American Revolution before coming to Kentucky. Born in 1750, Dudley attained the rank of captain in the Revolutionary army. By the war's end, he had professed faith in Christ and received baptism. Upon returning to his home in Spottsylvania, he united with the Baptist church there, and, to his surprise, he learned that they had been praying for a pastor. Dudley had been thinking about entering the ministry. The church took his desire as an answer to their prayers.[58] According to one biographer, "His manner was zealous, yet dignified, and, under the persecutions which characterized those times, he exhibited the most fearless intrepidity; soon the church became satisfied with his call to the ministry."[59] Others claimed that Dudley possessed both a commanding presence and an exemplary character. One of his contemporaries, James E. Welsh, described Dudley as a solemn preacher who convinced his hearers that he genuinely believed what he preached. "His manners and general habits," claimed Welsh, "seem to indicate that he was born for discipline. The very glance of his pierc-ing eye was often sufficient to awe into silence. In his personal appearance he was unusually erect and neat, so that once when a stranger asked, in Lexing-ton, where he could be found, he was told to walk down the street, and the first man he met having on a superfine black coat, without a single mote upon it, would be Ambrose Dudley."[60] Dudley relocated to Kentucky in 1786.

David Barrow also served as a chaplain during the Revolution. He be-came one of the better-known Baptist ministers of Revolutionary Era Virginia and later Kentucky. Although little is known of his early life, Barrow began preaching about 1771 and became "regularly employed in the pastoral office" in 1774.[61] He built a remarkable career in a brief time. He was an outspoken proponent of religious liberty, in part because he had been persecuted on nu-merous occasions. In addition to his pulpit skills, his peers found him to be an intelligent, articulate, and fair-minded person.[62] Barrow's life also furnished a key to the inner workings of the Elkhorn Association.

Notwithstanding his skills and giftedness, few of Virginia's persecuted ministers had been treated as badly as David Barrow. An ardent republican, Barrow freed his slaves in 1784, and his disdain for slavery only increased over time. He had moved to Kentucky from Virginia in 1798 and quickly became a regular at Elkhorn Association meetings. Barrow had been a well-loved co-laborer in Virginia. None of his fellow ministers doubted his courage or his commitment to Christian principles. They had seen him endure per-secution under Virginia's standing order for preaching without governmental approval, and they believed him to be sound in the faith.[63]

Barrow visited Kentucky between May 5 and August 31, 1795, before he moved his family. Even though Kentucky had been a state for three years, his diary records sundry dangers he encountered en route, including unfa-miliar terrain, unpredictable weather, and possible attack from hostile Native Americans. On July 16, he preached at Town Fork Church in Lexington and went home with Thomas Lewis. Barrow found Lewis and his wife "humble, pious people and withal very rich." Later that evening, "There came to me and converse with me Elder John Price and a Bro. Ashby, with whom I was glad to become acquainted." He welcomed the fellowship of like-minded folk noting, "Here I was treated with every degree of civility."[64]

David Barrow was known to be an ardent Jeffersonian Republican. In fact, his Revolutionary War experiences profoundly shaped his political thought. His trip to Kentucky convinced him that moving west was in his and his family's best interest, but before he left Virginia, he wrote an open letter ex-plaining why he was moving. "On long, and very serious deliberation," he said, "I have come to a determination under Divine Providence, to move my residence from this country to the state of Kentucky."[65] He stipulated that he was not running away from any difficulties or looking to get rich. Rather, he was experiencing difficulties supporting his family, and Kentucky offered him the opportunity to pay off his debts and provide for his family without engaging in land speculation, a practice he found "incompatible with the work of ministry."[66]

Barrow's letter offered a carefully articulated statement of his theological beliefs and what he styled as his "political creed." He summarized his theology in fifteen points that reflected his commitment to Calvinism and generally affirmed the Philadelphia Confession of Faith. Curiously, his political creed featured twenty-six points and reflected a deep commitment to the sort of republicanism found in the Declaration of Independence. That is, he believed that all men are created equal and endowed with certain rights:

> 1st. I believe the natural equality of man, except in some monstrous cases.
>
> 2nd. I believe that liberty, with a right to a good character, of acquiring and possessing property, with the enjoyment of life and members, and the means of defending them, is the unalienable privilege of all complexions, shapes, and sizes of men who have not forfeited those blessings by their own personal misdemeanors.
>
> 3rd. I believe that Government is an evil, as it cannot be supported without making considerable sacrifices of natural liberty; but, in our present state of depravity, it is to be preferred to a state of nature.
>
> 4th. That Government, is a civil compact, of a people emerging from a state of nature, contrived by themselves for their own severity, and is subject to the controul, and liable to alteration, when thought proper by a majority of such community.[67]

Barrow's political philosophy had no place for religious tests, "long, unnecessary imprisonments," or "exclusive privileges" for anyone. Article 25 urged, "That no community can long enjoy tranquility, but by strict adherence to virtue, and frequent recourse to fundamental principles." Perhaps for good measure, Article 26 affirmed honesty as the best policy.[68]

Finally, Barrow prayed for the prosperity of the "true Church of Jesus Christ." This prosperity required keeping the ordinances and maintaining well-disciplined congregations. He also prayed that God would send the kind of revival that would eradicate theological error and produce harmony among all believers. "I most ardently wish," he said, "that all those unhappy divisions, animosities, janglings, groundless criticisms, heart-burnings, evil-speaking, love of pre-eminence and persecution, which have for so many ages torn and mangled the Church of Christ, may happily and entirely subside. . . ."[69] As for his ministerial brethren, Barrow offered a blessing upon all faithful ministers of the gospel. He also prayed that they might receive adequate provision, and "That they may be upheld, directed, and supported under all their difficulties and temptations, and be taught to walk regularly before the people, and to *feed the Church of God which he has purchased with his own blood*. And that God would increase their number, as he shall see fit, making all *able Ministers of the New Testament*, and *examples to the flock*."[70]

As he put the finishing touches on his farewell letter in 1798, David Barrow may not have known how clearly he was speaking to Baptist life in Kentucky. Moving to Kentucky had indeed offered settlers a fresh start but balancing theology, politics, and economics was at least as difficult for the Elkhorn Association as it had been for any association in Virginia. In the end, relocating to the lands west of the Appalachian Mountains did little to ease the problems that plagued Baptists in the Old Dominion. Rather, it seemed to accentuate existing problems and create new ones.

In Pursuit of Happiness?

In 1790 Baptist minister and self-described "Swede" John Asplund conducted a survey of the known Baptists in the United States. After eighteen months on the trail and logging 7,000 miles, he reported 35 associations, 868 churches, 1,137 ministers, and 64,546 members. Kentucky claimed 42 churches, 61 ministers, and 3,105 members.[71] These numbers are remarkable, since Baptists had only begun to occupy the territory in 1781, and the Elkhorn Association was not organized until 1785. In less than a decade, and two years before Kentucky attained statehood, Baptists accounted for about 5 percent of Asplund's total number of ministers and about 4.8 percent of the total church members. Little wonder that Robert B. Semple saw Kentucky as a vortex of Baptist preachers.

Within the territory, Asplund's numbers tell a slightly different story. Of Kentucky's 42 churches, 14 affiliated with the Elkhorn Association; 20 affiliated with the South Kentucky Association; 8 affiliated with the Salem Association. South Kentucky may have claimed more churches, but 29 of the state's 61 ministers maintained membership in Elkhorn churches. Some of the Elkhorn churches had more than one minister in their fellowship. For instance, in 1790 Clear Creek Church tallied 5 ministers; Great Crossing Church had 4; Bryan Station had 3. Stated another way, 3 of Elkhorn's 14 churches claimed just under 20 percent of the association's ministers.[72] It did not take long for certain churches to emerge as associational standard bearers.

These Baptist ministers who settled in Kentucky before its statehood—Lewis, Elijah, and Joseph Craig, John Taylor, William Hickman, John Gano, Ambrose Dudley, and others—were making history. Some had been persecuted for their faith, others had fought to secure independence. All embraced religious liberty, American patriotism, and sought a better life in the West, however that life might be defined. Of course, Baptists could never claim to be greater patriots than any other American religious group. As Jewell Spangler observes, "To be sure, it would be overstating the case to argue that Baptists participated in the Revolutionary War at a greater rate than their non-Baptist counterparts, or that their patriotism was more solid or more passionate. . . . But, in the fighting of the war, Baptists did find common cause. They had opportunities to recognize a shared struggle in the Revolution."[73]

As settlers poured into early Kentucky, their numbers included a "vortex of Baptist preachers" indeed. Elkhorn quickly established itself as the Commonwealth's leading Baptist association, one that other associations looked to for guidance. But the ministers of the Elkhorn Association were not just any vortex. They shared a common theology and a commitment to Jeffersonian Republicanism. By the late 1790s the Elkhorn Association's ministerial roll boasted a Revolutionary War colonel, a captain, two chaplains, and numerous individuals cited for various acts of "patriotic service." They all wanted religious freedom, but there was more at stake in crossing the mountains. These pioneers came to Kentucky searching for a better life, but, as subsequent events demonstrated, there was no singular expression of what that better life looked like. As one author put it, "Jefferson's phrase, 'the pursuit of happiness,' bound the pietist and the rationalist, the deist and the dissenter, the Congregationalist and the Baptist together more surely than any concept of constitutional liberty or the rights of Englishmen, for each could define happiness in his own way."[74]

It was no strain for many Early National Baptists, especially in Elkhorn's ranks, to see how easily representative government and personal liberty dovetailed with Baptist polity.[75] Over time, most of these Baptists would modify their theology in response to changing conditions, but their desire for land and wealth would reveal deep-seated political differences that their religion could not overcome. They were men on the make and men of faith seeking moral and material advancement in the "dark and bloody ground" of Kentucky. Some found what they sought; others did not.

An example of "shingled" land claims. Eastern Kentucky University Special Collections and Archives, Richmond, Kentucky.

2

Between Backwoods Brethren and Bluegrass Barons

"Those who labor in the earth," declared Thomas Jefferson, "are the chosen people of God if ever He had a chosen people, whose breasts He has made His peculiar deposit for substantial and genuine virtue."[1] Jefferson's well-known affinity for America's "sturdy yeoman" farmers stands alongside his aversion to large urban areas. In addition to corrupting good morals and accentuating class differences, cities, he argued, bred a class of essentially nonproductive people who depended on others to sustain them, and such citizens stood at the mercy of the ambitious. He further believed that a state's rural population, its "husbandmen," could not be separated from its relative virtue. Thus, comparing a state's husbandmen to the other parts of society yielded a "good enough barometer whereby to measure its degree of corruption."[2]

The Elkhorn Baptists embraced Jefferson's vision for an agrarian America. They shared his understanding of religious freedom too, even if they did not share his religious views.[3] In Virginia much of the land had been overfarmed and the best land was too expensive to purchase. Middling farmers faced limited social and economic mobility. Besides, Baptists had endured persecution in the Old Dominion in the years leading up to the American Revolution. But for those who emigrated to the west, Kentucky's promise represented more than land or freedom. Kentucky represented opportunity. Lewis Craig, one of Elkhorn's most celebrated ministers and leader of the "Travelling Church," was known to describe heaven as "a mere Kentucky of a place."[4] Unfortunately, Kentucky land claims and their associated issues present almost as many challenges for modern historians as they did for the Commonwealth's first settlers.[5] However, a brief overview of early settlement and its associated land issues will help establish context for later events that seriously affected the Elkhorn Association.

Rumors of Eden

If early scouting reports are any indicator, it is easy to see why those seeking opportunity would risk their lives to cross the mountains. Gilbert Imlay, an early explorer and land speculator, could scarcely contain his enthusiasm when he wrote, "Flowers full and perfect, as if they had been cultivated by the hand of a florist, with all their captivating odors, and with all the variegated charms which color and nature can produce here, in the lap of elegance and beauty, decorate the smiling groves." He went on to say that Kentucky's air "gives the voluptuous glow of health and vigor," while the birds, those "sweet songsters of the forest . . . warble[d] their tender notes in unison with love and nature."[6] Imlay knew he spoke hyperbolically and he asked his readers' forgiveness. He had crossed the Alleghenies in March only to find Pittsburgh still in the throes of winter. Even so, as he reflected on Pittsburgh in the winter and springtime in Kentucky, there was no comparison.

For those accustomed to leaning on the Bible for guidance and strength, such descriptions made Kentucky sound like a New Eden. Even better, the land was available for a price. Even before Kentucky could be wrested from the Native Americans who had long claimed it as their hunting grounds, land speculators had begun amassing fortunes by selling "Eden" by the acre. For most, coming to Kentucky meant obtaining and, hopefully, holding on to one's land. Baptists were no exception. Perhaps more significant, even before Kentucky could petition for statehood, there was increasing momentum to guarantee religious freedom. Given their prospects west of the mountains, the Elkhorn Baptists had every reason to be hopeful. But before they could reap the benefits of their New Eden, they had to arrive safely.

There were essentially two ways, equally perilous, for pioneers to reach Kentucky. One could either float down the Ohio River or travel overland through the Cumberland Gap. River travel depended largely on flatboats and favorable currents. Travelers could lose all of their belongings if their flatboats sank and, of course, one was virtually defenseless against Indian attacks while on the river. Daniel Drake, who would later rise to prominence as a physician, moved to Kentucky as a small boy. He and his family came down the Ohio River by flatboat in a flotilla that included future Elkhorn leader John Gano and his family. The Drakes, Ganos, and their fellow travelers were fortunate. They survived the journey and landed at Limestone on June 10, 1788.[7]

Traveling overland was cheaper than making the trip by river, but it was no less perilous. William Hickman, who later served as pastor of Forks of Elkhorn Baptist Church, saw Kentucky as a land of opportunity and relocated from Virginia. He hoped to secure a comfortable future for his children, but it was a miserable transition that Hickman could not forget. It began in mid-August 1784. His pregnant wife did not want to leave Virginia. A horse kicked his son, Thomas, on the second day out and "laid him up several days." His other children were sick and unhappy throughout the trip. It rained for most of the eighty or so days they spent in transit and hostile Native Americans posed a serious threat along the way. Once in Kentucky, however, they began to feel some relief. As Hickman recalled, he and his family arrived at George Stokes Smith's cabin on November 9. Tired, dirty, and trail weary, they dried out and rested.[8]

Moving to Kentucky proved difficult but getting settled could be just as problematic, if not more so. John Taylor ultimately rose to prominence and considerable wealth among the state's earliest Baptists, but he faced tough conditions when he arrived in 1784. His first cabin measured sixteen by sixteen and had only a dirt floor. He had "no table, no bedstead, no stool," and he lived forty miles from the nearest mill.[9]

Kentucky's land may have been as beautiful and fertile as promised, but it did not yield crops on its own. In many cases the land needed to be cleared and even then, farmers were at the mercy of unpredictable weather. Upon securing land, Drake remembered his father planting a corn crop in the autumn of 1789 that "would have brought forth a sufficient abundance but that on the night of the last day of August there came so severe a frost as to kill the unripe corn, and almost break the hearts of those who had watched its growth from day to day in joyous anticipation."[10]

Even after settlement, Kentucky's first white pioneers faced threats from hostile Indians. As Daniel Drake recalled, those threats continued well into the 1790s. He noted, "I well remember that Indian wars, midnight butcheries, captivities, and horse stealing, were the daily topics of conversation. Volunteering to pursue marauding parties occasionally took place and sometimes men were drafted. This happened once to father. . . . He hired an unmarried man as a substitute and did not go. At that time, as at the present, there were many young men who delighted in war much more than work and, therefore preferred the tomahawk to the axe. I remember that when the substitute returned he had many wonderful tales to tell, but I am unable to rehearse a single one. . . ."[11] Likewise, the Wilderness Trail remained treacherous, especially in the winter months. One traveler, Moses Austin, noted that plodding into Kentucky through ice and snow created horrific images: "The situation of such can better be Imagined than described." He wondered what Kentucky might possibly offer "to make compensation for such accumulated Misery."[12]

Notwithstanding difficulties in uncertain weather, and the problems associated with frontier settlement, forward-thinking individuals saw such immense potential in Kentucky's land that they claimed acres by the thousands even though speculation was risky business. Under the right circumstances one could amass a fortune. The market, however, was as unstable as the weather and one could just as easily lose a fortune. As James Thomas

Flexner notes, "The laws dealing with land grants in the wilderness were self-contradictory, endlessly complicated, and subject to change without no-tice."[13] Even an experienced, well-connected surveyor/politician like George Washington understood the inherent peril in western land speculation. "No one," said Washington, "can lay off a foot of land and be sure of holding it."[14] Doubtless, the demand for western land created a number of problems re-gardless of where those lands might be, but the issues related to land acquisi-tion and retention in Kentucky were so problematic that one scholar describes the situation as a "Pandora's Box of evils."[15]

Any number of factors contributed to Kentucky's land difficulties. Begin-ning in the late 1740s two rival land companies, the Ohio Company and the Loyal Company, had received land grants totaling at least 1 million acres for settlement and, hopefully, trade with the east. Unfortunately, by the mid 1760s, the Ohio and Loyal Companies had neither developed their land nor developed trade with Native Americans. "After eighteen years of effort," observes Thomas Perkins Abernethy, "these rival companies were left without an acre of land that was legally theirs. In both cases their grants were made with certain conditions attached, and both had failed to meet terms."[16] Of course, the French and In-dian War had hampered western settlement as had the Proclamation of 1763 which halted land grants beyond the Appalachian Mountains. Free trade with Native Americans was permissible, but those settlers already in the land were to leave. A number of colonies, particularly Virginia, claimed that they were entitled to western land by virtue of their colonial charters. Whether the British wanted to protect settlers from hostile Native Americans or simply protect the lucrative fur trade for themselves is open to debate, but one thing is certain: Virginia was not about to give up its claim on western land, and the Common-wealth's Baptists maintained a close watch on the situation.[17]

As hostilities between England and the colonies increased, settlers contin-ued to defy the Crown and settle the trans-Appalachian region anyway. In 1768 the British government purchased land rights from the Iroquois thanks to the Treaty of Fort Stanwix. Sensing a significant opportunity, a number of investors and speculators formed the Grand Ohio Company in late 1769. Ini-tially, this group wanted to settle lands in the western reaches of Virginia and what would become eastern Kentucky. The British favored developing the land into a new colony, Vandalia. Virginia, however, claimed jurisdiction over the land and retaliated by renewing old land grants and encouraging western settlement until 1774.[18] Ultimately, Virginia rewrote its constitution in 1776 and claimed all lands from "sea to sea" as stipulated in its original charter.[19]

In the meantime, Richard Henderson dreamed of founding America's fourteenth colony. Born in Virginia in 1735, he was reared in North Carolina.

As a young man Henderson studied law and by 1768 he had become an associate justice of North Carolina's superior court, where he served until 1773. The following year Henderson formed the Louisa Company for the purpose of purchasing a tract of some 20 million acres of land bounded by the Ohio, Cumberland, and Kentucky Rivers. He negotiated with the Cherokee Nation for rights to the land in the fall of 1774, and in January 1775 he reorganized the Louisa Company and renamed it the Transylvania Company. He had begun advertising for settlers as early as December 1774, even though he would not finalize his negotiations with the Cherokees until the Treaty of Sycamore Shoals on March 17, 1775. With his negotiations concluded, Henderson quickly moved to create his colony with its capital at Boonesborough.

Upon affirming a minimal legal structure, the colony's proprietors sent James Hogg to the Continental Congress as their representative. Hogg's petition for official recognition of Transylvania as America's fourteenth colony failed to gain traction. As historian Daniel Blake Smith observes, "Trying to establish and legitimate Transylvania on the eve of the American Revolution was, to say the least, an exercise in bad timing."[20] Virginia claimed jurisdiction over Kentucky land and nullified the Treaty of Sycamore Shoals in November 1775. North Carolinians likewise objected to the treaty, seeing that it claimed jurisdiction over a significant portion of land that they claimed. The governor of North Carolina pronounced Henderson and his Transylvania group "an infamous Company of land pirates."[21]

Undaunted, the Transylvania Company petitioned Virginia for recognition in March 1776. Later that year, George Rogers Clark appeared before the Virginia legislature representing a different group of settlers from Harrodstown, later known as Harrodsburg. The Harrodstown faction knew they would lose their land to Henderson's Transylvania Company if Virginia recognized Transylvania's legitimacy. Clark called upon Virginia to assume control over western land and bring it under Virginia's dominion.[22]

No one could say what would happen next as curious souls filtered into Kentucky for a glimpse of this storied land. William Hickman numbered among the first Baptists to visit Kentucky. In his memoirs he recalled that he had heard of a place called Kentucky and determined to see it for himself. On February 23, 1776, he, along with George S. Smith, Edmund Wooldridge, William Davis, Thomas Wooldridge, and Jesse Low, struck out for the rumored western paradise. Three others joined them in "the back parts of Virginia."[23]

The small party made it to central Kentucky without serious incident. Upon reaching Crab Orchard, the explorers divided into two groups so they might visit the rival hamlets claiming territorial supremacy. One group went to Henderson's settlement in Boonesborough; Hickman's group went to

Clark's rival settlement in Harrodstown. Kentucky was beautiful beyond his imagination, though Harrodstown failed to make a positive impression. As Hickman recalled, it was a "poor town . . . a row or two of smoky cabins, dirty women, men with their britch clouts, greasy hunting shirts, leggings, and moccasins. I ate there some of the first corn raised in the country, but little of it, as they had a very poor way to make into meal."[24]

Despite the obvious difficulties of pioneer life, Hickman understood that setting up house on unimproved land was easier than nailing down one's claim to the land itself. Determining who held legal claim to western land during the Revolutionary Era was anyone's guess. Ultimately, Hickman concluded that apart from seeing the land for himself his tour of Kentucky did him little good. No one knew who held legal title to the land, much less how to obtain it or secure it once it had been claimed. As he began his long return trip back to Virginia on June 1, 1776, he wondered "whether Henderson's rights would stand good in law, or whether the cabin rights would stand."[25]

Hickman had good reason to wonder who would control the land. Clark's proposal won the day with support from Patrick Henry, and on December 1, 1776, Virginia created Kentucky County, thereby annulling the Treaty of Sycamore Shoals. In late November 1780, Kentucky County became Kentucky District with three counties, Jefferson, Lincoln, and Fayette, thanks largely to Thomas Jefferson's influence.[26] As for Richard Henderson, there would be no Transylvania Colony, but he salved his wounded spirit with the 200,000 acres on the Green River in western Kentucky that he received as part of the land settlement.[27]

With the prospect of a Transylvania colony no longer viable, Virginians faced a new set of problems with respect to land ownership. While the question remained the same—namely who owned the land, or more tangibly, who held the rights to divvying up the land—the anxious settlers now had to figure out who would have the best opportunity to claim and/or settle the land.

Virginia's claim to Kentucky neither secured clear title to the land nor opened the west to easy settlement. As Virginians vied for territorial advantage, yet another issue arose in the west when Spain refused to allow settlers to use the Mississippi River to ship their goods to New Orleans. This posed a serious problem. It was a long trip back to Virginia markets, and building a road through the mountains would have been an expensive, time-consuming proposition. Even if someone had been willing to construct such a road, the trip was so long that perishable goods could not make it to market. With Spain's refusal to allow free use of the Mississippi River, Kentuckians faced a serious threat to economic progress.

James Wilkinson and Spanish Intrigue

Once Virginia secured control over Kentucky, settlers like the Craigs and the "Travelling Church" began moving into Kentucky in significant numbers. Still, those moving west faced significant obstacles. Virginia may have claimed territorial sovereignty, but they were not prepared to provide militia to protect against Indian attacks. Neither were they in a position to build the economic infrastructure frontier folk needed to market their goods. Moreover Spain claimed most of the southland, including both banks of the Mississippi River, as its own, and they intended to keep it as a buffer between themselves and the American Confederation. It was a tenuous claim but given the fledgling nation's debt-ridden status after the Revolution, it was a claim that America could ill afford to contest militarily.

Virginia's failure to protect and develop the west left early Kentuckians in a bind. On one hand, they could petition for statehood knowing that building roads and creating trade networks would be a slow process. On the other hand, there may have been an assumption that Kentuckians would join the Union, but they were not obligated to do so. In fact, some claimed that westerners would be better off severing ties with Virginia and allying with Spain. Between roughly 1787 and 1791 James Wilkinson allegedly led what came to be known as the "Spanish Conspiracy," a plot to turn Kentucky over to the Spanish even as the Commonwealth pondered entering the federal union.

On its surface, the plan seemed plausible, and if anyone could have pulled it off it would have been Wilkinson. By all accounts, Wilkinson was as handsome and debonair as he was ruthless and self-serving. One writer describes him as "the most designing, plausible, treacherous, and amazingly successful scoundrel in American history."[28] Allegedly, the Spanish Conspiracy involved Wilkinson and some of Kentucky's most prominent citizens. Spain controlled the Mississippi River and refused to allow anyone to use either the river or the Port of New Orleans. Kentuckians needed the river to get their goods to New Orleans. As of the 1780s overland transportation of goods to eastern markets was out of the question, seeing that hostile Native Americans might attack along the way. Besides, the trip from Kentucky to Richmond, Virginia, would take two to three months. Without the right to navigate the Mississippi River and trade through the Port of New Orleans, America's western lands were tantalizing but of little value to settlers.[29] Those Baptists who had already filtered into Kentucky could only watch as subsequent events unfolded.

In 1786 Secretary of Foreign Affairs, John Jay, began negotiations with his Spanish counterpart, Diego de Gardoqui, to settle American issues with Spain. At one point, Jay expressed willingness to concede use of the

Mississippi River for twenty-five years. Wilkinson called for immediate separation from the eastern states, and in the following year he reached an agreement with Spanish governor of New Orleans, Esteban Miro, whereby Kentuckians could use the Mississippi River provided that Kentucky obtained its independence. As leader of an independent Kentucky, Wilkinson would then negotiate an alliance with Spain. Support for independence evaporated when Congress failed to ratify the Jay-Gardoqui Treaty.[30] Ultimately, the Spanish Conspiracy never amounted to a great threat to Kentucky or national interests.

When it was clear that his Spanish intrigues had come to naught, Wilkinson tried to make a go of it as one of the region's "Bluegrass barons." But as sometimes happened to self-appointed squires, Wilkinson lost a fortune. "Wilkinson invested too heavily in tobacco during the summers of 1790 and 1791," writes Patricia Watlington, "and his shipments to New Orleans were plagued with misfortune. One of his boats sprang a leak and sank; three ran aground in the Kentucky River and could not be sent down the Mississippi River with the others; and, of the 591,000 pounds he sent south in 1790, only 262,000 pounds passed the royal inspection."[31] His shipment for 1791 fared no better, and he faced financial ruin until George Nicholas and John Brown helped him secure a commission in the army as a lieutenant commander. Wilkinson left the area just a few months before Kentucky entered the Union as the fifteenth state. Harry Innes liquidated Wilkinson's remaining assets and managed to pay off his creditors, leaving Wilkinson to lament, "I am unfortunate and distressed but I have ever deserved the Character of a Man of honor."[32]

Honor, Evangelicalism, and Upward Mobility

Likely few of his peers agreed with James Wilkinson's self-assessment. Nonetheless, the fact that he saw himself as a "man of honor" is highly significant. First, Wilkinson's words suggest that he lived in a culture that recognized honor as a code of conduct for society. Second, if honor existed among early Kentuckians, and the Elkhorners had planted themselves in the middle of it all, how did the honor culture interact with evangelicalism and the Baptist expression thereof?

Easterners coveted Kentucky's rich, fertile land, but the trip overland was difficult and dangerous. The fact that pioneers traveled far and risked much to settle in a land of marked uncertainty suggests that something more than affordable land motivated settlers and speculators alike. "The Bluegrass lands were the best available within the confines of Virginia," Abernethy maintains, "and they were sought by strong and determined men."[33] The demand pushed prices to extremes, and "it was obvious that the Bluegrass country was never a poor man's frontier, despite the fact that Daniel Boone was its first famous citizen."[34] Most men came to Kentucky's Bluegrass Region because they either intended or hoped to become Bluegrass barons. It was no accident that the Elkhorn Baptists settled in a part of Kentucky that attracted wealthy, powerful men, and, radical frontier stereotypes aside, Elkhorn's Baptists wanted to advance their status, too.

Honor and evangelicalism in Kentucky might be regarded as mutually exclusive. Indeed, some scholars tend to see evangelicalism as feminine while honor supposedly epitomizes manliness. Early American religious census data indicates that evangelical religions claimed more female than male members. That is, women found comfort in the church while men opted for more masculine pursuits. In her study of Methodism Cynthia Lynn Lyerly claims that whereas Methodism's demand for holiness led to an "inner directed morality," honor concentrated on outward, "other-directed" behavior.[35] Moreover, an honor culture that values personal reputation and pride of social position over humility seems contrary to St. Paul's admonition for Christians to be Christ-like.[36]

While it may be true that certain elements of honor and evangelicalism clashed, there is reason to believe that the two cultures were frequently more complementary than competitive. In *A Sacred Mirror: Evangelicalism, Honor, and Identity in the Deep South, 1790–1860,* historian Robert Elder maintains that honor and evangelicalism tended to reinforce one another as citizens worked toward common goals.[37] Although his analysis focuses on South Carolina, similar conditions existed in Kentucky well before the 1820s. That is, Kentucky's seemingly boundless opportunities called for certain mediating influences that tempered materialism and liberty. This need afforded well-placed men of means like Baptist James Garrard an opportunity to lead the Commonwealth from frontier status to statehood. To be sure, Elkhorn had its share of "gentlemen" who interacted with their political peers as "gentlemen among gentlemen." The dynamic between honor and evangelicalism often blurred the distinctions between the two, and a number of Elkhorn Association ministers were comfortable in both realms.

Kentucky represented a new land and a new beginning. On the most basic level, Baptists came into the territory committed to recreate familiar communal forms in their churches and associations. Yet, balancing personal liberty with opportunity would be tricky. The question was not so much what kind of world they would create, but rather *how* they would create it. Baptists never constituted a numerical majority in Kentucky, but they were never "voiceless" in the Commonwealth's earliest days. James Garrard, a well-known Elkhorn

minister, would become Kentucky's second governor. A number of evangelicals played a role in framing the state's first constitution. Of course, they were
not uncontested. Early on Kentucky may have been known as much for its
freethinking population as its evangelicals. There was much at stake. Kentuckians of all persuasions had vested interests in securing the Commonwealth
toward their own ends. But no one can have all they want. Thus, the state's
disparate elements worked together to impose a measure of order on the frontier. In the Elkhorners, a nascent honor culture met an evangelical culture in a
decidedly Jeffersonian/republican context. As religious men, they would police
themselves according to well-established rules of church decorum. As men
who aspired to be more than farmers, they needed to interact with Kentucky's
planters and politicians to gain respect and approval. Only a few Elkhorn ministers had negotiated such pathways prior to the Revolution, and the Association would rely on them to represent their interests. It was clearly a hierarchical
arrangement, but one the Elkhorn Baptists willingly accepted.

The Elkhorn Association offers a lens by which one might see the synthesis
of two distinct cultures, namely, a ministry culture grounded exclusively in
the churches and an honor culture whose influence frequently overlapped the
spiritual and material realms. That is to say, honor primarily dealt with one's
personal conduct in the material world, but it was not limited to materialism. One's reputation frequently operated as a metaphysical value, determining one's moral standing in the community. Elkhorn's ministers practiced
a straightforward piety that confronted and demanded changes in societal
practices they deemed ungodly. The Elkhorn ministers exhibited honor
among themselves and they relied on their leaders to represent them before
the nonreligious. By wielding a kind of "holy honor," Elkhorn ministers exercised their faith and enhanced their reputations on the southern frontier.

Unfortunately, there is no rubric for assessing relative degrees of honor.
Southerners may have maintained some sort of honor code among themselves, but, as historian Edward Ayers observes, they never bothered to define
precisely what it meant. "In large part," writes Ayers, "this was because the
meaning of honor depended on its immediate context, on who claimed and
who acknowledged it."[38] Hence, honor exhibited a certain fluidity that did
not confine its influence to worldly matters. One could summon an implied
honor code if the situation called for it. Seeing honor in this way helps explain
why Elkhorn's ministers conducted themselves in the ways they did.

Nonetheless, a careful examination of the Elkhorners' hybridized honor
culture reveals several things. First, honor was not interracial. That is, honor
did not flow from the white community to the black community in a peer-
to-peer sense. Black men might share honor among themselves, but whites

did not extend honor to African Americans. Second, honor was a male-only domain, seeing that women possessed virtue, not honor. Third, honor typically applied to social equals, even though white men of all ranks could see themselves as honorable. In sum, "Honor thrives in a rural society of face-to-face contact, of a limited number of relationships, of one system of values. Honor depends upon a hierarchical society, where one is defined by who is above or below him."[39] Ayers' description of honor resonates with the Elkhorn Association's earliest history as well as the state's earliest history.

Many of Kentucky's early Baptist immigrants embodied the outlook of yeoman farmers. They wanted to be land-owning, self-sufficient farmers, "citizen Christians," so to speak. Some wanted to be more. The Elkhorn Association reinforced both of these concepts. The Bluegrass Region's early settlers hoped to reap some tangible benefit from their labors but opportunities for land and wealth, coupled with significant social and cultural changes, forced certain modifications to their early vision for life and ministry. The Association's stalwarts soon discovered that religion and economic opportunity did not always make congenial bedfellows. Synthesizing the two would tax their spiritual resourcefulness in ways they might never have anticipated.

The Move Toward Statehood and Article IX

Once the Spanish Conspiracy had been laid to rest, Kentuckians still faced a host of issues bearing on land and government. Absentee ownership and land speculation remained serious issues. In the Commonwealth's earliest days, one scholar estimates, "one quarter of the entire state was claimed by twenty-one extensive speculators."[40] Worse, others blamed inexperienced land speculators and inept surveyors for conflicting, "shingled" land claims.

Born in Fauquier County, Virginia, in 1760, Humphrey Marshall had served as an officer in the Revolutionary War thus earning him 4,000 acres of Kentucky land. He moved to Fayette County after the war where he became deputy surveyor. Upon the formation of Woodford County, he became the county's primary surveyor and amassed a fortune in land that ultimately totaled some 400,000 acres. Marshall may have been Kentucky's most outspoken Federalist and according to one writer he was so antireligious that his family burned his papers after his death out of embarrassment.[41]

Marshall's Federalism and his antireligious sentiments put him at odds with Elkhorn Baptists who made no secret of their Jeffersonianism or their religious zeal. Perhaps that is why Marshall singled them out as objects of his special wrath in his 1824 *History of Kentucky*. Well-connected landowners whose claims were more secure than others tended to blame poor surveys for the confusion over territorial land claims. Marshall complained, "As in 1780, so now, the public attention was turned to the acquisition of land, by locating treasury warrants: And now, as then, the business was very much engrossed by the hunters. These were generally illiterate, and ignorant of what the law required to constitute a good location. They nevertheless proceeded to make entries, urged upon by their employers, with all the avidity of men, fearful of loss, and intent on gain. Hence, they strewed the locations over the face of the country, as autumn distributes its falling leaves; heedless of those which had previously fallen; and almost as destitute of intelligent design, as they were ignorant of the legal consequences."[42]

Challenging a claim based on a survey was apparently not difficult. Kentucky surveyors followed the Virginia system of surveying land which meant they followed natural topographic features like watercourses and large trees. Unscrupulous surveyors might add watercourses that did not exist. Inexperienced surveyors might not be as specific as they should in describing plots of land. Poor surveys almost always guaranteed faulty claims.[43]

Entering a clear claim also posed certain challenges. Humphrey Marshall singled out Lewis Craig for sloppiness and inattention to detail: "Lewis Craig enters five hundred acres of land upon a treasury warrant, adjoining his former entry on the north side, and running along northwardly with Christian's and Todd's line for quantity."[44] Clearly annoyed, Marshall notes that Craig offers no referent watercourse, and even though Craig and his kin claimed numerous tracts of land in Kentucky, in this case there is no way to know precisely which tract of land Craig had claimed. "Again: it does not appear what former entry of Craig's is meant," intoned Marshall, "neither is it certain what line of Christian and Todd, is intended; or who, among many of the name, they are; or what line of theirs is to be followed—or where it is to be found—or if one be found, whether it be the same called for by Craig, or not."[45] In another example, Marshall blamed George Smith for recording the kind of imprecise claim that caused confusion:

> The same day, 'George Smith enters five hundred acres of land
> on a treasury warrant, lying on the north side of Kentucky, a
> mile below a creek, beginning about twenty poles below a lick,
> running down the river, westerly, and north-westwardly; for
> quantity.'
>   It is obvious that the locative calls in this entry are all
> vague and uncertain to a subsequent locator. The north side of
> Kentucky comprehended the whole of the county of Fayette,
> and more than one-third of the whole country. The next call

is a mile below a creek—but which, of the five hundred creeks on the north side of the Kentucky, does not appear, either by name or description. And finally—it is to begin about twenty poles below a lick: But what lick? or where? are questions all important to the locator of the adjoining land, but which are left unanswered, and unanswerable, by any thing in Mr. Smith's entry. It is presumable that the person who made Smith's location knew the place which he intended to include, but certainly those holding unlocated warrants were not bound to find him; nor could his verbal explanation, if seen, aid an entry which the law required should be in writing. The holder of a warrant, which he desired to locate, with a copy of Mr. Smith's entry in his hand, could not know how to adjoin it, nor yet how to avoid an interference: he would however proceed to make his entry, and possibly, with a similar degree of vagueness. When they came to be surveyed, very probably, and to the very great surprise of both owners, the two interfered.[46]

In the end, such "vague entries" were responsible for a general state of unhappiness, endless litigation, and keeping "neighbours at variance."[47]

Kentucky land claims were so tenuous that some individuals bought their own land more than once simply to avoid conflict with "attorneys and agents of absentee landlords, or by swindlers with defective titles. . . ."[48] Anxious landowners wanted every advantage possible if they were called upon to defend their claims in court and they took extreme measure to protect themselves. One scholar claims, "Many Kentucky owners permitted their taxes to become delinquent and paid the penalties in order to obtain tax titles for the purpose of strengthening their own claims against which there were adverse interests."[49]

As Kentuckians struggled to establish and certify title to their land, they faced yet another challenge. Citizens of the future Commonwealth needed to draft and ratify a constitution before they could enter the Union. In all, there had been nine previous conventions called to discuss Kentucky's status, but the tenth convention was set for the spring of 1792. In the proceedings that followed, one sees the intersection of honor and evangelical impulses. One also sees that it was nearly impossible to separate land issues from slavery.

In 1791 Kentucky was well on its way to becoming a state. In crafting the state's first constitution, delegates would be forced to consider slavery. On August 27, 1791, the Elkhorn Association Minutes indicate that forty-two messengers from thirteen churches appointed a committee consisting of James

Garrard, Augustin Eastin, and Ambrose Dudley to draft a memorial to the constitutional convention "requesting them to take up the subject of religious liberty and perpetual slavery in the constitution of this district and that they make a report to this association at the Great Crossing the 8th of next month. . . ."[50] The minutes for the September meeting indicate that the memorial was read and approved. The association met again in December but this time reversed itself: "Resolved that this association disapproves of the memorial which the last Association sent to the convention on the subject of Religious liberty and the abolition of slavery."[51]

The Elkhorn Association Minutes do not specify what transpired between September and December. They do not include the memorial's text, nor do they explain why the association rejected the memorial in its December meeting. It seems likely that a majority of Kentucky's settlers sought land, including the Baptists of the Elkhorn Association's churches. Many either brought slaves with them or expected to purchase them on-site. In the end, Kentucky's state constitution would allow for slavery and the Baptists would never speak against it with a unified voice.

Two features of Elkhorn's actions in late 1791 frequently go unnoticed. At first glance, these Baptists appeared to have shied away from the political arena, opting to remain detached from state affairs. A closer examination suggests other possibilities. By linking religious liberty and slavery, the Elkhorn Association voiced their two most pressing concerns, namely, the pursuit of wealth and freedom of worship without state interference. By 1791, however, it is highly unlikely that religious liberty for Kentuckians was ever in serious doubt. A closer look at the association's messenger list reveals a shift in the group's composition. Prior to the early 1790s ordained ministers comprised a majority at associational meetings. As early as 1788, nonordained messengers began outnumbering ordained ministers at associational meetings. These "ministering brethren" represented a diverse lot. They ranged from wealthy and powerful men like Thomas Lewis to more middling sorts. As Kentucky inched closer to statehood, powerful laymen came to have greater say in associational affairs.[52]

The August 27 resolution doubtless precipitated informal conversations that identified three broad factions in the association. On one hand, a number of influential Elkhorn Baptists already owned slaves and many others had no objections to the "peculiar institution," perhaps because they wanted to purchase slaves themselves. They moved to Kentucky seeking economic gain for themselves and their families and as long as slavery was legal, they intended to capitalize on it. On the other hand, some Elkhorn Baptists favored emancipation of all slaves. They did not want to see slavery advance west of the Appalachian Mountains and they prayed slavery would soon die out. Finally, a third group found themselves caught in the middle between the other parties with varying degrees of sympathy for either side. Garrard, Eastin, and Dudley occupied a prime position to hear "public opinion" as they prepared the association's memorial. [53]

It appears that powerful, landed individuals banded together to protect their property, including their slaves. Elkhorners had good reason to be optimistic about religious liberty. Thomas Jefferson and James Madison favored it. They had defeated the General Assessment Bill and Jefferson was especially proud of Virginia's Statute for Religious Liberty. Despite favorable circumstances, Elkhorners had no guarantee that Kentucky would follow suit. Consequently, they may have backed away from overt political pressure to a more passive kind of politics. That is, they let the constitutional convention run its course with a good idea of where it was going. They all wanted religious freedom, and even though some Elkhorn ministers favored emancipation in some form, a significant number favored slavery. Their "passive politics" amounted to friendly cooperation with a political system from which they wanted to distance themselves. If religious liberty really was a "sacred cause" it could assume a variety of forms, as the Elkhorn Association would discover.[54]

Powerful forces swiftly quashed emancipation impulses. Settlers were pouring into Kentucky, especially from Virginia, and many brought their slaves with them. According to the state's census records Kentucky claimed 76,677 inhabitants in 1790, 12,430 of whom were slaves and those numbers were increasing. By 1800 those numbers had ballooned to 220,955, of whom 40,343 were slaves.[55] Additionally, Kentucky did not have a clear road to statehood in 1790. Some feared a "Spanish Conspiracy" that would move the entire territory under Spain's dominion. A more pressing matter concerned land claims for squatters, and what constituted a "clear" claim to land remained open for dispute. According to historian Robert Ireland, "The first constitutional convention represented the best opportunity before the Civil War for Kentucky's antislavery advocates to abolish the 'peculiar institution,' seven emancipationist Protestant ministers having been elected delegates to the convocation."[56] It is possible that the Elkhorn Association abandoned their memorial because they knew they could not win, for the majority of Kentucky slave owners, Baptist or otherwise, were not about to surrender their property without a fight.[57]

This foray into politics demonstrates that Elkhorn's Baptists were neither averse to nor completely beyond the process. There were forty-five delegates to the constitutional convention, seven of whom were ministers, three were Baptists (one of whom was James Garrard) with emancipationist sentiments. Of the constitution's sundry provisions slavery may have presented the most difficulties. It had existed from the Commonwealth's earliest days with especially heavy concentrations of slaves in the Bluegrass Region. By one account, 22.8 percent of white households owned slaves in 1792.[58] Abolitionists were scarce in early Kentucky; most antislavery advocates favored gradual emancipation.[59]

Kentucky's best-known Presbyterian, David Rice, emerged as the convention's leading emancipationist. Originally from Virginia, "Father Rice," as he was popularly known, first visited Kentucky in 1783. His preaching made a lasting impression on a number of individuals and they pleaded with him to relocate to Kentucky permanently. He returned in late 1783 and quickly established himself as one of Kentucky's leading ministers and intellectuals.[60]

Rice maintained that slavery was inconsistent with justice and good policy and he explained his position in great detail to his fellow conventioneers. He defined a slave as "a human creature made by law the property of another human creature, and reduced by mere power to an absolute unconditional subjugation to his will." Rice believed that all are equal before God and therefore enslaving someone against their will amounted to thievery, because the one who kept another in bondage profited from another's labor. Worse, they deprived enslaved people of their rightful standing before God, leaving them "a free moral agent legally deprived of free agency."[61]

As for good policy, Rice argued that slavery was bad for blacks and whites alike. Slavery forced a significant portion of the population to obey laws they had not written under a government to which they really owed no allegiance. It amounted to a state of "perpetual war with the avowed purpose of never making peace." But if slavery bred discontent in the slave quarters, it led to laziness and indolence among upper class whites who lived off of slave labor. "Young gentlemen," he intoned, "who ought to be the honour and support of the state, when they have in prospect an independent fortune consisting in land and slaves, which they can easily devolve on a faithful overseer or steward, become the most useless and insignificant members of society."[62] Either way, a republic could only survive if its people maintained their virtue.

In summary, David Rice saw numerous problems with slavery. He believed a pronounced gap existed between the post-Revolutionary rhetoric of freedom and the reality of slavery. It amounted to hypocrisy, and who could trust a hypocrite? It was time to right a serious wrong and keeping slavery out of Kentucky was a step in the right direction. Otherwise, Rice foresaw great problems. Almost prophetically he warned, "The slavery of Negroes began in antiquity; a curse has attended it, and a curse will follow it. National vices will be punished with national calamities. Let us avoid these vices, that we may avoid the punishment they deserve; and endeavor to so act, as to secure the approbation and smiles of heaven."[63] Honorable men needed to lead the way in eliminating slavery and he called upon his fellows to take measures to eliminate it in Kentucky. Elkhorn's emancipationists could heartily agree.

Proslavery forces found their champion in George Nicholas. A Virginian by birth, he studied law as a young man and served as an officer in the American Revolution. Nicholas came to Kentucky in 1788, but not before he had served both as a member of Virginia's legislature and the convention that ratified the Constitution of the United States.[64] He was a seasoned politician, but Nicholas's physical stature did not match his professional ability. One writer described him as "low" in stature, "ungainly, and deformed with fat. His head was bald, his nose was curved; a grey eye glanced from beneath his shaggy brows; and his voice, though strong and clear, was without modulation."[65] A contemporary caricature depicted him as a "plum pudding with legs."[66] But he more than compensated for whatever he lacked in physical stature with his legal shrewdness, his experience in Virginia politics, and his friendship with leading figures like James Madison. His political acumen virtually assured him a leading role in framing Kentucky's first constitution.

The Tenth Convention produced a document largely based on the Pennsylvania state constitution, regarded as one of the most radically liberal constitutions of its day. But when it came to property rights, Nicholas referred to the Virginia law and maintained that property could not be taken without compensation. Individual property rights had been guaranteed in Virginia's cession of its western lands, and since slaves were legally considered property, no emancipation could occur without compensation to slave owners. Upon this point, he would not budge. Of course, with no money available for compensation, there could be no constitutionally mandated emancipation. Individuals could liberate their slaves, but they would receive no compensation. As Nicholas saw it, emancipation posed a host of problems, while maintaining that continuing the "peculiar institution" would serve the Commonwealth's best economic interests.[67] As subsequent events would demonstrate, the majority of Baptists in the Elkhorn Association agreed.[68]

Notwithstanding individual property rights, Nicholas made a telling point with respect to Kentucky's economic interests. Immediately to the south, Tennesseans were also discussing their future. North Carolina ceded its western lands on December 22, 1789, and from the outset, it was clear that Tennessee would be a slave state.[69] Upon ceding their western land claims, North Carolinians listed ten provisions designed to protect property rights and provide sufficient lands for its military reserve. North Carolinians called for the region to be governed according to the same terms as the Northwest Ordinance with one notable exception, namely, "that Congress should pass no regulations to emancipate slaves."[70]

By the late 1780s and early 1790s, certain North Carolinians began reenslaving freed people of color. A study of Perquimans County notes that a number of the county's Quakers freed their slaves only to find whites eager to reenslave them.[71] The freed slaves were "taken up" for allegedly being freed illegally. Some feared that a significant number of freed slaves might inspire other slaves to revolt. Consequently, some were "taken up" for fear that they "intended to disturb the peace."[72] In the end, one scholar concludes, "In the last quarter of the eighteenth century, these Quakers chose an inopportune historical moment to free their slaves. And because they refused either to acknowledge or to follow a legally defined process for manumitting their slaves, it is likely that they ended up doing more to entrench slavery in North Carolina than to advance awareness among North Carolinians of the inherent evils of slavery."[73] Kentucky's religious leaders, both at the convention and outside it, observed such actions as they tried to craft both a new government and a new way of life.

George Nicholas understood that slavery defined Kentucky's constitutional proceedings. The Northwest Territory's millions of acres were free by legal definition. But Kentucky was poised to be the first "western" state to enter the Union. By April 1792 the Tenth Convention had produced a draft of Kentucky's first state constitution, and while it is difficult to say with certainty that Kentuckians kept abreast of North Carolina's and Tennessee's political machinations, this much is clear: Kentucky would be the first "western" state admitted to the Union where slavery's fate had not already been determined by the Northwest Ordinance of 1787. Emancipating slaves by constitutional fiat in 1792 would have slowed the plantation-style economic development that had prompted western migration. Kentucky was in a position to establish a precedent on slavery; Tennessee would soon follow Kentucky into the Union as a slave state.

Of the constitution's various provisions, Article IX legalized slavery. The convention actually voted on a motion to eliminate Article IX altogether, but the motion lost 16 to 26 thanks largely to Nicholas's influence. The ministers present all voted to eliminate it.[74]

> The legislature shall have no power to pass laws for the emancipation of slaves without the consent of their owners, or without paying their owners previous to such emancipation a full equivalent in money for the slaves so emancipated. They shall have no power to prevent immigrants to this state from bringing with them such persons as are deemed slaves by the laws of any one of the United States, so long as any person of the same age of description shall be continued in Slavery by the laws of this

state. That they shall pass laws to permit the owners of slaves to emancipate them, saving the rights of creditors and preventing them from becoming a charge to the County in which they reside. They shall have full power to prevent slaves being brought into this state as merchandize. They shall have full power to prevent any slaves being brought into this state from a foreign country and to prevent those from being brought into this state, who have been since the first day of January one thousand, seven hundred and eighty-nine, or may hereafter be imported into any of the United States from a foreign country. And they shall have full power to pass such laws as may be necessary to oblige the owners of slaves to treat them with humanity to provide for them necessary clothing and provision to abstain from all injuries to them extending to life or limb, and in case of their neglect or refusal to comply with the directions of such laws, to have such slave or slaves sold for the benefit of their owner or owners.[75]

There were other features of the constitution, but none proved as contentious as slavery and its place in Kentucky's immediate future. Balancing republican idealism and democracy with property right was a tall order and the final product amounted to a compromise. As one scholar put it, "Thus, the constitution was an *accommodative* document, one that mediated between democratic and aristocratic demands."[76] And by balancing slavery with guaranteeing religious freedom, the document also represented a compromise for religious leaders as well. It was precisely where the majority of Elkhorn's Baptists wanted to be.

Overall, George Nicholas was relatively pleased with Kentucky's constitution, and he said as much to James Madison in a letter dated 2 May 1792. He took great pains to explain his take on Article IX. Personally, he saw no problem with slavery, and he never hid the fact that his interests rested firmly with landed property owners. Moreover, his own sense of honor demanded that he look out for the interests of his class. Beyond that, Nicholas believed that Kentucky simply *had* to enter the Union as a slave state. Otherwise, he mused, they could never attract "valuable emigrants" from other southern states. Ultimately, he believed that no one could really object to importing slaves into Kentucky according to Article IX's terms. Such action "will not add one to the number of slaves in the world; the only difference being that they will be slaves in Kentucky instead of Virgia. or Maryland."[77]

George Nicholas went one step further and actually blamed emancipationists for Article IX's inclusion in the constitution. Perhaps it was the sort of post-Revolutionary idealism that stressed equality among all men. Perhaps it represented guilt or a religious impulse that extolled freedom. Either way, emancipationists made no secret of their desire to see slaves freed, but their enthusiasm may have cost them. After the constitution was completed, Nicholas feared that some would be especially critical of Article IX and its sundry stipulations on slavery. "The clause respecting slaves will," he intoned, "I expect bring on us the severe animadversions of our N. brethren."[78] But he fumed that the article would probably not even be in the constitution if emancipationists "had not been so clamorous on that subject." As Nicholas saw it, their stridency in public debate and private conversations forced the convention's delegates to choose between emancipation and protecting property rights.[79]

If emancipationists had indeed forced the issue, they had also demonstrated how divided early Kentuckians were on slavery in 1792. Before Article IX became part of the constitution, the committee took a vote to eliminate the article, but the motion lost 16 to 26. Had six people changed their vote, Kentucky's first constitution would not have defined slavery by property laws and emancipation may have passed as a constitutional amendment at a later point. Significantly, each of the minister-delegates voted to remove Article IX from the constitution, and assuming that each delegate's vote reflected their constituency's sentiments, a significant minority of Kentuckians favored emancipation.[80]

In the end, Article IX was not a total defeat for emancipationists. True, it promoted slavery. As Ireland put it, "Article IX represented a powerful endorsement of slavery, which would not be diminished until rendered invalid by the Thirteenth Amendment of the federal constitution."[81] Even so, the emancipationists won two significant concessions from proslavery forces. First, masters who wanted to emancipate their slaves without compensation could do so without recrimination. Second and even more significant, emancipationists secured a constitutional provision protecting slaves from mistreatment, a feature that dovetailed with honor and the "proper" treatment of slaves.

Eden's Reality Behind the Rhetoric

Prior to 1792 and even beyond that for a time, the political, economic, and moral culture of Kentucky was in flux. That is, no one knew precisely how Kentuckians would choose to govern themselves. Some among the common folk held the aristocracy in contempt; lawyers, too, were sometimes objects of special derision. Among the upper classes, some believed that common farmers were not equipped to run the affairs of state. But as one writer succinctly put it, "Agriculture did not ordinarily bring classes into conflict even where slavery existed, but land speculation and insecure land titles did."[82] Insecurity, land issues, and the politics bearing on each kept Kentuckians—of a religious bent or not—on edge until well into the nineteenth century.

How much land was divvied up, sold, resold, stolen, or re-stolen is impossible to say. The amount may not even matter. "As Lord Macaulay pointed out," observed one historian, "it is unimportant where Hannibal crossed the Alps or whether Mary of Scotland blew up Darnley. The inquiry may amuse us but the decision leaves us no wiser. It is of no moment, then, just how many acres various individuals and companies acquired or tried to acquire during the exploitation of public lands. But it does matter that usually the most successful speculators and traders were those who betrayed public trust and used official position to bilk the people. It matters that the specters of Vandalia and Indiana and Ohio could never be banished from the halls of council."[83]

As men of faith, the ministers of the Elkhorn Association should have occupied a strong position from which to confront the greed and the lust for power that seemed to permeate early Kentucky, but as historian Everett Dick observes, "the steady flow of American settlers to the West was not primarily the result of political oppression; it was rather an economic response to the call of opportunity."[84] The Elkhorn faithful likely recognized that economic opportunity could not be separated from the emerging reality that would become Kentucky politics. There can be no doubt that they wanted space to exercise influence in framing their world. Over time, however, they proved to be at best reluctant activists and reformers, if they became such at all.

Lewis Craig surely overstated the matter when he described heaven as "a mere Kentucky of a place." Visions of heaven and the reality of Kentucky differed greatly. No earthly pattern existed for balancing issues like individual rights, religious freedom, and economic prosperity in a post-Revolutionary era. There were many paths to becoming a baron of the Bluegrass and some of them were less honorable than others. Pretension, greed, avarice, and a host of other vices exposed spiritual fault lines among early Kentuckians, and Baptists were not above them.

3

Good Old Virginia Doctrine

Ministers and Ministry
in the Elkhorn Association

Toward the end of his life William Hickman reflected upon leaving Virginia and moving his family to Kentucky. The early days proved especially difficult. He recollected the hardships they encountered as they moved west. He remembered the joy of meeting up with John Stokes Smith once they were in Kentucky. He vividly recalled that a number of people gathered informally at Smith's cabin for worship. There were at least three other ministers present, including a Methodist preacher, a Mr. Swope. This informal meeting served as an opportunity for Hickman to meet others who had preceded him to Kentucky. It may also have reminded him that he and his family needed to find a church to join. He knew there was a church at Gilberts Creek, but he was new to Kentucky and he was in no hurry to join. The Hickmans stayed with the Smith family while they adjusted to life in the Commonwealth.[1]

After an unspecified number of days, Hickman recalled a meeting at "brother Robertson's." Even though he wrote forty-four years after the fact, Hickman reminisced about the event in some detail. He recalled the sermon's text, "Christ is all and in all" (Colossians 3:11), and perhaps more significantly, Hickman remembered that fellow minister and relocated Virginian, William Bledsoe, was present and that John Taylor, a well-known minister and friend from Virginia, preached the sermon. The scene reminded him of the home he had left behind, and over forty years later he savored the memory. "I fed on the food," he said. "It was like the good old Virginia doctrine."[2]

The Hickman family traveled to Kentucky with a large group of settlers, most of whom were Virginians, and doubtless the group heard preaching along the way. But, as Hickman listened to John Taylor preach at Bro. Robertson's, he experienced something beyond merely hearing a sermon. William Hickman rejoiced to be reunited with friends in a worship form that had been absent on the trail, and if he felt a sense of mutual respect and affinity for his fellow ministers, he was not alone. As others moved to Kentucky, they, too, would seek fellowship with like-minded believers who had relocated before them. Many shared a style, or common framework, for life and ministry, and they tried to replicate that framework in the Elkhorn Association.

Association as Community

The early Baptists who formed the Elkhorn Association sought to recreate familiar patterns of religious life and ministry through particular kinds of communities. Historian Thomas Bender defines a community as "a social network characterized by a distinctive kind of human interaction."[3] The Elkhorn Association consisted of a network of independent churches that held similar doctrinal beliefs and worked toward common goals, ranging from survival and economic viability to more spiritual pursuits. A church's "distinctive kind of human interaction" might include meeting regularly to hear preaching, bring fellowship and encouragement to one another, conduct church business, hear disputes, and maintain discipline among the faithful.[4]

Baptist associations represented a type of community that was different from their individual churches. And while Bender's definition of community is a good starting point, two questions remain; namely, why did the Elkhorn Association conduct its affairs the way or ways that it did, and to what end? In *The Genesis of Christian Doctrine: A Study in the Foundation of Doctrinal Criticism* historical theologian Alistair McGrath distinguished between doctrine and theology. "Doctrine," he maintains, "entails a sense of commitment to a community, and a sense of obligation to speak on its behalf, where the corporate mind of the community exercises a restraint over the individual's perception of truth. Doctrine is an activity, a process of transmission of the collective wisdom of a community, rather than a passive set of deliverances. The views of theologians are doctrinally significant, in so far as they have won acceptance within the community."[5] He further contends that doctrine may be "provisionally defined as communally authoritative teachings regarded as essential to the identity of the Christian community," and that distinguishing between doctrine and theology "serves to emphasize the social function associated with the former, yet denied to the latter. Doctrine identifies social communities."[6]

According to McGrath, doctrine rests on four foundational theses. First, doctrine provides social demarcation in that communities define themselves in contrast both to other religious groups and the world. Second, doctrine is generated by and subsequently interprets the Christian narrative. Third, doctrine interprets experience. Fourth, doctrine makes truth claims. Given these four theses, McGrath concludes that doctrine is "not a static representation, but an invitation to the dynamic transformation of the human situation. It is this recognition of the power of doctrine to effect what it signifies—to convert *homo peccator* to *homo iustus*—that underlies its significance."[7]

Since a Baptist association amounted to a church network, associational meetings allowed like-minded ministers and concerned laymen to meet and discuss issues pertaining to the churches.[8] That is, associations met to uphold and sustain their doctrine. The most cursory reading of associational minutes demonstrates that meetings provided forums for discussing issues ranging from theology and church life to current affairs and politics. Baptist polity did not allow for associations to exercise control over their constituent churches, but they did conduct a certain amount of business relating to the churches comprising the association. Even though associational decisions, pronouncements, and opinions were not binding on churches, they carried considerable weight. One went against the association's collective wisdom at the risk of rebuke or disfellowship.

Associations governed themselves by common consensus, especially in church matters and to a lesser extent in social and political matters. An association represented a "community of communities" that reflected common goals and beliefs. As such, associations helped shape religious life on at least three fronts. First, they helped oversee the general health of its churches. As historian Robert B. Semple explained it, associations served as "mediums" for gospel advancement. "When assembled," Semple said, "their chief employment was preaching, exhortation, singing and conversing about various exertions in the Redeemer's service and the attendant success. These things so inflamed the hearts of the ministers that they would leave the Association with a zeal and courage which no obstacles could impede."[9] But associations tended to emphasize church-related issues rather than address specific issues bearing on individual ministers. For instance, they could refuse to seat a minister or church messengers at an associational meeting, thereby depriving him and his church of a voice in associational matters. Conversely, a church might decline to send messengers to the association if they found themselves in serious disagreement with the body.

Second, associations conducted business related to ministry and maintaining the theological integrity of affiliated churches. If a theological issue (e.g., Unitarianism) arose at a meeting, the association might communicate pertinent information to the churches in a circular letter. Baptist associations commonly shared information with other like-minded associations by exchanging annual letters or reports on the general life and health of affiliated congregations. Such information might be communicated to other associations by traveling representatives chosen at the association's annual meeting.

Such interassociational fellowship provided mutual encouragement and offered resources for associations who requested it.

Finally, even though associations were voluntary communities with no coercive ecclesiastical power, they maintained a structure that recognized ministerial giftedness and legitimized lines of authority among regular associational
participants. Stated simply, some ministers possessed more *gravitas* than others
and thereby commanded more respect from their peers. In its earliest days, the
Elkhorn Association included many ministers who had fought in the American Revolution and they were respected for their service. Some like Lewis
and Elijah Craig had been persecuted for preaching the gospel and they, too,
received honor for their commitment to the gospel. Some had an education, or
had more education than others. David Barrow was unique among Elkhorn's
early ministers in that he had been well educated, he had fought in the American Revolution, and he had been persecuted for his preaching. The association's more popular ministers, or those otherwise recognized for their pulpit
skills, usually preached at associational meetings. The more literate ministers
usually produced the association's circular letter, a written document designed
to encourage churches or inform them of issues they faced. Over time young
ministers might gain respect and stature in the association by consistency in
caring for their flocks or by faithfully participating in associational life. By the
same token, more established ministers might lose stature by becoming slack
in their duties or engaging in activities the association did not sanction.

This approach to interchurch business relied on a certain amount of deference and fostered a "ministry culture" that resonated with honor culture.
Associations created their own ministerial "pecking order" by conferring status on ministers who had "proven" themselves. The lines of authority in such
a system were informal but clear, and ministers knew their respective place.
Everyone had a voice, but some voices carried more weight than others. That
is, honor among ministers at the associational level mirrored honor culture
in the broader society and therefore allowed for interaction between the two.
The voices that spoke most eloquently at the associational level usually spoke
eloquently beyond the association as well.

Conducting ministry within accepted parameters created common issues
for Baptist associations in the late eighteenth and early nineteenth centuries.
The real problems came as churches and associations adjusted to broader cultural shifts. America's religious culture was changing even before the American
Revolution, but with the promise of religious liberty previously marginalized
groups like Baptists stood to reap great benefits in a place like Kentucky.[10] No
Baptist in the Elkhorn Association would face the persecution that some had
experienced in Virginia. On the other hand, each of Elkhorn's faithful faced the

challenge of striking a balance between maintaining a Christian witness and capitalizing on the unprecedented opportunities that had lured them westward.

The "Philadelphia Way"

Once in Kentucky, the so-called "Travelling Church" spawned other congregations. On June 25, 1785, representatives from four churches formed the Elkhorn Association. The Philadelphia Baptist Association (PBA) set the tone for associational life among America's late-colonial and Early National Baptists, especially those who espoused a Calvinistic theology. Elkhorn's founders styled their association after the PBA. Those who convened Elkhorn's organizational meeting considered whether or not they would strictly abide by the Philadelphia Confession of Faith. The answer: "It is agreed that the said recited confession of faith be strictly adhered to."[11]

The Philadelphia Association became especially prominent among America's early associations. Organized in 1707 by five churches in or near Philadelphia, this association introduced a measure of stability and organization among certain of America's Baptists and, before long, it had extended its influence along the eastern seaboard. Once organized, the fledgling association chose the Second London Confession as their theological standard, thereby identifying themselves as Calvinistic Particular Baptists. In addition to its emphasis on God's sovereignty over human affairs, the Second London Confession's twenty-sixth chapter, "Of the Church," articulated a nuanced ecclesiology, or doctrine of the church. In fifteen subpoints, the confession defined the church and sketched out church life on a host of issues ranging from officers to interchurch relationships.[12]

The confession's first article, "Of the Holy Scriptures," subpoint 6, stipulated that the Bible recorded everything humanity needed to know about God's glory, salvation, and holy living. But while the Bible was an all-sufficient guide to faith and practice, subpoint 6 also noted, "Nevertheless, we acknowledge the inward illumination of the Spirit of God, to be necessary for the saving understanding of such things as are revealed in the Word, *and that there are some circumstances concerning the worship of god, and government of the Church common to humane actions and societies; which are to be ordered by the light of nature, and Christian prudence according to the general rules of the Word*, which are always to be observed."[13] The Second London Confession allowed for a degree of latitude in certain aspects of worship and church government. So, on one hand, PBA Baptists recognized a degree of freedom between churches and associations in conducting their business. On the other hand, they knew that differing understandings of how to apply Scripture to specific situations left room for disagreement and disorder. All agreed that the Bible addressed spiritual and temporal issues, but with certain circumstances left to "the light of nature and Christian prudence," the association continually faced calls for clarification.

In 1742, the Philadelphia Association modified the Second London Confession to include statements affirming the imposition of hands and hymn singing.[14] Individuals who believed that God had set them apart for ministry were expected to frame their theological convictions according to the confession. One year later, Benjamin Griffith penned *A Short Treatise Concerning a True and Orderly Gospel Church* which immediately became the association's official polity statement.[15]

Griffith's *Short Treatise* differed from earlier understandings of church polity in a couple of noteworthy respects. First, Griffith admonished churches seeking pastors to look first in their own fellowship.[16] If they could find no suitable pastor in their own ranks, they could seek help from other congregations. If they had a potential minister who was not ready for the task, Griffith urged, "let such as they have, if they have any that seem hopeful, to be awhile upon trial; and the Lord shall choose, will flourish in some good measure with Aaron's rod among the rods of the tribes."[17] In any event, Griffith encouraged churches not to set unrealistic expectations for either their preaching skills or conduct.

In addition to its advice on where to search for ministers, Griffith's *Short Treatise* also contained an article on ruling elders. Some Baptists dismissed ruling elders as an apostolic office but Griffith included them among officers needed for orderly churches. By definition, "Ruling Elders are such persons as are endued with gifts to assist the pastor or teacher in the government of the church. . . ."[18] Griffith recognized both teaching and ruling as pastoral duties, "but in case he [the pastor] be unable; or the work of ruling too great for him, God hath provided such for his assistance, and they are called ruling elders."[19] Griffith further stipulated that ruling elders served in administrative capacities only, unless they were gifted to be teachers. In the event that a ruling elder was found to be a capable teacher, Griffith recommended ordination, with the understanding that such ordination was unto "a distinct office from the former, which was only to rule well, and not to labor in the word and doctrine."[20] For Baptists, establishing ministerial standards and determining who might preach raised issues that became especially pronounced toward the end of the eighteenth century. The Elkhorn Baptists encountered the same kinds of issues as soon as they reached Kentucky.

Griffith concluded his *Short Treatise* with a detailed section titled, "Of the Communion of the Churches," in which he detailed the terms of intrachurch fellowship. At the associational level, he noted that all churches were "equal in power and dignity, and we read of no disparity between them, or subordination among them." Griffith also said that churches may exercise close fellowship but "the officers of one particular church, may not act as officers in another church, in any act of government, without a particular call thereunto from the other church where they occasionally come."[21]

As for associations such as Philadelphia or Elkhorn, Griffith's *Short Treatise* suggests that churches had a collective responsibility toward one another in maintaining gospel order. While churches were independent and autonomous, Griffith argued that a general fellowship benefited all concerned. Associations facilitated such fellowship and were available for counsel should a church need advice. However, Griffith stipulated, "such delegates thus assembled, are not intrusted or armed with any coercive power, or any superior jurisdiction over the churches concerned, so as to impose their determinations on them or their officers, under the penalty of excommunication, or the like."[22]

Conducting church life became increasingly difficult throughout the eighteenth century, and particularly so by the time of Elkhorn's founding. Notwithstanding the PBA's endorsement, Griffith's take on church polity did not supply the final word on associational authority. In 1744 one Simon Butler petitioned the PBA for help in settling an unspecified dispute in the Montgomery church. The minutes for the following year indicate that the association's four-man deputation had indeed settled the earlier dispute, but not to Butler's satisfaction. Later, in 1746, the association answered five queries on a variety of issues ranging from who could preach lawfully to who could receive communion. Once again, the association's answers irked certain constituent churches. The PBA's 1747 circular letter noted, "As to the sneers and reflections cast by some on our answers to questions sent us last year, we leave the authors to delight themselves in the product of their admiring fancies, seeing no cause to alter our apprehension, being persuaded that it is the duty of the churches to call and prove their candidates for the ministry, whom we judge ought to wait with self denying meekness, humbleness, and lowliness of mind to a further approbation from the churches of their ordination and investiture Into the sacred functions, and not, urge or hasten it themselves, contrary to the mind and judgment of the church which gave them a call to exercise their gifts."[23]

By 1748 it was obvious that the association needed to stake the limits of its own authority. In 1749 Griffith produced an essay that clarified his earlier writing. He noted that while associations did not have extensive power, they bore a collective responsibility for maintaining theological integrity and church stability. To that end, churches formed associations based on mutual cooperation for the good of all. He clarified his earlier assertion that associations had no coercive power by stipulating that churches could not exclude other churches from the association. The association could, however, "disown and withdraw from a defective or disorderly church, and advise the churches related to them to withdraw from, and to discountenance such as aforesaid, without exceeding the bounds of their power."[24]

Griffith's *Short Treatise* and his follow-up essay on the limits of associational authority raise a number of important issues. These writings along with the PBA's minutes suggest that churches struggled to secure competent ministers. Churches without pastors naturally wanted capable ministers who would model Christianity for the flock. The PBA's churches agreed that gospel order mandated that churches have ministers. Moreover, empty pulpits exposed churches to sham preachers.

The association may have been still smarting from the Piscataway Church's tawdry dealings with Henry Loveall even as Griffith wrote *Short Treatise*. About 1729 the church ordained Loveall to the ministry despite the association's suggestion not to rush the ordination. Unfortunately, within a year the church learned that Henry Loveall was actually Desolate Baker, a syphilitic bigamist.[25] To make matters worse, the church had bypassed associational ministers and ordained Loveall with assistance from Paul Palmer, a theologically Arminian Baptist minister visiting from South Carolina.[26] Ultimately, the Piscataway Church found a more reliable minister, but their experience with Henry Loveall served as a pointed reminder that the association's advice, while not binding, represented collective wisdom and experience. One ignored such advice at their peril.

Beyond the difficulty of finding suitable preachers, Griffith's inclusion of ruling elders as a valid office for his contemporaries suggests that administration of local churches was becoming increasingly difficult. Existing sources do not specify if ministers had too many people to visit or if church members lived too far apart. Ministers may have been simply struggling to eke out a meager living. Regardless, by 1743 ruling elders had become an accepted way of insuring pastoral assistance beyond the deaconate for some Baptist churches.

Griffith's phrasing may also shed light on mid-eighteenth-century church life. His admonition for churches not to be too picky in selecting their preachers hints at changing perceptions of ministers and rising expectations from congregations. Historian E. Brooks Holifield has observed that the eighteenth century witnessed a transition in popular perception of ministerial roles, thanks in part to the Great Awakening, changing concepts of sin, and the degree to which ministers comforted the afflicted.[27] As mid-century revivals spread, Baptist numbers increased markedly, and gradually they gained a measure of grudging acceptance in society. Fresh converts led to new churches and as the number of churches increased, so did the number of Baptist associations. As their numbers increased throughout the colonies, Baptists faced new challenges in maintaining local church independence while drawing the boundary lines of associational authority.[28]

When Elkhorn organized in 1785, associations had long been a standard feature of Baptist life. Those modeled after the Philadelphia Association claimed a theology detailed in the Philadelphia Confession of Faith by way of Second London. Ministers served churches with appropriate aid from non-ordained congregants when needed, and the churches looked to the association for general guidance and fellowship. Obviously, ministers shouldered great responsibility, and seasoned ministers exercised great caution in recognizing their fellows.

Ministers and Ministry

The ministry included more than preaching once or twice per month. Ministers in any Baptist association were also responsible for their personal conduct, for preaching and teaching proper theology, and maintaining a certain amount of order both in their churches and across the association. Ideally, ordination represented one way whereby ministers guarded churches from theological uncertainty and bad moral character.

Individual churches within associations like Elkhorn usually assumed responsibility for ordaining their ministers. Consequently, there was no predetermined pattern for determining an individual's qualifications for ministry. In 1774 Morgan Edwards offered one possible ordination scenario in *The Customs of Primitive Churches*, a work that focused on church decorum and polity. Edwards listed fifty-four particular aspects of polity and included extensive footnotes. Articles 6 through 11 discussed the ministerial office in careful detail. Generally, ministers were responsible for "every sacred thing that is of official nature: nevertheless where there are ruling elders etc. his office is, chiefly, to convene the church; pray; read the Scripture; preach, break bread; dismiss and bless the people; govern, in conjunction with the ruling elders; take into the church; bind or retain sin; admonish; cast out of the church; loose or remit sin; lay on hands; baptize; visit; give good example; anoint the sick; bury the dead; perform marriages; catechize; bless infants; defend the faith; assist at associations, and other public meetings; &c."[29] With such an extensive list of responsibilities, little wonder that seasoned ministers urged churches to be cautious in ordination.

Edwards maintained that becoming a minister rested primarily with God performing three operations. First, God impressed upon an individual's mind an internal sense of divine urgency that Edwards labeled the "inward call." Second, God provided the individual with ability to teach, preach, and lead congregations. But, an individual's "call" to ministry was subjective, and potential ministers were expected to prove themselves worthy of the office. Thus, it was necessary for a church to confirm a minister's sense of calling, which they did by listening to them preach and teach and by observing their character over time to insure they exhibited moral integrity. Finally, upon establishing their ability and character, ministers needed an "outward call," or a church inviting them to take charge of the congregation under God's leadership.[30]

Determining who qualified as a "proper" minister ultimately rested with one's church. Once a church deemed individuals capable of ministry, they were usually ordained to the gospel ministry. Ideally, several ministers formed an "ordination council." Whereas a church with multiple ministers could rely exclusively on their own preachers to form the council, ministers from sister congregations might also be invited to participate. Once formed, the council asked the candidate a host of questions ranging from a recitation of their conversion experience to explaining specific aspects of the Christian faith. The council might also ask the candidate to describe their "call" to the ministry, that is, how they concluded they were divinely suited to the ministry.

In Elkhorn and elsewhere, there was no single ceremony for ordaining Baptist ministers once they passed muster with their council. Some ceremonies could be elaborate and formal. For example, when Samuel Jones received ordination to the ministry on January 2, 1763, Morgan Edwards, Samuel Stilman, and Isaac Eaton, three of the most respected ministers in the Philadelphia Association formed the ordination council. The services began with prayer and a song, followed by an ordination sermon prepared specifically for the occasion by one Morgan Edwards. When Edwards finished his sermon, Stilman briefly interrogated Jones on issues ranging from his calling to the ministry to his affirmation of the Philadelphia Confession of Faith. After Jones answered the interrogator's questions to everyone's satisfaction, the council laid their hands on Jones. Eaton then charged Jones to be diligent to fulfill his ministry and to serve faithfully.[31]

While it is true that the form varied from ordination to ordination, Edwards's sermon doubtless reflected sentiments held by nearly all Baptist ministers at the time, including frontier Baptists like the Elkhorners. Preaching from Romans 11:13, "I will magnify my office, or ministry," Edwards exhorted Jones to magnify his own ministry by conducting himself in a manner worthy of his calling. After detailing proper ministerial comportment, Edwards challenged Jones to study, because without adequate preparation he would remain "an Ignoramus in his profession . . . [performing] his ministry in a little circle, ending at the point where he began, and beginning again where he ended. . . ."[32] The ministry involved single-minded dedication, and Edwards wanted Jones to understand that there were no shortcuts to success.

Ordinations in rural areas tended to be less formal, but they were no less rigorous. Once James Ireland determined to seek ordination as a Separate Baptist, he set out for North Carolina. The Sandy Creek Association, a Separate Baptist association, planned to meet with a number of Baptists from the Carolinas and Virginia to see if they might agree on terms of union that would unite their various groups. Ireland traveled with a group of Baptist ministers and quickly learned that ordination entailed more than answering theological questions before an ordination presbytery. As they made their way south, Ireland's compatriots allowed him to "exercise his gift" by calling on him to preach, usually without preparation. Older, more seasoned ministers deferred to Ireland for explanation of difficult points of doctrine, just to see how he would respond.[33]

By the time they reached Sandy Creek, Ireland had convinced everyone that he was fit for baptism and ordination. Likely, both would have proceeded smoothly but associational business occupied more time than anyone anticipated. Ireland returned to Virginia where he at last received baptism and ordination to the ministry under the watchful eye of fellow Virginian, Samuel Harris. He remarked, "Next morning I had taken leave of that church, and I obtained my credentials, signed by eleven ministers in order to go forward as an itinerant preacher without any hesitation until further occasion."[34]

Elkhorn stalwart John Taylor experienced a similar path to ordination. Taylor was about twenty-two when he sought ordination. He had already established himself as a capable preacher when he and his pastor, Joseph Redding, approached a gathering of ministers at the Shenandoah Church with a request from Lunies Creek Church for Taylor's ordination. He had been licensed to preach for about four years and he estimated that he had traveled about eight thousand miles to meet his preaching appointments. "The design of my ordination, was in the Itenerant way," he recalled, "and to administer ordinances where the Churches were destitute of a Pastor, and called for my service."[35]

The ministers meeting at Shenandoah agreed to ordain Taylor. His council consisted of Lewis Craig, Joseph Redding, John Picket, John Cunes, and Theodoric Noel, men well-acquainted with Taylor and his ministry. After a brief examination, the ordination continued as everyone knelt and Craig, Redding, Picket, Cunes, and Noel placed their right hands on his head. Taylor recalled that "two or three of them prayed, [and] Lewis Craig, I think, gave me a pertinent charge, while holding me by the right hand, with the right hand of fellowship, from them and all the brethren present; with me it was an awful solemn time." The ceremony concluded when "young Mr. Noel though an older man than myself, wrote the credentials they were pleased to give me."[36] Once ordained, Taylor assumed his place among other ordained preachers in a quest to preach Christ and build churches.

Comparing the ordinations of Samuel Jones, James Ireland, and John Taylor is suggestive on several levels. First, ordination reflected a measure of acceptance among one's fellow ministers. Jones had earned the respect of ministers in Philadelphia. Ireland proved his mettle on a long and ultimately unsuccessful trip to North Carolina. Yet, he received baptism and proper ministerial credentials upon returning to Virginia. Taylor logged several thousand miles as a preacher before receiving ordination as a minister. All three had "proven themselves" in the presence of other ministers. Second, ordination amounted to a public recognition by other recognized ministers that Jones, Ireland, and Taylor had demonstrated their ministerial aptitude both publicly and privately. All three demonstrated their commitment to ministry goals and objectives. All three demonstrated biblical knowledge and the ability to preach effectively. Consequently, ordination legitimized them before others. Ordination meant that Jones, Ireland, and Taylor had been recognized by a select peer group and were bona fide ministers in every respect. Other would-be ministers followed a similar path. Before receiving ordination, they verbalized their call to vocational service, demonstrated their ability to strike a balance between orthodoxy and orthopraxy, and had been evaluated by others.

White ministers maintained an especially watchful eye on religion among slaves, and prospective black ministers received close scrutiny. In April 1790, the Bryan Station church near Lexington, Kentucky, considered "Brother Boswell's Simon," a slave who claimed to be called to preach. Apparently, Simon had been holding informal religious gatherings with other slaves, and while it is not clear who raised the issue, Simon's unsanctioned preaching had caught someone's eye. The church considered the matter and "concluded to Stop him from holding Publick meetings."[37] The church did not specify why he could no longer hold public meetings, but the decision clearly upset Simon and he made the mistake of complaining to his master. At a church meeting on May 15, 1790, the Bryan Station Church's minutes indicate that Bro. George Boswell brought a charge against Simon "for Speaking reproachfully of this Church, and dispiseing the Government and Authority thereof. . . ." Simon confessed his guilt, but when he could not convince the church of his sorrow, they excluded him from their fellowship.[38]

Not all black ministers ran afoul of the honor code. Unlike Simon, the church approved of "Bro. Sam's" work, and in September 1791 allowed him to "appoint meetings" and to exercise his gift of exhortation under church supervision. Yet, in the same meeting the congregation considered another, more troubling matter. John Rogers's "James" was a member of Bryan Station Church who had been convening irregular meetings. James had also been officiating marriage ceremonies for slaves.[39] The reasons are unspecified, but the Bryan Station Church took no immediate action against James. The church may have been conducting its own investigation into the matter. More likely, the entire association faced the same quandary; namely, what to do about slave marriages. As property, slaves could not marry; but as human beings, they desired the comfort of marriage and family. The Elkhorn Association wrestled with the issue, and James appeared before the Bryan Station Church in July 1792. He confessed that he had held "disorderly" meetings and "agreed to sissest [desist]." The church accepted his confession and "acquitted" him apparently without further sanction.[40]

Notwithstanding their similarities, one important distinction marked the ordinations of white ministers. Both Ireland and Taylor identified themselves as itinerants. In Elkhorn's earliest days most of their ministers saw themselves as itinerants of some sort. Itinerancy in principle—though never a reality for slave preachers—allowed for great freedom of movement and flexibility, especially as settlers flooded the Commonwealth. While the itinerancy system created the circumstances for a modicum of stability for frontier churches, it also set the stage for serious internal conflict.

In the late-eighteenth century, churches usually met once per month, leaving ministers free to serve more than one congregation at a time. Many ministers took advantage of this opportunity. Usually, under-shepherds who tended more than one flock maintained a "primary allegiance" to one congregation over the others. Consider Ambrose Dudley and the Bryan Station Church. Organized in 1786, Bryan Station had a membership scattered over such an expansive territory that they decided to build another worship site at David's Fork, near Winchester, Kentucky. The congregation alternated worshipping between these two sites with Elder Dudley serving as pastor in both locations. The church prospered under Dudley's leadership, and in 1801 Bryan Station Church organized David's Fork into a separate congregation. Dudley remained pastor of both congregations until 1806, when Bryan Station Church wanted to begin meeting twice per month. They asked David's Fork to consider changing their meeting time to accommodate their new schedule, but when David's Fork refused to change, Dudley resigned to serve Bryan Station exclusively.[41]

While membership in Elkhorn's constituent churches may have been scattered over a wide swath of central Kentucky, itinerancy did not always stem from a shortage of preachers. Some churches claimed several ordained ministers as members who were not serving as pastors. This could present a number of challenges, especially when it came to important decisions. For instance, Clear Creek Church near Versailles was organized in 1785. Lewis Craig preached at the church for about a year before the church began searching for a regular pastor. According to John Taylor, Clear Creek's membership roll included four ordained ministers, but to Taylor's thinking, "all of us did not make one Lewis Craig." Taylor feared the church would divide into factions, seeing that each minister had friends who held them in special esteem. To his astonishment, the church chose Taylor as their pastor. One person voted against him, claiming that his coat was "too fine," but they changed their vote after some friendly persuasion from Craig.[42]

Clear Creek apparently enjoyed a season of growth with Taylor at the helm, but their prosperity was short-lived. After about a year, the church faced controversy from settlers who were pouring into Kentucky. As Taylor explained it, "[W]e began with ruling elders, according to *the Virginia custom,* and Griffith's plan in the confession of faith; those men were useful among us. The emigrants from distant parts, *brought their former customs with them,* so that factions began in the Church. We were now about a hundred and fifty in number, and the more the worse, in case of confusion."[43]

In the meantime, James Dupuy had joined the Clear Creek Church, bringing the number of minister-members to five. With that many ministers, who served as the primary leader? Taylor maintained that congregational leadership could—indeed, should—be shared between any number of leaders. However, some within the church believed the church ought to have a singular leader, and with five ordained ministers in the congregation, the fault lines appeared clearly drawn. Ultimately, two ministers left to form a new congregation, but even that did not quiet the discontent. Taylor found himself in the middle of the controversy, with everyone claiming him for their side. Taylor stepped down as pastor after about three years of service at Clear Creek, a move that stunned the entire congregation. After assuring them that he only wanted what he believed to be best for them, the congregation rallied around their three remaining ministers, James Rucker, Richard Cave, and Taylor, with each sharing pastoral responsibilities as equals.[44]

Griffith's supplemental essay on associational authority clarified what associations could and could not do, but it did not answer all questions bearing on Baptist polity. Ordination offered a measure of assurance that potential ministers had been properly vetted, but beyond that, many questions remained as

PBA churches sought clarity on procedure. For instance, between 1707 and 1807, the association heard at least 105 queries from its churches—15 of them between 1744 and 1749, and 65 between 1750 and 1807.[45] Obviously, Griffith's *Short Treatise* left many practical questions bearing on Christian ministry open for different approaches.

Beyond Sunday preaching, ministers were called up for advice, aid, and comfort. There was no single, specified method for accomplishing pastoral responsibilities and expectations, for ministers varied from congregation to congregation. Ironically, John Taylor hit upon a successful approach to tending the flock at Clear Creek only after he "stepped down" as pastor. As the congregation warmed to his leadership, he noticed that the church seemed more confident that he had their best interests in mind. With Clear Creek's situation stabilized, Taylor developed a simple plan to visit each home in his community. Richard Cave, James Rucker, and Taylor each lived near a ruling elder in the church. Each of the ministers would team up with the elder that lived closest to them "so that we were six men, making three couple, a preacher and elder, to go one after another to visit; each couple to go through the whole neighborhood." Of course, Taylor could not force his fellow ministers to follow his plan, but he was so determined to visit his neighbors that he would go by himself if necessary. His fears proved ungrounded. Taylor's plan met with unanimous approval, everyone in the neighborhood received a ministerial visit, and Clear Creek Church enjoyed a season of revival.[46]

With so many open questions, Baptists in America consulted a variety of sources to answer their polity questions. While Morgan Edwards's *Customs of the Primitive Churches* offers a measure of insight into eighteenth-century Baptist church life, the PBA never affirmed it as their official standard.[47] While the association did not deny the work's possible benefit, they wanted all concerned to know that they had neither commissioned it nor officially affirmed it. Thus, churches usually turned to their association for guidance.

Ministers, Ministry, and the "Elkhorn Way"

Baptists were well positioned to reap the windfall of religious liberty. They maintained a unique ecclesiology that allowed for a flexible church polity. They believed churches were independent and autonomous. As such, churches of like faith and order could form associations for the well-being of member churches. Associations like Philadelphia and Elkhorn maintained a theological consensus based on a common confession of faith.[48] Group consensus determined specific interpretation and application of the confession. Churches participated in associations voluntarily. Such flexibility should have served

Baptists well, especially those pushing westward. However, independence and the tantalizing opportunities for wealth and advancement the frontier offered only accentuated earlier difficulties.

The social, cultural, and political upheaval of the Revolutionary Era did nothing to bolster the Philadelphia Association's already strained polity consensus. As early as 1783 the PBA began hearing calls for something to supplement or replace Griffith's *Short Treatise*. After considering several options, the association appointed Samuel Jones to revise the existing discipline, a task he completed in 1797. The new polity echoed much of what had been said earlier, especially with respect to brotherly love. However, Jones introduced new material under the headings, "Of Settling a Minister Over a Church," and "Of Dissolving the Connection between a Pastor and His Church." Of course, churches were free to choose their own ministers, but Jones likened the relationship between a minister and his church to a marriage. If the association wanted its affiliate churches to maintain gospel order, they needed long-term ministers shepherding the flocks, a point Jones made with great care.[49]

Unfortunately, not all ministers stayed in their churches for the long haul. Some left for better prospects. Others espoused doctrines Baptists deemed heretical, while some faced issues that could not be resolved through regular channels. By the mid-1790s the issue warranted its own treatment in the new discipline. Jones reiterated that ideally, churches and pastors maintained a binding relationship. However, should a minister's situation become untenable it really did not matter who shouldered the blame. It was best for ministers to leave their church once their position as minister had been compromised. In the event of a separation, Jones noted that a council of surrounding churches should be called to insure an amicable separation. If the church could not dismiss their pastor with a positive recommendation, Jones maintained the council should list the differences between the pastor and church and give their judgment for the sake of the minister's next pastorate.[50]

Finally, Jones concluded his *Discipline* with a thoughtful statement on associational life. Among other things, he maintained that delegates or messengers from cooperating churches met in association "to gain acquaintance with, and knowledge of one another—to preserve uniformity in faith and practice (Phil. 3:16)—to detect and discountenance heresies—to curb licentiousness in the wanton abuse of church power—to afford assistance and advice in all difficult cases—to contribute pecuniary aid when necessary—to make appointments of supplies for destitute churches—And every way advance and secure the interest of religion, and strengthen and draw closer the bonds of union and fellowship." He quickly added, "The delegates thus assembled are, properly speaking only an advisory council. They are not armed with coercive power, to compel the churches to submit to their decisions, nor have they any controul over the acts or doings of the churches."[51] Of course, the association maintained the right to withdraw fellowship from churches they deemed irregular. The Elkhorn Association styled itself on the Philadelphia Association, and while it may not have copied it in every respect, a considerable portion of the "Philadelphia Way" became the "Elkhorn Way."

Post-Revolutionary America witnessed profound changes in religious expectations that cut two ways. With religious liberty on the horizon and unprecedented opportunity in the West, millions of acres lay primed for settlement. But such opportunity came at a price. In the late-seventeenth and early-eighteenth centuries, religious life in North America, and in Kentucky as well, rested on a relatively fixed social order. Ministers and their congregants lived in a close reciprocal relationship where ministers tended their flocks, who, in turn, followed Christ under the minister's leadership. Members were accountable to one another for living holy lives.[52] That was about to change as America lurched toward a market-oriented economy.

Settling Kentucky demanded resourcefulness, and building churches in areas that had never seen or heard Christian preaching would prove especially daunting. The Baptists of the Elkhorn Association rose to the challenge by relying on familiar forms at the church and associational levels. The rapid increase in frontier churches coupled with economic and social mobility presented challenges in defining a minister's role in Kentucky's earliest days. They were under greater pressure than ever to guard the ministry, provide order, and apply biblical teaching to daily life. Ironically, the same associational structure that furnished stability and order also revealed flaws in the association's leaders.

Kentucky's early Baptists needed leadership that everyone knew and trusted if they hoped to preserve theological integrity and church vitality. Baptist associations relied on informal power structures that allowed for certain men to emerge as first among equals. Such leadership status and credibility stemmed from several sources. For instance, some ministers commanded respect based on their service during the American Revolution. Nearly everyone affiliated with Elkhorn in its earliest days boasted a patriot connection of some type, but some were more noteworthy than others. Some had established themselves as military leaders during the Revolutionary War. Other ministers distinguished themselves by ministerial giftedness, education, or plain common sense. Well-educated ministers were in short supply on the Kentucky frontier, especially those who tended their flocks well and promoted associational harmony. Early Elkhorn ministers were especially mindful of their brethren who had been persecuted for the faith. They respected "ministerial courage." Thus, with the right combination of piety, patriotism, and personal ability, a minister could go far.

Religious life might have been unsettled on the frontier, but some things did not change. Even on the frontier, Baptist church members were expected to maintain circumspect lives. Theodrick Boulware grew up in the Forks of Elkhorn Church under William Hickman's preaching. In his memoirs Boulware recalled that churches guarded their membership carefully. "Candidates for membership," he recalled, "had to comply with New Testament requisitions, Matt. 3:8, 'Bring forth therefore fruits meet for repentance.' 1 Pet. 3:15, 'Be ready always to give an answer of the reason for the hope within you.' Without this experimental and practical recommendation, candidates were advised to wait and examine themselves."[53] Ministers functioned as watchful undershepherds, and church disciplinary records demonstrate that flocks maintained a watchful eye over each other.

The relationship between eighteenth-century ministers and their congregations had begun to change even before settlers pushed west. Benjamin Griffith's polity had not addressed the amicable separation of pastors and churches, much less forced termination. Ideally, pastors would serve their congregation for a lifetime, much like a marriage. Jones' *Discipline*, however, suggests that by 1800 a more fluid relationship had developed between pastors and churches that belied the lifelong-marriage metaphor. Stated simply, churches could oust their pastors and pastors could voluntarily leave their congregations so long as everything was done in peace.[54] The Elkhorn Association experienced the collision of church expectations and frontier opportunity in three episodes involving John Gano, slavery, and Elijah Craig.

With the prospect of social and economic mobility, capable ministers had options to assume prominent pulpits or relocate to areas where growth seemed certain. Such was the case with John Gano. Unfortunately, Gano emerged from the Revolution in debt. Consequently, he moved to Kentucky in 1787 at the behest of a certain William Wood who enticed him to the frontier with the prospect of "useful" ministry in Kentucky's new churches. Equally tantalizing, Wood hinted that Gano's move might prove lucrative. "For these reasons," Gano recalled, "I concluded to move. Besides, I was considerably in debt, and saw no way of being released, but by selling my house and lot. This I concluded would clear me, and enable me to purchase waggons and horses to carry me to Kentucky."[55] His decision stunned the New York congregation. Notwithstanding their pleading and their offer to raise his salary if he would stay, Gano was resolved to leave. As he recalled, "I told them, if they had desired me to stay before I had put it out of my own power, I should have given it up."[56]

William Wood was right. Capable ministers *could* position themselves to reap the benefits of America's emerging "religious market" in various ways. Once in Kentucky, John Gano's stature as a well-established, credible minister created many opportunities for "usefulness." For instance, the Minutes for the Elkhorn Association indicate that by 1788 Gano had assumed the pastorate of the Town Fork Church, a congregation strategically located between Lexington and Frankfort. The Elkhorn Minutes also indicate that the association capitalized on his leadership skills immediately. The association chose him as their moderator in 1788 and he preached the associational message the next year. Prior to his death in 1804, Gano served as association moderator five times, he preached to the association four times, he drafted or assisted in drafting two circular letters, and he served on at least three committees.[57]

Education marked another way by which ministers might distinguish themselves. The PBA became increasingly interested in ministerial education throughout the eighteenth century. Some of the association's earliest ministers received their training in British institutions, but few options existed for Americans who could not relocate abroad.[58] Some received training informally at the hands of ministers. Others went to American institutions like Hopewell Academy. Things changed in 1764 with the charter of Rhode Island College. Under James Manning's leadership, the college quickly became the flagship Baptist college in America and the Philadelphia Association funneled many of its aspiring ministers there to receive ministerial and theological training.[59]

Securing an education could be difficult on Kentucky's frontier. Theodrick Boulware was approached by unnamed persons to teach in a school. He "cheerfully consented" largely because he saw teaching as an opportunity for his "own improvement." After a brief stint teaching, Boulware's health weakened and he left the school. But once he recovered, he "went thirty miles to a grammar school, taught by Elder John Price in his own house." Price fine-tuned Boulware's education and encouraged him to enter the ministry. Ultimately, Boulware resumed teaching in his former school and placed himself under the tutelage of three "pious men," spending "one evening in each week with one or another of these men, in reading and instructive conversation."[60]

John Gano established a kind of school dedicated exclusively to church-related matters about the time of Kentucky's frontier revivals. Boulware referred to it as a "'Religious Polemical Society,' in which were investigated doctrine, experience, practice, discipline, ordinances, qualifications and duty of a church to her minister, &c., &c." Although Boulware does not specify where the society convened, he says that interested parties met "semi monthly" for two years, and in his estimation Gano led the society well. Participants increased in "Bible knowledge, oneness of sentiments, and qualifications to transact business in the church with neatness and dispatch."[61]

David Barrow maintained a school for children. Barrow knew that education would provide opportunities for his students. Literacy would open many doors by providing a degree of uplift—uplift which, in turn, would prepare them to function in society. There were many such schools in early Kentucky with varying degrees of formality.[62] Barrow began his school on Lulbegrud Creek in January 1801. Rates were reasonable and somewhat negotiable. From the school's inception, it seems clear that Barrow intended to teach more than the three Rs. He listed nineteen rules for his students, at least five of which addressed personal conduct:

> 4th. The pupils are to be kind and civil to each other, and by no Means to call one another out of their Proper names.
>
> 5th. In school Time, each one is to keep his or her Seat, without necessary Reasons or Orders require the contrary. [T]wo are not to be absent at one Time, without Leave obtained or Orders given; nor even one, without he or she bears the Token of Absence.
>
> 8th. When the Scholars, whether in or out of School, have an Occasion to speak to or of the Master, it shall be with the Title of Mr. Barrow, and in like Manner to or of all married Persons and grown unmarried ones. Master & Miss, with only their g[i]ven Names, and when in Conversation with all such, the Terms Sir & Madam are to be used.
>
> 11th. Quarreling, Swearing, or Cursing, Lieing, using Obscene Conversation, giving one another the Lie, and Fighting, will demerit the severest Kind of Punishment.
>
> 14th. If after all necessary Means have been made use of, and there should be any Scholar that cannot be broken of Quarreling, Swearing, Cursing, &c, he shall with advise of a Majority of the trustees be expelled [from] School.[63]

Barrow's rules suggest that he believed a good environment was conducive to good education. It also suggests that he expected his "Scholars" to conduct themselves with proper decorum at all times. His school would be a training ground for learning educational fundamentals, as well as "proper" social and cultural skills. His tenth rule stipulated that running, jumping, prison-base, and cat, were acceptable games during "Diversion Time," but wrestling, climbing, and other activities that might destroy one's clothes were not. Females students were expected to "exercise inosent Diversion to themselves."[64] It was not uncommon for ministers to maintain elementary schools or academies.

Elijah Craig's name could also be added to the list of Elkhorn ministers who maintained a school. Unfortunately, the name "Craig" tended to spark a mixed reaction among the association's faithful. Lewis Craig and his brother, Elijah, were among the first Baptists to settle in Kentucky. Lewis had been instrumental in organizing the Elkhorn Association while Elijah looked on. Back in Virginia both men had been known as staunch gospel preachers who were willing to suffer persecution for their faith. Equally significant, Joseph and Elijah Craig demonstrated consistently good business sense. Supremely confident, opinionated, and occasionally quick-tempered, Elijah Craig frequently irked his brethren as he became embroiled in one squabble after another.

One Craig controversy began at the same August 1791 associational meeting that formed a committee to petition the state constitutional convention to prohibit slavery. The trouble focused on Great Crossing Baptist Church (GCBC), the church's pastor Elijah Craig, and Joseph Redding, another influential Elkhorn preacher. Redding had moved to Kentucky from South Carolina and quickly established himself as one of the association's most sought-after speakers. Details are a bit fuzzy, but contention arose in the church soon after Redding arrived. Perhaps GCBC's membership believed Elijah Craig spent too much time minding business matters and too little time tending his flock. Redding possessed good people skills and may have tried to supply the congregation with the attention they did not receive from Craig. Ultimately, a majority wanted Redding to be their pastor. The ensuing conflict led to Elijah Craig's excommunication from his own church![65]

In assessing the situation, the association found plenty of blame to go around but agreed with the church's decision to exclude Craig from its fellowship. Not surprisingly, the church called Joseph Redding as pastor in 1793, a position he held until 1810.[66] Meanwhile, Craig made amends for his misconduct and the church restored him to fellowship, but in September 1795 Craig left GCBC and organized McConnell's Run Baptist Church (MRBC) with thirty-five GCBC members. He fired a parting shot not long after, when he published a booklet denouncing "settled," that is, salaried ministers.

Elijah Craig's booklet, *A Few Remarks on the Errors That Are Maintained in the Christian Churches of the Present Day; and Also, On the Movements of Divine Providence Respecting Them*, denounced salaried ministers as a bane to churches. Craig began his screed by affirming his commitment to a kind of Jeffersonianism that he gleaned from an unnamed minister whose memory he revered. This same minister taught Craig not to receive money for preaching, and God blessed his church with many members. "The treatment I met with under the old government, and men in some degree of a similar disposition not in power, rivetted in me the firm disposition of a republican, in things civil and religious, which has remained invariable, and has kept my eyes open in some degree to both the liberties of the church and state. . . ."[67] For Craig, Baptist ministry as he and his fellow Elkhorn itinerants initially practiced it reflected a nearly ideal form of republicanism and biblical fidelity.

Unfortunately, Craig saw a number of problems developing among Elkhorn's ministers, problems that threatened the association's harmony. He believed that Baptist ministry rested upon two central tenets. First, ministers should be one with their flocks. While one's calling and ordination set a person apart in a spiritual sense, it also meant that church members saw potential in a candidate and that other bona fide ministers affirmed the candidate's ability. Otherwise, in Craig's mind, ministers were supposed to be like everyone else in their church. "But those local preachers who have the real call and cause of God at heart," Craig intoned, "being no longer tempted to please men, will put off that garb of feigned sanctity they are now insensible of; and having in simplicity to travel the same thorny way of the laity, of labor, cares of this life, &c. and depending on the God of mercy and not their expositors for their preaching, will preach the christian trials much more certain and feelingly, and no doubt to me, with much greater benefit to the churches."[68]

The second tenet of ministry was more difficult to explain, even though for Craig it amounted to one word: money. Ministers, he claimed, were beginning to demand payment for their services, another betrayal of republican principle. For Craig, paying a clergyman amounted to "priestcraft" and he was astonished that his Elkhorn brethren could have forgotten so quickly the persecution meted out by paid clergymen in Virginia. Now, he argued, his friends and colaborers were apparently falling into the same snare. The Revolution had presented Baptists with an opportunity to gain their liberty. A petition calling for disestablishment coincided with a memorial with Jefferson's intervention: "At the same time a memorial was presented from the Presbytery of Virginia, I believe to the same effect; and by steady exertions the friends of the liberties of mankind, with the great mr. Jefferson at their head, worried the tobacco from under the church, and she fell as I believe and many of her lovers."[69]

Of course, there were obvious differences between clergymen paid by tax revenue and those paid by free will offerings, but Craig either did not see them or he simply ignored them. The point he was making was simple: The preachers of his generation had paid a high price for ridding themselves of persecution at the hands of state clergy and their henchmen, and a paid ministry in any form looked like a return to that same kind of bondage.

Craig conceded that certain ministers should be paid. Those who traveled extensively and dedicated themselves to a traveling ministry should be paid by the churches where they labored. After all, "these men cannot take their farms with them, therefore, nature and scripture both agree in fixing the meaning of those sacred. . . ."[70] All other ministers would best care for their flocks by "exhortation, feeding, preaching, ruling, &c." which left ample time to provide "things honest in the sight of all men, as other members has. . . ."[71]

By associating a minister's livelihood with agricultural yeomanry, Craig identified what he saw as the real problem among his brethren. A growing number of ministers were not earning their living by farming. Some were becoming "settled" ministers who served one church exclusively as their pastor. It was an issue that all churches faced and no one seemed to have an answer. With the frontier open, ministers who sensed opportunities could capitalize on any number of them. Capable ministers, those recognized by others as gifted preachers or leaders, had the option of conducting itinerant ministry in different churches or serving one church.

This shift away from itinerancy to settled, localized ministry led to other problems. For instance, Craig claimed that certain ministers had begun to rely on "expositors" rather than the Holy Spirit for sermonic inspiration. Worse, these men were interpreting Scripture to suit their own purposes in order to make a comfortable living for themselves. These ministers seemed to attract fairly large crowds, and in some cases they claimed several ministers as members. It was not right, Craig maintained, for one church to claim multiple ministers or even potential ministers while some churches had no pastoral leadership. Finally, Craig indicated that certain churches had betrayed their own republican values by allowing themselves to become powerful. Several churches had built "good meeting houses" and become so powerful that they actually stifled other congregations."[72]

Of course, Craig said nothing about ministry, celebrity ministers, or powerful churches until he was safely away from Great Crossing Church. As he wrote in 1801, Craig still felt the sting of his dealings with his former congregation, and given his temperament, it would have been natural to assume that *A Few Remarks* was a slap at his rival, Joseph Redding. But Craig probably had a number of other ministers in his sights, especially Jacob Creath.

Like many Elkhorn ministers, Creath had grown up in Virginia, but he was Canadian by birth. He was born on February 22, 1777, to Samuel and Susan Creath, both of whom sympathized with the American Revolution.[73] The Creaths enjoyed few luxuries and the family could not afford to educate Jacob. Fortunately, a neighbor noticed his potential and taught him. Creath fell in love with his benefactor's daughter, and the two were married in 1799. By all accounts, Creath may not have been born into a wealthy family, but he took to a privileged lifestyle quickly. One writer described him as "inclined to be foppish in dress."[74] Creath's extravagant dress and demeanor gave the impression that he was a dandy—and trading on his father-in-law's money and reputation, at that.

Beyond the young man's pretentious manner, there may have been other reasons why some of the Elkhorn brethren looked askance at Jacob Creath. He was baptized in 1795 under the authority of Grassy Creek Baptist Church in North Carolina, and ordained three years later by John Poindexter and William Basket at a place known as the "Roundabout Meetinghouse" in Louisa County, Virginia, in 1798.[75] Thus, Creath was relatively young when he began his ministry. This was certainly not uncommon, but the Elkhorn brethren scarcely knew him when he moved to Kentucky. Even more significant, they had not ordained him and could only wait for him to prove himself to their complete satisfaction.

If that were not enough, Creath gave no indication that he identified himself as an itinerant. In fact, he appears to have looked upon itinerancy with disdain. For instance, Theodrick Boulware boarded with Jacob Creath and his family when he began attending Georgetown Academy in 1806. Boulware showed such academic and spiritual promise that several ministers, including Creath, suggested that he consider vocational ministry. Boulware appreciated Creath's hospitality, but Creath's manner, particularly his attitude toward ministry left him cold. As he recalled, "After flattering my vanity; he proposed some inducements, viz.: 'I would be introduced into the best society, live upon the fat of the land, freed from the drudgery of hard labor; and very likely marry a lady of family and fortune.'"[76] Appalled, Boulware retorted that the devil accused Job of serving God for the same reasons. When Creath asked Boulware for what he deemed "proper inducements and qualifications for a minister," Boulware offered four qualifications beginning with the minister's spiritual condition. He believed that ministers need to be "born of God" and well acquainted with "spiritual things." From there, Boulware believed that ministers should desire "God's honor" as well as "the encouragement, peace, and comfort of God's children, and the salvation of men." Next, it was not enough for a minister to understand spiritual matters. Genuine ministers, he maintained, should be able to teach them to others. Moreover, ministers should practice "both at home and abroad what he preaches."[77] Boulware was not finished. He further noted, "Without these qualifications, Sir, I have no confidence in the Preacher or his religion."[78] Young Boulware's forthright answer must have taken Creath aback; they never discussed the issue again.[79]

Upon arrival in Kentucky, Creath quickly established himself as one of Elkhorn's better preachers, but few considered him a good pastor. According to some sources, churches actually declined while under his care. For instance, William Hickman succeeded Elijah Craig as pastor of McConnell's Run

Church shortly after its constitution, and he enjoyed considerable success there. In 1801 alone, the church welcomed 156 new members. By contrast, Jacob Creath succeeded William Hickman in 1805, and over the next four years Creath baptized two, and the church declined in membership from 177 to 150.[80]

If these things were not bad enough, Creath appears to have been a polarizing figure who engendered strife wherever he went. Shortly after assuming the pastorate at McConnell's Run, Creath found himself in the middle of a controversy involving two laymen, John Cook and Lewis Denny. The strife escalated and MRBC asked several local churches for help in mediating an equitable solution. When pressed for reasons why the minority party was offended with the majority, the minority responded with three specific grievances, including the church calling Jacob Creath "against the will of a minority—contrary to a standard rule in said church—and with said Creath for his absurd attempts to explain away the force of said rule."[81] The controversy ultimately died down, but Creath left the church in 1809. As one writer put it, "At the height of the controversy over Jacob Creath, he slipped away almost unnoticed in the turmoil. . . ."[82] When it came to creating turmoil in churches, Elijah Craig was in a league by himself, but Jacob Creath did not lag far behind.

As ministers wrestled with their changing roles, they agreed that churches needed to remain pure. Yet, balancing local church gatekeeping and building mutual love and respect between church members frequently proved difficult. William Hickman's "good old Virginia doctrine" featured a broad-based theological consensus and a deferential political system that allowed those regarded as the association's "best men" to lead everyone else. They could scarcely imagine it any other way. Yet, strong cultural and economic forces were challenging deferential politics at all levels, and religious organizations were not exempt. Personal piety, patriotism, and politics of the most Jeffersonian persuasion, the very tenets upon which Elkhorn rested, would soon be put to the test by the two things the association esteemed most—namely, theology and revival.

Theological disturbances and occasional wranglings aside, the ministers-fraternal of the Elkhorn Association had reason to smile as the eighteenth century gave way to the nineteenth. Their numbers were increasing, they had garnered a measure of social acceptance, and they were prospering. Ministers tended their flocks, ever vigilant for signs of heresy and corrupting influences. Even so, the strictest discipline cannot forestall every crisis. Unitarianism proved to be a significant issue, and slavery continued to simmer beneath the surface as settlers flooded the Commonwealth. Some brought slaves with them; others demanding them upon arrival. There was trouble ahead for Elkhorn, but not, ironically, before a season of reunion and revival.

4

Revive Us Again

The summer of 1801 found Kentuckians in a season of unprecedented religious fervor.[1] Led by men like James "Preaching Jim" McGready, the Great Revival's fire spread quickly throughout the Commonwealth. Scores of anxious Kentuckians left their crops and shops to mind their spiritual estates. Some estimate that the famous Cane Ridge Revival alone drew in excess of 20,000 souls, as the revivals claimed converts by the hundreds. As historian Paul Conkin describes it, Cane Ridge was "America's Pentecost."[2]

Contemporary accounts describe individuals engaging in activities ranging from laughing and crying to rolling on the ground and convulsing. Some even claimed they had "treed the devil."[3] Scholars seem irresistibly drawn to such religious exercises, perhaps because they were so common—and so unusual. Regardless of the reason, toward the end of the twentieth century so many good works on American awakenings and revivals appeared that it is tempting to see all late eighteenth- and early nineteenth-century revivals through a "Cane Ridge lens."[4] Yet, Elkhorn's faithful were well-acquainted with revival long before "Preaching Jim" or Cane Ridge. In fact, revival, complete with religious exercises, was a regular feature of religious life for Kentucky's earliest Baptists. Nearly all of them had been converted during a revival season in Virginia before the American Revolution, and they hoped for a similar season of spiritual awakening in frontier Kentucky.

Revival and Union

Given the emerging synergy between religion and politics in the Early Republic, it is tempting to think that Baptists would bolster their position once in Kentucky. With Thomas Jefferson and James Madison advocating complete religious liberty, the Commonwealth's Baptists were poised to capitalize on their seemingly endless opportunities with no state-sanctioned church to bedevil them. But first, there were hurdles to clear.

Theological similarities and personal ties did not automatically lead to unity among America's Separate and Regular Baptists.[5] In Virginia, however, the interaction between the two groups played a crucial role in shaping life for their Kentucky brethren. In August 1787, delegates from six Virginia Baptist associations met in Goochland County. Among other things, they discussed a possible union between the state's Regular and Separate Baptists. Both sides held the same reservations about the other as they always had, but things had changed since 1767 and sentiments were softening. The Regulars claimed that Separates were not sufficiently explicit in articulating their beliefs, a failure that had led some Separates to embrace Arminianism. The Separates countered that a majority of them held the same theological principles as the Regulars, but they balked at being bound by a confession. True, some had embraced Arminianism, but they overlooked such variances because "they were generally men of exemplary character and great usefulness in the Redeemer's kingdom." Besides, those who chose to articulate their theological convictions frequently did so in their church covenants, and the Separates claimed that it was "better to bear some diversity of opinion in doctrines than to break with men whose Christian comportment rendered them amiable in the estimation of all true lovers of genuine godliness."[6]

After spirited debate, Virginia's Baptists finally hammered out acceptable terms of union. Everyone agreed that the Philadelphia Confession of Faith reflected gospel truth. They further agreed that salvation was by grace through faith in Christ. They also agreed to accept the confession, at least in principle, but neither party wanted it to be used as a war club over trivial matters. "To prevent the confession of faith from usurping a tyrannical power over the conscience of any," they said, "we do not mean that every person is bound to the strict observance of everything contained therein."[7] They further agreed to drop the descriptors "Separate" and "Regular." Instead, they agreed to become the United Baptist Churches of Christ in Virginia. Twenty-three years later, Robert Semple observed that the union effectively laid aside the "party spirit" that formerly plagued them. He also noted, "It is worthy of remark that this conjunction of disjoined brethren took place at a time when a great revival of religion had commenced, and not far from the time when it burst forth on the right hand and on the left throughout the state."[8]

The process by which Kentucky's Baptists achieved their union is an equally compelling story but would not be complete it until 1801. In fact, the Union of 1801 actually constituted the fourth attempt to unify Kentucky's Separate and Regular Baptists since 1785. Offering a plausible explanation for how they finally achieved union is not easy but this much is clear: between 1785 and 1801 many among Kentucky's Baptists wanted some sort of union. Ultimately, they achieved it thanks to a combination of trusted leadership, precedent, their numerous similarities, and revival. Consequently, Kentucky's frontier revivals represented more than large, emotional gatherings where preachers demanded repentance and faith. The Great Revival signaled the beginning of a shift in Baptist identity. As Separates and Regulars jettisoned their respective descriptors, they modified their respective theologies to create a doctrinal consensus agreeable to both. This new consensus facilitated mutual recognition of both church members and ministers. Even more, the new consensus fostered cooperation between the two groups. Beyond religious fraternity, the Union of 1801 indicates that Kentucky's late-eighteenth- and early nineteenth-century Baptists were determined to frame any such fellowship around carefully articulated theological parameters.

If citizens of the Early Republic craved liberty, it is fair to say that Baptists craved unity. Virginia's Baptists laid aside their differences and achieved union thanks in large part to a revival that swept through Virginia after the American Revolution. Late eighteenth-century settlers trekked westward searching for a variety of things, particularly opportunity. Baptists from Virginia and North Carolina wasted no time in moving to Kentucky. Many had suffered persecution, and they hoped Kentucky would provide both economic opportunity and a place where they might worship free from ecclesiastical interference with others of like faith.

Upon reaching Kentucky, these early Baptists began building churches. On June 25, 1785, several churches met together for fellowship. John Taylor recalled, "We soon began to contemplate an association; for that purpose, and partly to bring about a union, with the South Kentucky Baptists, we held a conference at South Elkhorn, in June 1785."[9] The meeting minutes focused on the proposed union, with the delegates agreeing to be ruled by simple majority vote.

Even though this group had not officially constituted itself, they heard one query: "Whether the Philadelphia confession of faith adopted by the Baptists shall be strictly adhered to as the rule of our communion or whether suppression thereof for the sake of Society be best? Answer—It is agreed that the said recited confession of faith be strictly adhered to."[10]

Unable to achieve this union, those insisting on "strict adherence" to the Philadelphia Confession met later in the year and formed the Elkhorn Association. The new association chose Lewis Craig, pastor of South Elkhorn Baptist Church, as its session's moderator. Craig had been a leading voice among Virginia's revivalistic Separate Baptists. He and his brothers Elijah, Joseph, and Benjamin became key leaders in the Elkhorn Association, prominent Kentucky citizens, and land speculators. In forming their constitution, the new association reaffirmed their commitment to a Baptist confession of faith from 1643. More likely, however, they meant the Philadelphia Confession which was based on the Second London Confession of 1689. It was the same one they had debated earlier in the year.[11] Their constitution stipulated

that the Elkhorn Association would be dedicated to advancing God's kingdom and committed members' energies to the mutual comfort and happiness of the association's churches. In addition to adopting the Philadelphia
Confession, the Elkhorn Baptists stipulated two points. First, they acknowledged God's sovereignty but categorically rejected any suggestion that God
was responsible for human sinfulness. Second, they deemed the laying on of
hands on newly baptized people—often a prerequisite for church membership—to be a matter of congregational choice. They concluded their business
by agreeing that the term "Regular Baptist" best described them and their
new association.[12] It appears that Elkhorn's founders knew little of the Philadelphia Association apart from the fact that it was the most prominent Baptist association in North America, and that it was well connected with other
associations of like faith and order. Their insistence on "strict adherence" to a
staunchly Calvinistic confession suggests that they were deliberately distanc-
ing themselves from their Separate Baptist brethren.

Those who had rejected "strict adherence" to the Philadelphia Confession
met on the "first fryday in October" 1787 and organized a competing association. They styled themselves "Separate Baptists" and since their congregations
were all located south of the Kentucky River, they named themselves the
South Kentucky Association. The new group wasted no time in delineating
the proper bounds of associational decorum. They affirmed the association's
right to meet as well as its solemn duty to protect doctrinal integrity as they
understood it. They agreed to resolve their ministerial differences among
themselves, and they affirmed individual church autonomy.[13] At their next
meeting, the South Kentucky Baptists entertained five specific queries. They
first considered "whether the washing of Saints feet is a duty injoined on
Christians," which they answered in the affirmative. The next three questions
addressed procedural issues, but the fifth asked whether or not a select committee might screen potentially divisive queries before any public discussion.
Ultimately, they decided it was a good idea to screen queries before public
debate, but they affirmed the association's right to override the committee's
suggestion and debate whatever issues they deemed appropriate.[14]

It is difficult to say what happened between the time the "Travelling
Church" arrived in Kentucky in 1781 and Elkhorn formed in 1785. Nonetheless, it is apparent that as a group, the Baptists found fellowship elusive.
J. H. Spencer claims that several churches split, and in some cases, one locale
hosted two churches with the same name—one Separate, one Regular. For
example, the Gilberts Creek Church sent representatives to the first Elkhorn
meeting in June 1785, but when the association met again in August 1786,
the minutes indicate that the church had been dissolved. By contrast, South

Kentucky's minutes show that in 1789 the association met at "Gilberds Creek Meetinghouse."[15]

Describing church and associational dynamics is difficult. Explaining why two groups who had numerous reasons to unite with each other failed to do so is even more difficult. One reason may have involved perception. Prominent eastern ministers like John Gano were being courted for frontier service, and there may have been others. Thus, in identifying with a settled, well-established association like the Philadelphia Baptist Association, Elkhorn's earliest ministers may have hoped simultaneously to shed the stigma of Separate Baptists as ignorant enthusiasts and lure other well-known preachers to frontier Kentucky.[16]

Beyond any theological differences between Regular and Separate Baptists, politics likely prevented Kentucky's Separate and Regular Baptists from unifying in 1785. The Separates were well-known for their emotional, revivalistic services, but they may also have appeared as Tories to the Elkhorn ministers. As the colonies had inched toward the Revolution, certain western factions pushed back against eastern elites. In North Carolina, the so-called Regulators railed against paying taxes that they claimed did not benefit them. The Battle of Alamance in 1771 finally broke the Regulator movement but not before North Carolina's governor, William Tryon, developed a negative impression of Baptists.[17]

According to Morgan Edwards, Tryon saw the Regulators "as a faction of Quakers and Baptists who aimed at oversetting the church of England." An eighteenth-century Baptist minister and historian, Edwards claimed that out of four thousand known Regulators, only seven were Baptists. Moreover, those seven were not members in good standing of any Separate Baptist church. No matter. As early as 1769 the Sandy Creek Association had gone on record as opposing rebellion against duly constituted authority. On the second Saturday in October in 1769, the association resolved, "If any of our members shall take up arms against the legal authority or aid and abbet them that do so, he shall be excommunicated. etc."[18]

Elkhorn's earliest Baptists were all, almost to a person, ardent Jeffersonians who had enthusiastically supported the American Revolution. Ambrose Dudley, John Gano, James Garrard, and later, David Barrow, commanded respect from their fellow ministers in part because they had fought for American independence. Likewise, a number of women in Elkhorn churches received citation for patriotic service. Apparently, South Kentucky's ministers and their families could not make the same claims.[19]

Kentucky residents faced a host of serious issues in 1785. Kentucky had not yet been recognized as a state, and as outlandish as they proved to be,

Spanish land claims in the area doubtless weighed on many minds. If the Elkhorn Baptists had to go to war, they would want trustworthy allies. If South Kentucky's ministers had not fought for their own independence, would they fight to retain land in the territory? Acquiring and securing land presented significant challenges to early Kentuckians of all stripes. Who's claims would be honored? Again, Elkhorn had much at stake. Their political sympathies were clear, but they wanted to know precisely where South Kentucky stood. In a word, Elkhorn wanted trustworthy allies. While no one said it explicitly, it seems likely that Elkhorn patriots disdained their South Kentucky brethren for failing to support the Revolution. If so, Elkhorn declared itself to be Regular Baptist and insisted on a "strict adherence" to the Philadelphia Confession of Faith at least in part to self-consciously build a wall between themselves and South Kentucky.

Securing Union

The actual process for unifying America's Regular and Separate Baptists varied from state to state.[20] The South Kentucky Association had been organized for about a year when they received a letter from the General Committee of Baptists in Virginia. The letter indicated that Virginia's Regular and Separate Baptists had agreed to become "United Baptists" with positive results for all concerned. They hoped their brethren in Kentucky would become "united" as well and extended an invitation to South Kentucky to unite with them. Essentially, union implied that both groups viewed each other as equals.[21] Virginia's Baptists had been considering union since the 1760s, and in the wake of a recent revival, they had finally achieved it.

South Kentucky's union with the Virginia Baptists made sense on several levels. As Separate Baptists, they shared a common faith, and since the majority of Kentucky's earliest Baptists had relocated from Virginia, these two groups already knew each other. Moreover, Virginia's union allowed the state's Baptists to speak with a single, "united" voice in matters bearing on important issues like religious liberty. Since Kentucky was not yet a state, having a united voice in Richmond might prove politically beneficial. The South Kentucky Association agreed "as free men and Christians" to unite with Virginia's United Baptists, and the General Committee responded with gratitude.[22]

In this spirit of cooperation and mutual benefit among Baptists, the South Kentucky Association appealed to the Elkhorn Association for union in 1789. Unfortunately, they met unexpected resistance. The Elkhorn Baptists appointed a committee of five ministers to consider the matter, and after due deliberation they suggested a special meeting. The first sign of difficulty came when the Elkhorn Association gathered for its regular meeting in October. The association read several letters from corresponding associations but ordered the letter from the South Kentucky Association to "lie on the table." The Elkhorn Association did not recognize the South Kentucky Association, but they appointed a committee to respond to the letter. Elkhorn's minutes do not include a copy of the letter or details of their response, but according to the South Kentucky minutes, Elkhorn refused union because of unspecified theological irregularities. "As long As So Grate diversity of Sentiments prevailed with regard to the Bible," the minutes note, "a union that would be for their Mutual happyness Could Scarcely be hoped for."[23]

It is unknown precisely what the Elkhorn Baptists meant by "so Grate diversity of Sentiments" or "Mutual happyness." Strict subscription to the Philadelphia Confession doubtless remained a sticking point, but South Kentucky knew Elkhorn's position when they initiated the call for union, and Elkhorn knew that South Kentucky held a high view of the Bible. Politics aside, the problem may have stemmed from perceived theological inconsistencies in the South Kentucky Association. David Benedict claims that while Separate Baptists throughout America remained Calvinistic in theology, a number of the early Kentucky Separates were anti-Calvinistic and had "gone nearly the full length of the doctrine of Arminius."[24] J. H. Spencer went even further in noting, "The Arminian party of the Separates, constantly diverged farther and farther from the common standard of orthodoxy, till many grave heresies crept in among them. . . ."[25]

Worse still, certain South Kentucky ministers preached doctrines the Elkhorn Baptists rejected. The South Kentucky minutes for 1792 indicate that the association discussed the propriety of maintaining fellowship with someone who believed in "Restoration from hell," or the possibility that someone might repent after death. The association agreed they could not fellowship with any who maintained this view, and after an investigation, they expelled one John Bailey for heresy. Bailey, however, commanded a sizeable following, and South Kentucky received him back into fellowship less than a year later. Whether or not the Elkhorn Association knew of Bailey's case, they clearly questioned elements of the South Kentucky Association's orthodoxy.[26]

Talk of union filled the air once again in the spring of 1793, only this time the Regular Baptists approached the Separates. The Elkhorn Association sent a deputation of its most esteemed ministers to the South Kentucky Association hoping to secure union between the two associations. Ambrose Dudley and James Garrard led the group along with Augustine Eastin and John Price. The association charged these men to meet with the South Kentucky Association "with full power to confer freely on terms of union. . . ." If all went well, the Elkhorn Association authorized their delegation to set a time when both associations could meet and finalize their union.[27]

The two associations could not reach an accord at this meeting, but the South Kentucky Association agreed to hold a special meeting to see if they could establish appropriate terms for union. Desiring to live in harmony with their neighbors, they offered terms for union:

> Whereas there has been Some desire of a union between the two
> bodies of Baptists in Kentucky we the United Baptists Are wiling
> to Unite Upon the following terms (to wit) the Bible instead
> of the Philadelphia Confession of faith and that the Regular
> Baptist preaching As is commonly known Among them and
> perticular Election Shall be no Bar to communion Except when
> carried to the Extreme of Eternal Justifycation and Reprobation
> of Men or Angles. And that what is Cald the Separate or United
> Baptists preaching their doctrine As commonly known and that
> Christ died for All Men and Universal provision in him for the
> Salvation of all Shall be No bars to Communion Except when
> carried to the Extreme of Restoration of Men and Angles from
> the infernal Pit of fire and Brimstone.[28]

The Elkhorn Baptists rejected these one-sided terms of union, but subsequent events suggest that some in the South Kentucky camp wanted union more than others. Elkhorn apparently demanded some agreement on the Philadelphia Confession, which the Separates staunchly opposed. Stung by this latest rejection, South Kentucky reconsidered union at their annual meeting in October 1793 and reaffirmed their commitment to the Bible as a sufficient foundation for union. Further, since their union with the Virginia Baptists did not require submission to the Philadelphia Confession, they did not feel obliged to accept it for Elkhorn's sake. The South Kentucky Association believed it had made adequate concessions to Elkhorn and if there would be a union, Elkhorn knew the terms.[29]

As most Separates saw it, the problem between the two groups hinged on extremes. Elkhorn would not budge on the Philadelphia Confession, or more precisely, their understanding of it, and some South Kentuckians feared they would take certain doctrines too far. Even so, the South Kentucky Baptists believed that union was possible if both sides could agree not to become extreme on the doctrine of election and the extent of the atonement. In offering these terms of union, the first of their kind among the Kentucky Baptists, both sides had a starting point for any future negotiations.

Still, several of South Kentucky's ministers believed their association was guilty of its own extremism. The Virginia Baptists had united with the Philadelphia Confession as the confessional basis of their union with the stipulation that it would not be applied with absolute strictness; South Kentucky ruled it out entirely. According to one historian, the Virginia Baptists did not want the confession to exercise a "tyrannical" power over anyone and thus stipulated, "We do not mean that every person is bound to the strict observance of everything therein contained."[30] In other words, Virginia's union had allowed for churches to affirm the confession if they so chose but required no one to follow it too strictly. South Kentucky did not appear willing to extend the same courtesy to Elkhorn.

When the two sides could not reach a satisfactory agreement, four churches and five ministers left the South Kentucky Association and formed the Tates Creek United Baptist Association. This new association styled itself "United Baptist" because they were already in league with Virginia's United Baptists. Moreover, Tates Creek immediately requested union with Elkhorn under new terms. The Tates Creek Baptists stipulated that the Philadelphia Confession articulated the "essential truths of the Gospel," including the ultimate authority of Scripture, human depravity and need of divine grace, the necessity of repentance and faith, justification based on Christ's righteousness, and baptism by immersion. They also affirmed that "the supreme Judge by which all controversies of religion are to be determined, and, all decrees of Councils opinions of ancient writers doctrins of men and private spirits are to be examined and in whose sentance we are to rest, can be no other than the Holy Scriptures, delivered by the Spirit, into which scripture so delivered our faith is finally resolved."[31] Perhaps most significantly, Tates Creek used language that mirrored Virginia's terms of union: "To prevent its usurping a tiranical power over the Consciences of any, we do not mean that every person is to be bound to the strict observance of every thing therin Contained. . . ."[32] In the wake of the American Revolution and the debates leading to the Constitution's ratification, most Americans, including the Elkhorn brethren, had well-defined ideas about tyranny. Both sides agreed to these terms, whereupon Elkhorn forged a union with the Tates Creek Association.[33]

At first glance, it appears that Elkhorn would abandon their most basic principles if they agreed to unite with Tates Creek. The Philadelphia Confession articulated a number of doctrines in fine detail that the Tates Creek terms either mentioned tangentially, or in most cases, not at all. However, it is important to note that the Tates Creek Baptists had moved from "Bible only" language to specifying several key doctrines that both associations affirmed, albeit requiring Scripture to be the final arbiter in any religious dispute. If anyone opted for "strict adherence" to the Philadelphia Confession, well enough, but their union did not mandate that anyone follow it too closely. Both parties would be making serious concessions to the other for the sake of union.

Not everyone rejoiced over the union. When the Elkhorn Association met the following year, the new union with Tates Creek quickly became the first item on the agenda. A number of churches expressed dissatisfaction over procedural issues, claiming that the association had "departed from their constitutional principles" in agreeing to the union. Consequently, Elkhorn dissolved the union less than a year after its inception and tapped associational leaders John Price and Robert Frier to inform the affected churches of the decision.[34]

Elkhorn's minutes do not specify which constitutional principles the association had ignored in their union with Tates Creek. When first formed, the Elkhorn Association agreed that their purpose in forming an association centered on advancing the kingdom of God and promoting the "mutual comfort and happiness of the churches of Christ. . . ." They also affirmed strict adherence to the Philadelphia Confession of Faith.[35] Given Tates Creek's sudden departure from South Kentucky, it is possible that some saw the association as a group of schismatics and disapproved of the union out of personal scruples. It is also possible that some believed union with South Kentucky would be more difficult if Elkhorn recognized Tates Creek. Since Elkhorn backed out of the union, it could also be that a powerful minority of staunch Regulars considered any compromise regarding the Philadelphia Confession as unacceptable and not conducive to the association's general happiness. Or they could have rejected the union based on some narrow, unspecified procedural issue.

Like their fellow Baptists in Virginia, Elkhorn and South Kentucky apparently wanted union, but stalwarts on each side stood in the way. At least four churches had left the South Kentucky Association hoping to achieve it. Likewise, the majority of Regular Baptists were willing to look for common ground, even if it meant compromising strict subscription to the Philadelphia Confession. Moreover, the Elkhorn Baptists could scarcely complain that the Separates asked for too much, seeing that they had dropped the controversial term "Regular" from their outgoing correspondence in 1789. They had also agreed among themselves to several compromises on their own interpretation of the confession. As late as 1793, some of the Elkhorn brethren were wondering if the entire confession might be modified or recast "in words easier understood by weak minds. . . ."[36] If nothing else, Elkhorn's brief concord with Tates Creek demonstrated that union was possible and that a certain latitude existed for arranging satisfactory terms.

In the meantime, the "rescinded union" with Tates Creek posed a serious problem for Elkhorn. When the association convened in 1795, the Marble Creek Church immediately posed a troublesome query: "Was not the Association of 1794 guilty of covenant breaking in dissolving the union of the united Baptists upon the principle they did?"[37] The association referred the query to committee for special consideration, but everyone knew that the issue would not die quietly. Consequently, at their 1796 meeting Elkhorn received messengers from the Tates Creek Association, eager to restore the union. After careful discussion, Elkhorn agreed to avail themselves of every opportunity to "cultivate untimacy [intimacy] and harmony in conversing, praying and preaching together" in order to determine their compatibility.[38]

This time, John Gano, perhaps the best-educated and certainly one of the best-spoken of the Regular Baptists, led a committee with Augustine Eastin, Joseph Redding, and Ambrose Dudley to achieve the union that had proven so elusive. In 1797, the Tates Creek United Baptists and the Elkhorn Association once again reached accord, but not without carefully delineating the terms of union. Elkhorn's minutes indicate that their respective committees agreed on six essential doctrines: one on human nature, four related to salvation, and one on church discipline. A seventh item, the doctrine of a "general provision," or the extent of the atonement, was "not answered," probably because it had already been thoroughly discussed and each committee already knew where the other stood. The Elkhorn Association approved these terms, even though they did not even mention the Philadelphia Confession of Faith.[39]

From 1793 until 1797, the Tates Creek churches had provided a buffer between Elkhorn and South Kentucky. With their union finally secure, it remained to be seen if Elkhorn and South Kentucky could finally cooperate. Once again, revivalism apparently motivated Kentucky's Baptists to unite. America's Separate Baptists originated from revival and each of the four attempts to bring union to Kentucky's Baptists came as a result of revival. Kentucky Baptists experienced revivals in 1785 and 1788–89, again in Mason County in 1797, and throughout a considerable portion of the Bluegrass Region during the Great Revival. In each instance, the call for union loomed somewhere in the wings.[40]

The earliest writers do not speak of it in revivalist terms, but Elkhorn's minutes indicate that a number of churches apparently enjoyed a revival between 1791 and 1792. The associational statistics for 1791 report 171 baptisms in the thirteen reporting churches, 50 in South Elkhorn Church alone; the 1792 minutes report 114 baptisms from the twenty-three reporting churches, 35 at Bryant's Station, and 24 at Cooper's Run. While these numbers do not necessarily indicate widespread revival, certain churches in the Elkhorn Association grew substantially in the early 1790s. Curiously, the number of baptisms for 1793 fell to 41 for the entire association. If they kept a watchful eye on their statistical health, and assuming they gave heed to biblical exhortations to live in harmony, it is likely that Kentucky's Baptists may have desired union as a possible means of both conserving and possibly perpetuating revivalism on the one hand, while maintaining a theological consensus on the other.[41] Moreover, Kentucky's entrance into the Union in 1792 may have eased any lingering animosities with respect to Jeffersonian Republicanism.

The Commonwealth's Regular and Separate Baptists finally achieved union in 1801, during one of the most remarkable revival seasons in American religious history. The Elkhorn Association called for the union, and once again they turned to some of their most respected ministers to carry the day. David Barrow joined Ambrose Dudley, John Price, Joseph Redding, and William Payne to meet with South Kentucky's representatives Moses Bledsoe, Thomas J. Chilton, Daniel Ramey, Samuel Johnson, and Robert Elkin.[42] The two committees agreed on eleven points, the first eight of which bore a distinct resemblance to the first terms of union between Elkhorn and Tates Creek. The 1801 Terms of Union did not require churches to abide by the Philadelphia Confession. Rather, both associations agreed that the Scriptures would frame their faith and practice. Both associations agreed that beliefs about the extent of Christ's atonement would not be a bar to communion. Two points proved especially noteworthy: Item 8 stipulated "that it is our duty to be tender and affectionate to each other, and study the happiness of the children of God in general; to be engaged singly to promote the honor of God."[43] Item 10 clarified "that each may keep up their associational and church government as to them may seem best."[44] After three unsuccessful attempts and nearly sixteen years, Kentucky Baptists finally secured their union, leading J. H. Spencer to muse, "Now ensued a golden age of the Kentucky Baptists, their divisions had been healed."[45]

The Great Revival launched a spectacular grown spurt among Elkhorn churches, who had begun keeping associational statistics as early as 1788. They charted the previous year's baptisms, additions by letter, dismissions by letter, excommunications, and the total membership for each of churches.[46] Judging from Elkhorn's tabular data, the association experienced its most dramatic growth between 1800 and 1805, with 1801 and 1802 marking the revival's best years. In 1801 the association grew from 1,642 members to a whopping 4,853, of whom 3,011 had been received by baptism. Elkhorn's statistics record another banner year in 1802 with 488 baptisms and 275 received by letter, for a reported membership of 5,310 in its constituent churches.[47] Elkhorn's numbers are even more impressive when compared to the state's growth during the same period. Between 1790 and 1800, Kentucky's population grew from 73,677 to 220,955, nearly a 300 per cent increase. Elkhorn experienced a 295 percent growth in only one year.

As church rolls ballooned, the number of excommunications also increased dramatically. Whereas Elkhorn tallied 11 exclusions in 1800, they reported 47, 143, 138, 165, and 137 respectively for the next five years. Reasons for such numbers vary. Drunkenness and adultery claimed many; others had committed themselves to church membership from an emotional reaction to a dynamic preacher. Subsequently, these latter found the Baptist understanding of an orderly life too restrictive and refused to abide thereby.[48] Elkhorn's statistics indicate that excommunications outpaced baptisms after 1802, a trend that continued until 1807.[49]

Beyond the Union

No one could blame Kentucky's Baptists for celebrating the Union of 1801. They had finally achieved union and amidst large-scale revival, no less. Their regular fellowship promised relief from the grind of their routine, and these early Baptist ministers drew a certain collegial comfort from their camaraderie that they could not expect from others. Yet, the union's crowning achievement may have been interconnecting like-minded churches. Doctrinally, interchurch fellowship at the associational level helped maintain a relatively common orthodoxy. Union across associational lines paved the way for fellowship and cooperation based on that orthodoxy. Taken together, these Baptists could look upon revival as a guide to help them understand God's will. Revival seasons both indicated God's affirmation of their activities and provided a mandate to continue therein. Conversely, seasons without revival could indicate God's displeasure. In the first twenty years of its history, Elkhorn saw revival occur with sufficient frequency that the association's faithful likely never felt far from the divine favor they sought.

At its most practical level, union expedited interchurch transfer and even ensured continuity across state borders. Colonial and Early National Baptists guarded their ranks carefully and with the increasingly large numbers of Virginians moving westward, unity between Virginia's Baptists and Kentucky's Baptists simplified transferring one's church membership. Upon unifying with South Kentucky, the Virginia Baptists sent a letter. "With pleashure we heard your tenderness towards the Members who Moved from the Several Churches with us to reside Among you," they noted, "and that their letters of Admission were Received by your Minnisters and Churches without degrading them and us by exacting their Experience & Principles, we prayed to inable them to Act in line of Christian duty and that they maybe as dear to you as they have been to us and As Grate a blessing."[50] By affirming common beliefs and practices, South Kentucky and Virginia's Baptists validated each other as "authentic" Baptists. Union between South Kentucky and Elkhorn established standards of both theology and conduct for the vast majority of Baptists in Kentucky.

Since everyone involved wanted union in some form, the real question became how to achieve it. Here Kentucky Baptists relied on a number of means in forging their union beginning with their most trusted resource, their ministers of highest standing. That is, both associations deferred to their most capable spokesmen to achieve the union. In 1837 James Barnett Taylor published *Lives of Virginia Baptist Ministers*. This work featured biographical sketches of the ministers, who, in Taylor's estimation, had most influenced Virginia Baptist development. Not surprisingly, many of Taylor's Virginia ministers also ranked among Kentucky's leading ministers. Such renown inspired great confidence among the Elkhorn Baptists.[51]

The Virginia Baptist union established a precedent that Kentucky's Baptists used to their advantage. The minutes for the South Kentucky and Elkhorn Associations suggest that both associations corresponded with the General Association in Virginia. It was, after all, a logical thing to do, seeing that both associations knew the Virginia brethren well. The South Kentucky minutes carry the greatest detail about how the Virginia Baptists sought union, but Elkhorn seemed ready to cooperate. Both associations relied on their ablest ministers to affect the union. Each association sent their best-respected ministers to negotiations, men of stature who were esteemed for their biblical knowledge and ability to work with others. For instance, when Tates Creek sought union with Elkhorn, their proposed terms of union followed the same formula as the Virginia Baptists.[52] While the final terms of union around which the associations united contained no reference to the "tyrannical Power" of confessions, Virginia's union offered a starting point that ultimately facilitated union between Tates Creek and Elkhorn, and their representatives made it work.[53]

Ultimately, their commonalities allowed Kentucky's Separates and Regulars to maintain some sort of interchurch fellowship in the absence of an official union. Their pronounced theological similarities allowed the Separates and Regulars to modify both their doctrinal positions and their demands on one another. That is, they demonstrated a willingness to compromise their theological demands on each other by assigning key doctrines positions of primary and secondary importance. The Separates feared that an overly zealous attachment to the Philadelphia Confession might lead some to use it against others who did not interpret the confession the same way. In reflecting on the Virginia union, Baptist stalwart John Leland noted, "It is sometimes said that hereticks are always averse to confessions of faith. I wish I could say as much of tyrants. But, after all, if a confession of faith upon the whole, may be advantageous, the greater care should be taken not to sacradize, or make a petty Bible of it."[54]

Leland's sentiments capture in stunning relief the issues facing Kentucky's late-eighteenth- and early nineteenth-century Separates and Regulars. Both wanted union. Neither sought to subordinate the Bible to any confession of faith, so through their negotiations, both parties found common ground in affirming the Bible (both Old and New Testaments) as their sufficient guide in faith and practice. The Regulars ultimately surrendered their insistence on strict adherence to the Philadelphia Confession but lost little in the transaction, seeing that the confession itself affirmed the Old and New Testaments as authoritative, and interpretation of specific issues remained securely in local churches and associations. The Separates would not be bound by a rigid application of the confession, yet the terms of union specified certain doctrines that applied to every minister and church in the union. In other words, both camps came to believe that affirmation of the Bible's truthfulness along with certain cardinal doctrines constituted a better basis for union than rigorous compliance with the Philadelphia Confession.

Moreover, both parties knew that unity depended on a common understanding of salvation, but precisely what did that mean for each party? The Regulars were willing to accept brethren who did not hold to "limited atonement" and Separates were willing to accept "unconditional election," provided that one did not espouse eternal justification. Thus, union depended on an open agreement that hinged on neither camp taking any one doctrine to an extreme. When it came to other important doctrines, both affirmed Calvinistic assumptions, particularly humanity's inability to save itself and justification as God's gracious work. As a result, the United Baptists reached a doctrinal consensus that affirmed many Calvinistic tenets about human nature and salvation, but left explanations of precisely what Christ did open for disagreement. The confession remained available as a touchstone to clarify specific issues. No one really wanted to be "bound" by it, but individual churches and associations could make as much or as little of it as they wanted.

Yet a vague affirmation that the Bible somehow answered all theological issues could not secure the union by itself. Both Separates and Regulars understood that they needed some doctrinal consensus, if minimal, in order to sustain their union. Some cultural or political issue might buttress the union if each party could agree on what mattered. In the end, emancipation furnished just such an issue.

The 1792 Constitutional Convention produced Kentucky's first governing document with the understanding that voters could reconsider and alter their constitution as early as 1797. By the end of the eighteenth century several issues prompted concern. Kentucky's electoral system posed problems for many, and James Garrard's use or misuse of office concerned others. Critics claimed that all ills could be remedied by another constitution. In the broadest sense, Kentuckians had ratified a relatively liberal constitution in 1792, but by decade's end factions began pressing for reform that would address the perceived problems of the first constitution, while further democratizing the document.[55]

Emancipation remained an issue when the delegates met to redraw the state constitution in 1799. It could scarcely be otherwise. Kentucky was booming as the decade was ending, and the 1800 census would show that over the past ten years Kentucky's population almost tripled, from 73,677 to 220,995. Over the same period Kentucky's slave population grew from 12,430 to 40,343. Even more telling, of Kentucky's 42 counties, a fifth of the Commonwealth's slave population lived in 3 counties: Fayette, Bourbon, and Woodford—home for many of Elkhorn's churches.[56]

David Rice had never approved of slavery's inclusion in the original constitution through Article IX, and he wanted to see it amended. Others who had called for emancipation in 1792 still desired to see slavery's end. On the other hand, the same powerful forces that fought so hard to guarantee slavery's future in Kentucky were more than ready for any fight to keep it. Pro-slavery advocates once again linked human bondage to property rights. If the Commonwealth's voters gave in to the emancipationists, there would be no limit to the mischief they might cause in other areas of life. No one's property would be safe—or so the proslavery camp argued.[57]

Kentucky's emancipationists faced a daunting challenge. Whereas the first constitution stemmed from 43 delegates, 7 of whom were ministers, the second constitution would come from 58 delegates, only 3 of whom were ministers. The minister-delegates at the first constitution convention all favored emancipation. Of the three minister-delegates in 1799, all of whom were Baptists, John Price advocated slavery most strongly. On April 6, 1799, the East Hickman Baptist Church met in regular session. With the convention just over three months away, John Price asked the church "whether slavery was a Moral Evil, or whether slave holding be a sin against God. . . ." The church agreed not to discuss the issue "as Br. Price has declared that such as was in favor of Emancipation and yet held slaves, was Deists." The minutes do not specify who, but someone asked "whether the church could have fellowship with such members as were of the Deistical opinion." The church finally dropped the issue but not before a lengthy discussion "on the Tenants of a Deist."[58]

The remaining minister-delegates, John Bailey and Alexander Davidson, both favored emancipation. While little is known about Davidson, Bailey was as familiar to state politics as he was to state religious life. Bailey served on the committee that drafted the first constitution, and his views on emancipation had not changed since 1792. Nonetheless, whatever else might come from the second convention, slavery was not open for discussion. According to historian Joan Wells Coward's tally, most of the delegates were "men of substantial property," with about 75 percent of them having connections to the courts.[59] Emancipationists never had a chance when it came to reframing the constitution. Slavery was an integral part of Kentucky's economy, and well-positioned elites were determined to keep it that way.

If John Bailey's politics had not changed since 1792, neither had his religious convictions. He was articulate and well-liked by his fellow ministers. While it is true that he held to Universalism, he was such a gifted orator that the South Kentucky Association found it difficult to expel him from their fellowship. Besides, Bailey's gift of oratory served the association well in circumstances like the constitutional convention. Nonetheless, in the eyes of Elkhorn's stalwarts, his belief that all souls would eventually be in heaven was just as odious as his emancipationist leanings.

As Kentuckians faced uncertainty about their state constitution, the Regular and Separate Baptists were at an impasse with respect to their own terms of union. At this point, the Great Revival could not have come at a more opportune time. If the Great Revival helped forge a union between Kentucky's Separate and Regular Baptists, it also reflected a new consensus that may be described as part theological and part political. Theologically, both groups agreed on a number of issues ranging from biblical authority to agreeing not to refuse fellowship to those preaching that "Christ tasted death for every man."[60] In agreeing to eleven stated points, they also agreed in principle to deny fellowship to Unitarians like James Garrard and Augustin Eastin, and Universalists like John Bailey.

In agreeing to bar Universalists and Unitarians from their fellowship, Elkhorn's ministers could argue that they were simply enforcing doctrinal parameters they had maintained since their founding. One might also argue, theology notwithstanding, that union meant that South Kentucky and Elkhorn had also reached a soft political consensus. Elkhorn would no longer hold South Kentucky's apparent lack of revolutionary zeal against them, seeing that the heart of their noninvolvement lay in rebelling against established authority. For many, the Revolution had been about securing property rights as much or more than securing freedom. In Kentucky, land issues would jam the courts for decades to come. The second state constitution guaranteed

slaves as property for the foreseeable future. Given that their selective application of revolutionary ideology had prevailed, perhaps Elkhorn's ministers
now saw South Kentucky's ministers as allies in a war to protect land rights.
Regardless, by redefining themselves as "United" both camps seemed united
in their goal of preserving slavery. And, in articulating their common agreement with respect to the Bible and salvation, they also established orthodox
parameters for the churches to follow. In so doing, both associations faced a
certain amount of theological house cleaning.

In Kentucky's earliest days some feared the Commonwealth might fall
to Universalism or Unitarianism before other forms of faith could gain a
toehold. In 1803 Elkhorn appointed David Barrow, Carter Tarrant, Joseph
Redding, John Price, and Ambrose Dudley to visit the Cooper's Run Church,
along with Indian Creek, Flat Lick, and Union.[61] Kentucky's second governor, James Garrard, was a member of Cooper's Run, where Augustin Eastin
served as pastor. Kentucky's early Baptists knew both men as zealous advocates for orthodox Christianity, but by 1803 both abandoned orthodox, Trinitarian Christianity for Arianism.[62] Historian J. H. Spencer described Eastin
as "vain and [aspiring] to imitate distinguished men. He became a zealot
for Governor Garrard's religious tenets and wrote a pamphlet to prove that
Jesus Christ was inferior to the Father."[63] The United Baptists affirmed the
Trinity as a cardinal doctrine among themselves and held no fellowship with
non-Trinitarians.[64] The committee found Cooper's Run beyond reclamation.
Union, Indian Creek, and Flat Lick remained in Elkhorn's fold once they
addressed Arianism within the congregations. "Thus was the Socinian or Ar-
ian affair promptly nipped in the bud and speedily perished," noted Spencer,
"with the loss, to the Baptists, of a governor, a preacher, a church, and a few
private members."[65]

Purging South Kentucky of its aberrant theology proved more difficult.
Once again, the controversy focused on John Bailey. By all accounts, Bailey
may have been the most highly regarded man in the South Kentucky Association. An accomplished preacher, Bailey also served on the committees
that framed Kentucky's first two state constitutions. South Kentucky had
taken action against Bailey for espousing a form of Universalism then known
as "Hell Redemptionism," or the belief that all would be spared from hell
thanks to Christ's death on the cross. According to one contemporary, Re-
demptionists differed among themselves: "Some of them extend the doctrine
to fallen angels, others confine it to the human race—some believe there will
be no punishment after death, others conclude that torment will be inflicted
in *Hades* upon rebellious souls, even until the resurrection of the body; and
others that they will not all be restored, till the expiration of several periodical

eternities. Those who avow this doctrine are called *Universalists, Hell-redemptionists*, &c."[66]

No one specified exactly where Bailey stood, but his beliefs had hindered union with Elkhorn in the early 1790s. Consequently, his association disfellowshipped him along with several other ministers holding similar sentiments. For some reason, South Kentucky reversed itself in 1799 and admonished churches to restore those excluded under the earlier ruling "to their former standing, *without enquiring into their private sentiments*, provided their morals were good."[67] Several churches quickly followed the association's lead, including Rush Branch Church which reclaimed Bailey as both a member and pastor.

Apparently, Bailey was as likeable as he was capable. He ranked among Kentucky's leading citizens and both his sincerity and moral rectitude were beyond reproach. But if the terms of union meant anything, John Bailey was not welcome as a union minister. The South Kentucky Association became known as the South District Association after uniting with Elkhorn. When South District met in 1803, word leaked that John Bailey would be investigated for heresy. According to Spencer, "Bailey determined that this should not be done." Once the association convened, he defended himself by making "an impassioned plea to the messengers to guard against the usurpation of tyrannical power by associations. . . ." Bailey then invited those who shared his views to abandon the South District Association and follow him. "His personal popularity and power of his eloquence made the people forget his heresy," claimed Spencer, "and he drew after him a majority of the association. This caused an immediate division of that body. A majority of churches adhered to Mr. Bailey's party. Each party claimed the name and prerogatives of South District Association. The corresponding associations acknowledged the minority and rejected the correspondence of the majority. After this, Mr. Bailey's party resumed the name South Kentucky Association of Separate Baptists."[68]

Through it all, Bailey's friends claimed that he did not advance "Hell Restorationism" from the pulpit and they resented what they saw as Elkhorn's highhandedness. Even Spencer conceded that the churches that followed him did not seem to be affected by the teaching. Nonetheless, Elkhorn and its affiliated associations wanted nothing to do with the new association, and the feeling was mutual.

Likewise, the Elkhorn Association discovered that their "pragmatic Calvinism" could not quell political controversies in the association. The United Baptists were still basking in their achievement when emancipation became an issue in the person of David Barrow. One of their most revered ministers, Barrow had been one of the persecuted brethren from Virginia, where he had

opposed slavery from his earliest ministry days. Even though he was well respected for his willingness to suffer for the faith, he found himself out of favor
among the brethren in 1808 for his outspoken opposition to slavery.[69]

Looking Forward

From the mid-1780s until the early nineteenth century, revival played a significant role in shaping religious life for Kentucky's early Baptists. Most of
these pioneers had been converted in revival services before the American
Revolution. Revival in Virginia led to union between Kentucky's Separate
and Regular Baptists, while small-scale revivals kept the hope for union alive
as both parties negotiated their differences. Revivals called sinners to repentance and the faithful to service. If revivals served as a barometer of God's
relative pleasure or displeasure in a people, Kentucky's Baptists—particularly
those affiliated with the Elkhorn Association—must have been pleased with
the way things stood in 1805.

J. H. Spencer surely overstated the case when he proclaimed a "golden
age" for Kentucky's Baptists. In reflecting on revival and its ultimate significance, Robert Semple concluded that it had affected all Baptists for the better.
In his estimation, preachers had become "more correct in their manner of
preaching" as "whoops and awkward gestures" fell by the wayside. This more
restrained preaching style produced a more rational piety which, in turn, had
earned Baptists a measure of social respectability.[70] In time, increasing struc-
turalizing would allow for even greater mobility and recognition beyond the
associational level.

Conversely, the supreme irony of revival is its tendency to cause division.
The Great Awakening split Congregationalist and Presbyterian churches even
as scores of people claimed eternal life in Christ. Historian Robert Semple
observed that revivals produce growth which, in turn, seeks depth. That is,
revivals inspired new converts and mature Christians alike to explore the mysteries of their faith. Such explorations sometimes led to theological conclu-
sions that ran contrary to prevailing norms within a tradition. For instance, in
their effort to strike a proper balance between belief and behavior, Calvinists
saw some turn to Arminianism, while others became antinomian. Still others
abandoned "experiential religion" for more a more speculative faith. "To dive
deeply into the mysteries of the Gospel," wrote Semple, "to tell or to make a
plausible guess about what happened before the world was made or what will
happen before it shall end, looked more wise and excited more applause than
to travel on in the old track."[71]

The Elkhorn Baptists had supported the American Revolution and claimed their birthright in Kentucky. Revivals had seemingly affirmed their path in conversions and unity. Yet, as Semple wryly observed, "Speculators seldom make warm Christians."[72] If religion and politics make strange bedfellows, old controversies born from unpopular stances based on moral conviction such as emancipation die hard. Revivalism played a significant role in shaping the "good old Virginia doctrine" for which William Hickman yearned, but the revival that helped galvanize the Elkhorn Association was not strong enough to keep it together.

5

Ties That Would Not Bind

It was a most unusual trial; on that, everyone agreed. The plaintiff was a well-known local man, an entrepreneur who passionately advocated causes he believed to be right. He had accused the defendant, another well-known citizen, of fourteen specific crimes ranging from lying to theft. But this trial was unique in several respects. For starters, the trial was not held at the Fayette County courthouse, but at the Town Fork Baptist Church (TFBC), near Lexington. The defendant, Jacob Creath Sr., served as TFBC's pastor. The plaintiff, Elijah Craig, likewise a well-known local minister, neither attended TFBC nor was he involved in the incident that led to the trial. He did not even confront Creath to his face. Instead, he made his allegations in an inflammatory pamphlet titled, "A Portrait of Jacob Creath." The trial lasted four days, and perhaps to no one's surprise, the church acquitted their pastor of all charges. Yet no one breathed a sigh of relief, because this episode was far from over.

The issues surrounding Creath's "trial" are both complicated and intricate. In fact, this episode represented only part of a much larger story that played out in the Elkhorn Association between 1805 and 1811. Four different controversies flared up in the association that forever changed religious life for all concerned. Each controversy involved a leading associational figure, or figures. Two of the controversies revolved around conflict within individual churches. One conflict began as an interpersonal squabble that drew a combination of individuals and churches into the fray. Each of the problems involved slavery in some way, and considered together, they reveal smoldering resentments bearing on theological suspicion, personality conflicts, changing concepts of pastoral ministry, and personal honor. When the dust finally settled, the Elkhorn Association found itself fractured beyond repair.

Controversy One: David Barrow

Slavery had been a problem for Elkhorn's Baptists since Kentucky's earliest days. In August 1786, the association heard two separate queries regarding the "peculiar institution." The first query asked if slaves may be "proper gospel members" of churches the answer was clear: "A slave may be considered a proper Gospel member." The second, far more complicated query asked if it was lawful for a slave who was an "orderly member" to marry another wife if he had been forced to abandon his first wife and relocate a considerable distance with his master. The answer: "As an opinion cant be had at this time agreed to refer the query to the next Association and in the meantime advise the churches not to receive any more members under the above circumstance mentioned in said query."[1] True to their word, the association revisited the issue in 1787 with the answer, "Debated and withdrawn."[2] The issue resurfaced in 1789 when the Marble Creek Church asked "whether a woman slave that left a husband in the old Country and marry again here to a husband that has a wife twenty miles from him who also refuses to keep said man as a husband ought her marrying in such circumstances to be a bar to her membership? Ans[wer:] Debarred from membership."[3]

The queries from 1787 to 1789, and the aborted 1791 memorial on slavery and religious liberty, suggest a broad spectrum of thought within the Elkhorn Association. Everyone agreed that slaves could be church members, but they could not agree that slave marriages enjoyed the same status as white marriages. Nonetheless, everyone agreed that slaves could conduct themselves in such a way that disqualified them from church membership. In the end it appears that some opposed slavery, while others did not. A third group likely entertained mixed feelings on the matter with some leaning toward emancipation, while others leaned toward affirming slavery despite the moral problems it raised. Like it or not, by the end of 1791 the Elkhorn Association had sided with the Commonwealth's proslavery majority, and the problem simmered in the background until David Barrow denounced slavery as a moral evil.

Born in Brunswick County, Virginia, in 1753, Barrow began preaching in 1771. He served churches in Virginia and North Carolina until he and his family moved to Kentucky. Virginia Baptists revered him for his zeal and courage. On one occasion in 1778 a mob attacked and nearly drowned him.[4] Undaunted, Barrow continued to preach, much to the delight of his friends and congregants.

Once America secured independence from Great Britain, most individuals doubtless experienced mixed emotions over what it meant to be free. While some spoke openly of religious toleration, there seemed to be no clear consensus on precisely who would be free or what freedom entailed. As for slavery, Barrow numbered among those who were increasingly vexed by human bondage. In 1784 Barrow freed his slaves, and he encouraged others to do likewise.[5]

By the early 1790s Barrow had grown restless in Virginia and looked to Kentucky as a place where he might make a fresh start. He made a brief excursion into the Commonwealth in 1795 and moved his family there in 1798.

Before leaving Virginia, he penned a circular letter explaining his reasons for moving. He professed no ill will toward anyone, but rather claimed that moving to Kentucky would allow him to pay his debts, provide for his family, and furnish resources whereby he might practice Christian hospitality. In short, he believed Kentucky afforded more opportunity than Virginia.[6]

After explaining his reasons for moving to Kentucky, Barrow offered a fifteen-point summary of his theological convictions which affirmed his commitment to Calvinistic Regular Baptist principles, and a twenty-six-point summary of his political convictions which affirmed his commitment to Jeffersonian Republicanism. Of his twenty-six-point "Political Creed," six points are especially noteworthy with respect to Barrow's understanding of civil liberty:

> 3. I believe that Government is an evil, as it cannot be supported without making considerable sacrifices of natural liberty; but, in our present state of depravity, it is to be preferred to a state of nature.

> 4. That Government is a civil compact, of a people emerging from a state of nature, contrived by themselves for their own severity and is subject to the controul, and liable to alteration, when thought proper by a majority of such community.

> 6. That all natural born citizens, arriving at an age, the community may have a call for their services, with all emigrants, having conformed to the rules of naturalization, are entitled to the right of suffrage.

> 14. That civil rulers have nothing more to do with religion, in their public capacities, than private men; save only, they should protect its professors in the uninterrupted enjoyment of it, with life, property, and character, in common with other citizens.

> 15. That no man, or set of men, in a community, are entitled to special privileges.

> 21. That tortures, to force confession of suspected crimes, are cruel and heathenish.[7]

Barrow ended his letter with a prayer for peace and harmony among Virginia's population. He also prayed for fair, evenhanded justice in the courts and an end to all error, theological and nontheological.[8]

In concluding his remarks, Barrow expressed his concern about three things in particular. He prayed that "all masters, or owners of slaves, may consider how inconsistent that act with a Republican Government and whether in this particular, they are *doing as they would others should do to them. . . .*"[9] He anticipated negative backlash from slaveholders but he reminded his readers that even if some slave owners were benevolent, many others were not, and no one could predict what would happen when slaves were traded or sold. Even though he saw problems with human governments, he believed bad governments, and hence, bad laws, including those upholding slavery, could be changed if enough people demanded it. Until then, Barrow called upon ministers to be good shepherds to their flocks, and perhaps above all, he prayed that the churches would maintain "a regular and gospel discipline" and that God would bless the land with a great revival.[10]

In 1798 Barrow settled into his new home near Mt. Sterling and soon became pastor of the Mount Sterling Church, which united with the Elkhorn Association just before Kentucky's "Great Revival." Between 1801 and 1803 scores of people professed conversion and sought church membership as a series of revivals swept the Commonwealth. It should have been a time of great rejoicing and unity, but the rapid increase in conversions and baptisms coupled with the emergence of the United Baptists exposed a lingering resentment over slavery that would not die.

Slavery emerged as an issue again just ahead of the Great Revival. The issue had been relatively quiet at the associational level, but it continued to bedevil individual churches and certain ministers. Toward the end of the 1790s some preachers began to preach openly against slavery. A disapproving J. H. Spencer captured the sentiments of Elkhorn's proslavery ministers when he wrote, "Emancipation parties were formed in many of the churches, by which their peace was much disturbed. The imprudence of the abolition preachers, in declaiming against slavery, in the presence of the negroes, caused insubordination among the slaves, and thereby disturbed the peace of society. This, however, was true only of the ignorant and more excitable preachers among the emancipators. The better class of these preachers were men of wisdom and piety."[11]

As Baptist ranks swelled, sympathetic preachers renewed their call for emancipation, with mixed results. Some like Carter Tarrant sympathized with the emancipationists, while others wanted nothing to do with them. The pro-emancipation party looked to established preachers like David Barrow for leadership. With opinions ranging from ardent support for slavery to calls for immediate emancipation, the Elkhorn Association passed a pivotal resolution in 1805: "The Association judges it improper for ministers, churches, or associations, to meddle with emancipation from slavery, or any other political subject; and as such we advise ministers and churches to have nothing to do therewith in their religious capacities."[12] Slavery was becoming increasingly divisive, and this resolution was obviously aimed at curbing emancipationists. One month after Elkhorn passed their resolution, David Barrow discovered how serious the state's proslavery Baptists really were.

Each Baptist Association operated according to its own bylaws. The North District Association grew out of the South Kentucky Association. In Spencer's account, the South Kentucky Association ratified the Terms of Union in 1801 and immediately divided into the North and South Districts. Barrow's church in Mount Sterling had originally affiliated with the Elkhorn Association, but chose to join with the North District Association after 1804. Curiously, the North District Association allowed messengers from sister associations full associational privileges, including voting rights in their annual meetings. The Elkhorn Association had always enjoyed a kind of preeminent status among Kentucky's Baptist associations, and some took their admonition not to "meddle with emancipation" as a mandate to silence the antislavery voices in their midst. Thus, in October 1805, the Bracken Association's messengers to the North District's annual meeting preferred charges against Barrow for preaching emancipation.[13] The North District investigated the matter over the next year and in 1806 they expelled Barrow from their fellowship. Not content with this outrage, some tried to get Barrow ousted from his own church.

By 1807 a number of North District ministers experienced a change of heart and they sought to restore Barrow to their fellowship, but it was too late. Barrow and his fellow emancipationists formed a pro-emancipationist association, the Baptized Licking-Locust Association, Friends to Humanity. The new association constituted itself with seven churches and quickly added two others for a total of nine. They also chose Carter Tarrant to be their moderator.[14]

As the Friends to Humanity gathered momentum, David Barrow committed his thoughts about slavery to writing. In a small book titled *Involuntary, Unmerited, Perpetual, Absolute, Hereditary, Slavery Examined on the Principles of Nature, Reason, Justice, Policy, and Scripture*, he took his fellow ministers to task for supporting slavery, targeting their justifications one by one. It was a stinging denunciation of slavery on ethical, political, and scriptural grounds.[15] Emancipationists found a new home among the Friends to Humanity and Barrow's book provided them with a thoughtful counterargument to slavery advocates.[16] As for Elkhorn, by ridding themselves of their emancipationists they could resume living under the fiction that slavery was merely a political issue—but not for long.

Controversy Two: William Hickman
and the Forks of the Elkhorn Church

As associations across the state debated emancipation, several related inci-
dents occurred at the Forks of the Elkhorn Baptist Church (FEBC) that illus-
trate the increasingly hard line some Baptist churches took on slavery. In May
1806 the church minutes note that a member, or perhaps a group of members,
asked if the Bible authorized ministers to preach emancipation. This query
likely sought clarification on the Elkhorn resolution, to wit: Was it merely
improper to meddle with emancipation, or forbidden altogether? The church
referred the question to their next session and in their June business meeting
amended the query to read, "Does this Church think that Baptist Preachers
are Authorized from the Word of God to Preach Emancipation of Negroe
Slaves," then promptly "voted out" the amended query.[17] The church then
affirmed the Elkhorn Association's advice to leave emancipation alone. Then,
in December 1806, FEBC rebuked their pastor for allowing Carter Tarrant
to preach at his house. The church minutes read: "A charge against Brother
Hickman for inviting Carter Tarrant to preach at his house after being Excluded for disorder in the Hillsborough Church—the Church took the Question, is it right to Invite an Excommunicated Minister to preach? Answer'd by
a majority of three fourths it is not—2ndly five said Bro. Hickman had Erred
by so doing. Eight said he had not. Signed Mordecai Boulware M."[18]

The Hillsborough Church was in Woodford County, not far from the
Clear Creek Church. Doubtless, Tarrant's pro-emancipationist stance earned
his exclusion from that congregation, but there is no record detailing precisely
how Hickman erred. Had he erred in allowing an excommunicated preacher
to preach at his *home*, or was the error in allowing an *emancipationist* to preach
in his home? Likely, the real error lay in Hickman keeping company with an
emancipationist, but the church seemed uncertain. A three-fourths majority
of FEBC believed Hickman had acted in a disorderly manner by inviting
Tarrant to preach at his home, thus raising another issue: What did it mean
to be "disorderly"? In the ensuing discussion, eight members spoke in their
pastor's behalf, while five members spoke against him. The church minutes
specify no definition for "disorderly." Neither do they indicate the real depth
of the church's displeasure. However, this much is certain: William Hickman
had aligned himself with Kentucky's emancipationists by associating with
Carter Tarrant, and a majority of FEBC disapproved.

While the church mulled its December business session, another controversy erupted. In January 1807 FEBC heard the case of a slave woman
named Winney. The charges were preferred by Winney's owner, Sister Esther

Boulware, who complained, "she [Winney] once thought it her duty to serve her Master & Mistress but since the lord had converted her, she had never believed that any Christian kept Negroes or Slaves." Had she left the matter at that, Winney may not have been hauled before the church, but according to Sister Boulware, Winney also said "she believed there was Thousands of white people Wallowing in hell for their treatment to Negroes—and she did not care if there was as many more."[19]

The church excluded Winney for her insolence at their February 1807 business session, but their ordeal with slavery was by no means settled. In September William Hickman, the founding pastor of Forks of the Elkhorn Baptist Church tendered his resignation. In leaving he explained that he was troubled over slavery, as the church minutes state succinctly: "Bro. William Hickman came forward and informed the church that he was distressed on account of the practice of Slavery as being tolerated by the members of the Baptist Society, (and) therefore declared himself no more in Union with us, or the Elkhorn Association—Therefore, the Church considers him no more a member in fellowship."[20]

Of course, church minutes seldom capture an event's emotion or nuance, and not everyone remembered Hickman's resignation in such sterile terms. For example, Theodrick Boulware remembered the event vividly. Boulware had grown up in the church and would go on to make a name for himself as a preacher. One of his contemporaries, John Taylor, described him starkly: "He is much of a preacher," said Taylor, "and considered orthodox by all the high-toned predestinarians. His preaching bears the semblance of a man snuffing a candle, as if he would take away from true religion all the superfluities that could possibly mingle themselves with it. Some are of the opinion that he snuffs a little too deep. He has a greater aptitude to trim hypocrites than to invite poor sinners to come to Christ."[21] As an old man Boulware penned his memoirs, and Hickman's departure from FEBC had left quite an impression.

Some fifty years after the fact, Boulware still recalled that it was a day of fasting and prayer. Hickman preached from Isaiah 58:6: "Is not this the fast I have chosen? to loose the bands of wickedness, to undo the heavy burdens, and to let the oppressed go free, and that ye break every yoke?" (KJV). Whether Hickman was still stinging from the business session of December 1806 or not is anyone's guess; but as Boulware saw it, "The sermon was disingenuous and offensive, declaring a nonfellowship for all slave holders; and a few days after sent a lengthy and abusive letter to the Church, declaring his withdrawal."[22] The FEBC responded to Hickman's departure by calling John Shackleford as their new pastor in January 1808.

In the meantime, the Friends to Humanity wasted no time articulating their cause. In 1808 Carter Tarrant, the Friend's unofficial scribe, published *A History of the Baptized Ministers and Churches in Kentucky, &c. Friends to Humanity.* Tarrant wanted to set the record straight with respect to those Baptists who advocated emancipation. "I suppose," he began, "that I should not have thought of an history of this kind, had it not been for the abounding of misrepresentations. Although the Romans had a law which condemned no man until he was heard, yet the maxim does not hold good respecting us. I think I have had about twenty trials in this state, and never was at but one of them. . . ."[23] Tarrant further explained that he and his fellow emancipationists saw the right to liberty as an inalienable right, one that enslaved Africans had never forfeited. Further, he noted that emancipation had become the problem it was because of the Elkhorn's "aristocratical decree for ministers and churches not to 'meddle with emancipation.'"[24] Other associations, like Bracken, apparently took Elkhorn's suggestion as a mandate to purge their ranks of those who favored emancipation.

Tarrant listed a number of ministers who were friendly to the emancipationist cause, even if their churches were not, including William Hickman. Toward the end of his book, he affirmed the group's commitment to what they believed to be genuine republicanism, and appended minutes of the group's first meeting.[25] Significantly, these minutes contain a list of twelve queries posed by the assembled ministers. Question 2 asked, "Can any person be admitted a member of this meeting, whose practice appears friendly to perpetual slavery? Answer—we think not." Question 3 was equally straightforward, but suggests that emancipation was tricky, even for emancipationists: "Is there any case in which persons holding slaves may be admitted to membership into a church of Christ?" Generally, the answer was no, but there were five possible exceptions:

1. In the case of a person holding young slaves, and recording a deed of their emancipation at such an age as the church to which they offer, may agree to.

2. In the case of persons who have purchased in their ignorance—and are willing that the church shall say when the slave or slaves shall be free.

3. In the case of women whose husbands are opposed to emancipation.

4. In the case of a widow who had it not in her power to liberate them.

5. In the case of idiots, old age or any debility of body that

prevents such slave from procuring a sufficient support; and some other cases which we would wish the churches to be at liberty to judge of agreeably to the principles of humanity.[26]

As a rule, the Friends to Humanity held no fellowship with slaveholders, but they would make exceptions under well-defined circumstances. Ultimately, however, their main objective remained emancipation.

As the Friends to Humanity ironed out their associational details, the FEBC conducted their affairs under John Shackleford's watchful eye. However, the FEBC minutes suggest that the church faced some deep soul searching, if not turmoil. In October 1808 the church asked Shackleford to remain as their preacher for "one more year."[27] In December 1808 the church received and referred the following query: "Does this church think it right to open her doors to Bro. Smith, Barrow & Tarrant and all those that we believe preaches the Gospel, that are in good standing in their own Churches, and try to be as friendly as in days past." The minutes for the following business session simply state, "The Query referred to this meeting from our last, throw'd out."[28] After considering the discarded query, the church took up the matter of their preacher, John Shackleford. For reasons unspecified, some did not want him to remain as their minister. A faction within the congregation may have hoped that Hickman would return, but after discussing the matter, all agreed that the status quo was their best option.[29]

John Shackleford served the church for about two years until Hickman suddenly returned in November 1809, seeking restoration with his former congregation. But all was not forgiven—at least, not yet. Once again, Boulware's recollections are instructive. Before Hickman could be restored, Boulware asked the clerk to read the former's resignation letter. After the letter had been read, Boulware noted that nothing in the church had changed since Hickman's departure. If anything, his actions had done far more harm than good, seeing that he emboldened slaves to disobey their masters, to which masters responded with "double severity." There was little Hickman could say; but "the church, from sympathy received him."[30]

If Hickman left FEBC over slavery, why would he want to return? Boulware believed he knew the answer. He claimed that the church had always supported his "large and extravagant family" well. Obviously, some, perhaps most, of that support came from slave labor, and since his departure, Hickman was no longer supported as before. In Boulware's assessment, Hickman's return to FEBC was rooted in self-interest rather than God's leadership. Principles were one thing; survival was another. Boulware concluded by musing, "I have observed that the conscientious scruples of Emancipators and Abolitionists are much regulated by their party, or personal interest. In the New Testament, Jesus Christ enforced every duty, and warned of all evil. Servants and slavery are one thing, but inhumanity and barbarity is another matter."[31]

There may be good reason why Boulware's recollection of Hickman's departure and return are especially pointed. Theodrick's brother, Mordecai Boulware, had moderated the December 1806 business session that rebuked Hickman for his association with Carter Tarrant. As for Winney, the FEBC minutes for January 1807 identify her as belonging to Theodrick's mother, Esther Boulware.[32]

William Hickman's ambivalence toward slavery may not have been his only issue with the FEBC membership. True, this church was scarcely the place for an emancipationist, especially as pastor, but the animosity against William Hickman may have been simmering long before his stormy departure. If that is true, the Boulwares were not the only ones who had issues with their pastor. Even though he had been instrumental in establishing the church, for unspecified reasons Hickman was not the unanimous choice to lead the new congregation. During their earliest days, the membership chose Nathaniel Sanders and John Major as deacons, but they could not decide who to call as their minister. After two months the church finally settled on Hickman, and if his family really was as "large and extravagant" as Boulware claimed, a certain amount of continual friction between pastor and church might be understandable.[33]

The attempts to define the limits of nonfellowship with emancipationists and the call for restoring relationships with certain preachers "as before," indicates that a significant minority sympathized with their pastor and sought to extend an olive branch to their estranged brethren. One might also infer that many thought Hickman would ultimately return. The church apparently never became deeply attached to John Shackleford, choosing to address his tenure only in provisional terms. In any event, FEBC's faithful might "agree to disagree" on any number of issues, including William Hickman and his family, but the majority had spoken: FEBC was a proslavery congregation.

The details are sketchy as for how William Hickman the emancipationist reassumed the pastorate at FEBC. First, Hickman apparently spent sufficient time with the Friends to Humanity to be numbered among them. Tarrant's *History* lists Hickman as one of their ministers, but he also notes that slave owners who wanted to affiliate with the Friends to Humanity could only do so under extremely proscriptive circumstances. Therein lay the rub: Hickman owned a slave.[34] One historian for FEBC speculated that Hickman may have kept the slave as a benevolent act, rather than furnishing freedom without providing any means of support.[35] However, this suggestion seems unlikely for several reasons. The tax records for 1800 show that William Hickman owned over 1,500 acres, but no slaves. Ten years later the tax records show that he owned over 600 acres and one slave who was at least sixteen years old.[36] Thus, Hickman could not have been sheltering an old slave who could no longer work. Moreover, if he really was caring for an aged or infirmed slave, Hickman could have remained affiliated with the Friends to Humanity, seeing that they agreed to make provisions for slave owners who could not emancipate a slave for certain humanitarian reasons. While the tax records supply neither the details for when Hickman acquired the slave nor how this deal transpired, it seems more likely he had purchased a slave to help attend to his land.[37] If that is the case, Hickman allowed opportunity and the prospect for gain to trump his idealism.

There may have been other factors that contributed to Hickman's return to FEBC. In November 1809 a controversy in the Elkhorn Association had reached fever pitch, and the association would soon face a schism that would lead to the formation of a new association, the Licking Association. Assessing that controversy and its subsequent impact on Kentucky Baptist development is beyond the scope of this inquiry. But in seeking reconciliation with his former congregation, Hickman may have guessed that associational schism was coming and concluded that casting his lot with FEBC and the Elkhorn Association was his best option.

Controversy Three: Jacob Creath and Thomas Lewis

Amidst the flap surrounding Barrow and the problems at Forks of the Elkhorn Church, a third controversy erupted. This conflict pitted Jacob Creath, pastor of Town Fork Baptist Church (TFBC), against Thomas Lewis, a wealthy member of TFBC. Initially, the Creath-Lewis agitation did not even involve Elijah Craig, but he soon became a pivotal figure in a controversy that would soon divide the Elkhorn Association.

The problem began when Thomas Lewis exchanged slaves with Jacob Creath. Apparently, Creath's slave was not as valuable as Lewis's, so Lewis wrote a note for the balance due. Unfortunately, the slave Creath obtained from Lewis died within a short time of the transaction. Creath, in turn, did not feel like he had received his money's worth in the deal, and he refused to honor his debt for the outstanding balance. This led to a conflict between the two, and when they could not reach a mutually satisfactory resolution to their disagreement, they asked the church to arbitrate their differences. Upon hearing both sides, the church absolved Pastor Creath of any outstanding debt, reasoning that Lewis "was wealthy and Creath was poor."[38] This phase of the Creath-Lewis controversy clearly demonstrates that Baptists recognized the elites among them, and they had since Elkhorn's founding. Further, those who held prominent positions intended to curb any conflicting impulses.

According to Baptist polity, churches are independent, self-governing bodies and not bound by any ecclesiastical authority beyond the local congregation. Nonetheless, TFBC's decision sparked a sense of outrage among some in the Elkhorn Association, particularly Elijah Craig. Among Kentucky's earliest permanent settlers, Craig seemed particularly offended by the church's action. Craig had commanded great respect when he lived in Virginia, but one writer described him as a "bold, out-spoken man, whose honest candor disdained all policy, and who had in the decline of his life, become somewhat soured in his temper. . . ."[39]

After TFBC sided with their pastor, Craig's sour temper boiled over in a pamphlet titled, "A Portrait of Jacob Creath." This pamphlet was a defamatory screed that attacked nearly every facet of Creath's character and exploited preexisting internal divisions within the association. Craig's allegations were sufficiently serious for TFBC to call a special meeting, but since the majority of TFBC had sided with their pastor, one chronicler says the church met only to "pass upon" Craig's allegations rather than "investigating" their veracity. As it happened, failure to act against Creath only "intensified the party spirit" and ultimately led to a schism in the association, with the churches opposing Creath leaving Elkhorn to form the Licking Association.[40]

At this juncture it might appear that the impeding schism was a simple matter of personality conflict. If Craig really had become a hateful old man, perhaps other embittered souls merely followed his example in demanding some sort of retribution toward Creath. Several questions, however, merit closer attention. For example, precisely what action was TFBC supposed to take against their pastor? As an autonomous, duly constituted body, TFBC's ruling in Creath's favor should have ended the matter. If other associational churches had no say in another church's internal doings, why did they insinuate themselves in TFBC's business in such a public way? Finally, if the entire mess really was a matter of personality conflict, why was it so intense, so personal? What was it about Jacob Creath that brought out the worst in Elijah Craig, or anyone else for that matter? These questions defy simple answers, but some details are abundantly clear.

Never one to shy away from a controversy, Elijah Craig took it upon himself to expose Jacob Creath as a thoroughgoing scoundrel. As Craig saw it, the situation involved far more than one transaction gone bad. Creath had faced difficulties in all of the churches he served. He was an outsider who aspired to something greater than itinerant ministry. Even worse, he succeeded the venerable John Gano as pastor of Town Fork Baptist Church. Among Elkhorn ministers, Gano may have been the association's crown jewel. His popularity and reputation were unmatched, and he left a sizeable void when he died in 1805. The church called Creath to succeed their celebrated former pastor, a pulpit that many outside of TFBC likely esteemed Creath unworthy to assume.[41]

Outside opinion notwithstanding, a majority of TFBC members supported Creath. The Town Fork Church was not especially large, but its membership included several influential people, including Thomas Lewis. Long before Kentucky became a state, Lewis had established himself as one of the Commonwealth's most prominent citizens. In addition to serving as a colonel in the militia, Lewis had sworn in Isaac Shelby as Kentucky's first governor and he had amassed a fortune before he moved to Kentucky. He owned numerous slaves and the Virginia land book suggests that he originally held claim to over 5,000 acres in his own name, along with an additional 12,500 acres held jointly with Humphrey Marshall.[42] One writer described him as a very "intelligent, enterprising, old Kentucky gentleman" noted for "hospitality and high living."[43]

By contrast, Jacob Creath was the brash interloper. Creath had advised Theodrick Boulware that the ministry would furnish him with an easy life among society's upper crust. In assuming the pastorate of TFBC, Creath may have allowed himself to believe that he had achieved the status and recognition that he coveted. In the end, Creath's affirmation was not unanimous, but it did not matter; a clear majority sided with Creath and that should have settled the issue. Lewis, however, enjoyed a privileged social standing and powerful friends. Creath could not have encountered a worthier adversary.

A minority of TFBC members did not agree with the majority. In one of the more egregious examples of antidemocratic authoritarianism, they appealed to the association for help in settling a matter that should have already been settled. The minutes of the Elkhorn Association for 1806 state, "Received a letter from a minority of Town Fork church informing us of a distress among them; therefore we advise the following churches to send them two members each, to meet at said meetinghouse, the 1st Wednesday in October, and endeavor to settle said distress, vis. North Fork, Forks of Elkhorn, Dry run, Rockbridge, Tate's Creek, and Indian Creek."[44]

Unfortunately, the "helps" could not appease TFBC's aggrieved minority. The timeline is unclear, but Elijah Craig published his pamphlet, "A Portrait of Jacob Creath," soon after TFBC absolved Creath. Apparently, this pamphlet shattered all standards of public decency and civil discourse. One writer described it as "written in a style of inexcusable bitterness."[45]

The TFBC had already tendered their decision on the Creath-Lewis matter, and they did not owe anyone an explanation for their actions. Nonetheless, their pastor's character had been questioned, and a majority believed it was proper to hear the matter and settle things once and for all. In July 1807, the church convened a council composed of a total of forty-two delegates from sixteen different churches. This time the "trial" lasted four days, absolving Creath on all of Craig's charges.[46]

Without Craig's pamphlet it is impossible to say what charges Creath faced. But when the trial ended, the Committee on Helps published their results. The committee considered the following charges:

1. Charge of intrigue and cunning, dismembering society.

2. Charge of breaking rule.

3. Charge for stating that Craig's charges should be heard first.

4. Charge for saying that he did not know a minority, and for riding from house to house to prevent their signing a letter to the association.

5. Charge of falsehood in talking to Clifton Thompson.

6. Charge of not preaching to churches without pay.

7. Charge of falsehood in questioning Jim &c.

8. Charge of making havock and distress in the churches.

9. Charge of telling the judges to keep the $100.

10. Charge of intoxication.

11. Charge of grabbing the money &c. at Frankfort.

12. Charge of false claim to $11250.

13. Charge of impropriety and sin at Mrs. Carter's burial.

14. Charge of corruption used to get helps.

The committee considered each charge separately and cleared Creath of any wrongdoing. Toward the end of the proceedings, the moderator asked, "Is Brother Creath guilty of any of the charges contained in the Pamphlet aforesaid, which have not yet been voted on, supported by evidence brought against him?" Again, the committee found Creath innocent of Craig's allegations.[47] Satisfied with the unanimous ruling, TFBC agreed to publish the committee's report and ordered five hundred copies printed.[48]

Controversy Four: Associational Schism

With Creath in the clear, Elkhorn's faithful looked to return to their regular routines. Unfortunately, not everyone shared the majority's sentiments and clear battle lines were being drawn. The Elkhorn Association minutes for 1807 are somewhat vague, but three things stand out. First, the association heard a question from Mount Pleasant Church and answered, "We are happy in receiving those hints from Mount Pleasant, as they give us an opportunity of expressing our abhorrence of said conduct. We do utterly condemn the principle and practice of one member, in a religious society, publishing the crimes, or defaming the character of his brethren, either by speaking, writing, printing, or any other way whatsoever, except by a proper tribunal."[49] Second, the association tabled an unspecified remonstrance from East Hickman, Rockbridge, and Flat Lick Churches. These churches likely expressed their disapproval of the TFBC proceedings, seeing that the tabled remonstrance followed immediately after the association's strongly worded "disapproval" of public slandering of fellow ministers.[50] Third, and perhaps most telling, Peter Higbee's circular letter articulated an association-wide sense of foreboding. "The present complexion of things," he wrote, "seems to be gloomy and dark, as if it was midnight with the Church of Christ." The revival spirit that had swept the association just a few years earlier had been replaced by confusion, and Higbee believed he knew why. "Alas!" he cried, "we have sinned in departing from the spirit and rules of the gospel; we fear there is a lack of that fundamental principle of Christianity, amongst many of the professors of religion, and its benign influence too little felt among all, that is, charity, which is a grace highly spoken of in the scriptures. . . ."[51] Ironically, the same association that deemed it impolite to "meddle with emancipation" suddenly had no problem meddling in other churches' affairs.

Given the esteem afforded to favored ministers, it is easy to see how controversy could spill over into other churches. In this instance, reaction to Creath's acquittal ranged from relief to outrage. His supporters in TFBC sought to put the episode behind them, but other complaints surfaced, thereby escalating the conflict. Joseph Redding lodged three new allegations against Creath—one he dropped, while the church cleared Creath of the other two. The details are unknown, but Redding apparently alleged that Creath had besmirched Ambrose Dudley's honor. The Bryan Station Baptist Church (BSBC) minutes for October 1807 register a complaint by William Clarkson and Ambrose Dudley "for their [TFBC] improper decisions in a case wherein Bro. Joseph Redding charged Bro. Jacob Creath for slandering Bro. Dudley for which he was acquitted *without being called on for proof*. . . ."[52] The Elkhorn minutes do not specify, but given the circumstances it seems likely that the association viewed the accusations as a continuation of a conflict that should already have been settled. The BSBC minutes for December 1807 indicate that TFBC had responded to the complaint, but the response did not satisfy the BSBC fellowship. In June 1808, BSBC complained to the association regarding TFBC, and in September their grievance had not been removed.[53]

Soon the entire association was enmeshed in the turmoil, once again dragging the association's churches into a conflict that should not have existed. In late 1808 or early 1809, a broadside titled, "A Caution to the Churches Composing the Elkhorn Association," began circulating in Central Kentucky. The author styled himself "Peruse, Esquire," and he implied that the association was treading in areas they should avoid. As the writer saw it, Craig and others were undermining church independence, and having failed to impose their will on TFBC, they now wanted to focus attention on themselves. Peruse queried, "What has the association to do with the individual members of any Church? nothing: what have they to do with either Craig or his pamphlet? nothing: then those priests must mean something else—Is not Craig a member of a Church? yes: (and mores the pity). . . ." Assuming Craig to be a church member in good standing, Peruse suggested that the church should be the place for him to be tried, and in the event the church could not try him, they might turn to the "sister churches" for assistance. The association might disfellowship a wayward congregation, especially if it harbored a flagrant, unrepentant malcontent, but as Peruse wryly observed, "I hope no person would believe that any member of society professing Christianity, would offer to shelter the crime of E. Craig, which is a head and shoulders higher than any transgression I ever knew committed in the Baptist Society."[54]

To further underscore his point, Peruse chided the anti-Creath faction by comparing them to Herod the Great, who "decreed that all the children should be slain of such an age; but this decree has no bounds, slay old and young peradventure we may slay Jacob Creath."[55] Probably much closer to the truth, the broadside claimed that the anti-Creath faction was jealous because they were losing their power and position. Besides, Creath was right in this instance, and according to Peruse he was a better preacher than any of them: "Do not their acts testify the truth of this? Yes. Oh! you little ones, why envy the great? It is the gift of God. How can you expect good men to respect you, while you have E. Craig and his bag of filth in your bosom? A poor creature void of shame and feeling, that long since has been sunk into insignificance." Peruse ended with a pointed admonition that likely stung many: "Now brethren, stand firm; be your own judges of offences committed in your own churches: secure to every church her independence of judging her own members and never have your members torn from your bosom, to be slain by ambitious priests—and your liberties swallowed up in this great gulph of popery."[56] That is to say, TFBC had done due diligence in vindicating Creath and *that* should have settled the matter. Anything else smacked of Roman Catholicism.

Meanwhile, Elijah Craig had joined Marble Creek Baptist Church (MCBC) in south Fayette County, and he had brought his venom with him. According to the MCBC minutes, Craig joined the church in December 1806, and by February 1807 the MCBC had two separate conflicts to address. On the one hand, the minutes indicate that the church had received a letter "recomending the Different Churches to send Two of their members to meet At Bryans on the third munday to deliberate on the present distress in society—the Church fully Accorded in the same—"[57] On the other hand, with Creath supposedly in the clear, TFBC demanded satisfaction. Would Craig's new home church tolerate his outrageous conduct? The Marble Creek members agreed to answer TFBC's objections.

After considering the matter for about three months, MCBC held its own church council. This "hearing" was part of a regular church business session, and therefore not open to other associational churches. After a few preliminary remarks, including one David Baker's observation that he could not disprove any of Craig's allegations, Craig asked for and received permission to substantiate the charges he made in his pamphlet, "A Portrait of Jacob Creath." He gave names of witnesses who, if asked, would corroborate each of his previous allegations. Not surprisingly, Thomas Lewis and his wife figured prominently in Craig's defense. In the end, MCBC agreed that in their minds Elijah Craig had violated neither the "Rule of Society" nor "the Gospel" in publishing his pamphlet. They also agreed to inform TFBC of their proceedings, doubtless satisfied that their hearing for Craig had been at least as probing as the one TFBC held for Creath.[58]

Craig's vindication likely did more to galvanize Elkhorn's anti-Creath faction than it did to unify Creath's supporters. After all, TFBC had heard charges made against their pastor by a nonmember and cleared him in the presence of numerous witnesses. While some may have wished for a different outcome, the association's churches had no authority to overrule TFBC's decision. Besides, the Elkhorn Association had vindicated the embattled minister, and Creath's supporters wanted to move forward. Others had merely grown weary of it all. On the other hand, MCBC's support for Craig rallied others who believed TFBC's proceedings were little more than a whitewash covering up some rather serious breaches of ministerial ethics. They did not approve of Town Fork's or Elkhorn's actions, but they had no authority to overrule either's decision. However, they were not powerless to do something about it.

In 1808 Bryan Station Church escalated the conflict when they registered a complaint in an associational meeting. This complaint charged TFBC with "disorderly" conduct in its handling of the Creath-Lewis conflict. By now the association had grown weary of the turmoil and wanted to move forward. Upon hearing the complaint, they promptly dismissed it, which only fueled the animosity among those already grieved. They could do little else, and as David Benedict observed, "The association had imprudently intermeddled with a dispute, which it could not consistently decide, and after a lengthy and painful attention to it, its division appeared inevitable."[59]

Ten churches registered their displeasure with the Elkhorn Association by not sending messengers to the 1809 meeting. Disgruntled churches could either accept the association's actions or leave the association and form a new one. Ultimately, a minority opted to leave Elkhorn, but not before they tried to co-opt the existing association. The Bryan Station minutes for February 1810 tell a compelling story: "Received a letter signed by a number of our brethren who have thought it would be most for the peace and happiness of society, under our present distress, to call a meeting on the first Tuesday in March, to meet at the Forks of the Elkhorn, in order to dissolve the Elkhorn Association, which was agreed to. And brethren Ambrose Dudley and Leonard Young are chosen to attend said meeting, and let the brethren know that we chose to meet at what they call the New Elkhorn Association, at Bryants."[60] As J. H. Spencer saw it, "The meaning of this remarkable proceeding is this: That a minority of Elkhorn Association proposed to meet and dissolve that body, without consulting the majority, and then meet again, and reconstitute it, according to their own plans . . . apparently for no other purpose than that of leaving out Jacob Creath and those who failed to adjudge him guilty of the misdemeanors laid to his charge."[61]

Elkhorn learned of the rival meeting and sought to preempt schism by sending messengers to the splinter group. They expressed sorrow over all that had transpired. In an almost embarrassed tone they pleaded, "We can assure you, brethren, that it never was our wish wantonly to hurt the feelings of any of our brethren; we are sorry that such a thing should have taken place. . . ." They tried to extend an olive branch to their estranged brethren by assuring them of their willingness to "cast into the sea of forgetfulness, as much as possible, our former difficulties."[62]

The Elkhorn delegation received a swift response. The minority association refused to be reconciled. "You are in possession of our difficulties," they said, "[and] until they are removed we remain a distressed and grieved people."[63] There would be no reconciliation. The minority wrote, "Taking all things into consideration we are of the opinion that it will be for the happiness of each, to continue in two Associations."[64] They would conduct business much as they always had; they professed to be "warmly attached" to Elkhorn's rules and constitution. "As for names," they wrote, "we are not tenacious, we are willing to be known by the name of the 'Licking Association.'"[65]

The churches that met at Bryan Station posed a new set of problems for Elkhorn. Not everyone supported the schism, much less a new association. Churches divided into pro-Elkhorn and pro-Licking factions based largely on where their minister stood in the Creath-Lewis conflict. But which faction constituted the "real" church? The Elkhorn Association minutes for 1810 note the receipt of a request from a minority at Bryan Station—the latter requesting formal recognition because, in their thinking, the majority had "violated useage." Elkhorn recognized the minority, and soon Elkhorn and Licking began recognizing the faction that identified with them, even if it was a minority within the church.[66]

In 1811 the Elkhorn Association should have been celebrating its twenty-fifth anniversary. Instead, it marked the occasion with a schism and the formation of a new association. It is difficult to fathom how men who had fought for religious freedom and even suffered for their faith could not find enough common ground to forgive and forbear with one another over an issue that did not directly involve them. There were other attempts to reconcile the two groups after 1810, but with no success. Neither party seemed willing to admit any wrongdoing.[67]

The matter might have died quietly had it not been for a public exchange between Henry Toler and James Fishback. In 1821 Toler, pastor of Grier's Creek Particular Baptist Church, published a pamphlet titled, "Union—No Union," in which he lambasted the Elkhorn Association for abandoning their constitutional principles and confession of faith. Elkhorn and Licking may have gone their respective ways but each believed their version of what happened was right. The question remained: Whose version of the story would the public accept?

According to some, Toler had been a successful pastor in Virginia. In 1786 he started Nomini Church in Westmoreland County, Virginia. He served this congregation for twenty years and oversaw its growth from 17 to 875 members. He also preached in the surrounding area and distinguished himself as a pulpiteer. He came to Kentucky in 1816 but his career sputtered, and he never experienced the same level of success he enjoyed in Virginia. About 1821, the Grier's Creek Baptist Church called him as pastor. As a condition of assuming the pastorate, Toler demanded that the church identify itself as a "Particular Baptist Church." But when the church voted not to change its affiliation, Toler became so angry that he gathered a small band of disgruntled folk from neighboring churches and constituted a Particular Baptist church in Versailles, which then united with the Licking Association.[68]

Toler believed Elkhorn had deviated from its theological moorings; and he traced the problems to the Union of 1801, whereby Separate Baptists united with Regular Baptists and became "United Baptists."[69] As Toler saw it, the Separate Baptists were not Calvinistic enough in their doctrinal understanding of salvation, and they had eroded the association's doctrinal integrity. "Many regret the union ever happened," Toler claimed, "and many more rejoice in it, and make it supercede the constitution. . . . The dreadful division which happened in the Elk Horn Association was in a few years after the *Union* took place, and though different circumstances led to this distressing event, I have heard it said that that difference of doctrine had a bearing in the case."[70] In short, the Union of 1801 had corrupted Elkhorn's theological purity, and Licking claimed to be the legitimate heirs to the real Elkhorn of 1786.

Henry Toler did not specify who had decried the union on theological terms. Neither did he name names when accusing certain men in the Elkhorn Association of holding aberrant theology. "In the investigation of doctrines, let us recollect in that Introductory sermon four years ago, we heard a preacher say, 'as to *election*, if you are willing as I am, we will leave it for eternity to disclose whether it be true or not."[71] Upon hearing this, Toler claimed that a visiting preacher from Virginia told him that Kentucky Baptists were not sound in the faith. It took several years, but Toler reached a similar conclusion. He declared the Elkhorn Association guilty of numerous heresies ranging from holding to a general atonement to denying election and predestination. Further, he maintained that the association had no real theological center, seeing that they did not follow their own confession of faith. "And though many in the Association have heard this clamor against confessions," he noted, "of which no doubt their *Constitution* is one, they pass it all over softly, and declare they have not departed from the Constitution."[72]

Toler's main complaint centered on the 1801 Plan of Union that united Separate and Regular Baptists when both groups agreed to an eleven-point statement of faith. Article 4 stipulated, "The teaching that Christ tasted death for every man shall be no bar for communion."[73] As he noted, the Elkhorn Association had been established on the Second London Confession of Faith which the Philadelphia Association had modified in 1742 to include specific articles on the imposition of hands and hymn singing. The Second London / Philadelphia Confessions contained more specific statements on Christ's death and its intent. Toler believed the union's statement was much too general and had become a loophole by which all manner of ill had seeped into the association.[74]

Going further, Elkhorn's failure to maintain doctrinal standards had resulted in lax practices. At least, that is how Toler saw it. "By making the way into the church so wide and easy, as to increase the number of improper members; by incautiously ordaining Preachers; all these Preachers, inexperienced and unsound in the faith, and by even creating Preachers; all these Preachers will slide from the standard of Truth to be popular. . . ."[75] He ended his pamphlet by wishing the Elkhorn Association and its churches well, but he could not stay in good conscience.

It was James Fishback who had preached "that Introductory sermon four years ago [1817]" that Toler found so odious, and the former took pen in hand to defend his honor, his theology, and the Elkhorn Association. While Henry Toler did not mention James Fishback's name in his pamphlet, people in the association knew Toler was talking about him. Fishback served First Baptist Church, Lexington, as pastor, and in 1822 he answered Toler's complaints in a book titled, *A Defence of the Elkhorn Association; in Sixteen Letters Addressed to Elder Henry Toler, Pastor of Grier's Creek Particular Baptist Church; in Answer to His Publication, Entitled "Union—No Union."*[76]

If volume counts for anything, Fishback outwrote Toler better than 10 to 1.[77] He wasted no time in staking out his own ground. He accused Toler directly and the Licking Association indirectly of systematically attacking Elkhorn's ministers. "Regardless of plighted faith and covenant obligations," he claimed, "they have waged a predatory war upon Christian society, under the feigned pretence of errors in doctrine, &c.; and, to give to themselves a more imposing character, have assumed the name of *Particular* Baptists." As he saw it, someone needed to stand up against these theological hooligans, "and having myself shared largely in their misrepresentations, and, as far in their power, suffered injury of character as a preacher of the Gospel, I have felt it a duty to undertake it."[78] In defending himself and his fellow Elkhorn ministers, Fishback noted, "Schism and contention in religion always exist at the expense of gospel truth and practical godliness. The movers and leaders of schism and disorder abandon for the most part the preaching of the Gospel for the conversion of sinners, and rely for the building up their party, pulling down and disorganizing other churches; and they soon enlist all the worst principles of fallen human nature in their service."[79]

Fishback spent a good bit of time defending himself against charges of heresy. But, when it came to the Elkhorn Association, he took Toler to task for his loose generalization that doctrine had played a role in the schism. "Against the correctness of the statement that doctrine had any thing to do in the case, I must enter my unqualified protest, and rely upon the most unequivocal evidence to sustain me." According to Fishback, the real difficulty lay in "the Elkhorn Association sustaining the Town Fork Church against three charges of disorder brought against that church by the church at Bryan's, and the recognition of the minorities at Bryan's and Dry Run as competent parts of the Association."[80] He reminded his readers that Elkhorn and Licking had attempted reconciliation on several occasions since 1810, and in no instance did anyone mention doctrine or theology as a barrier to reunion. Further- more, Ambrose Dudley, John Price, and Joseph Redding, three key leaders in the Licking Association, had helped frame the Terms of Union in 1801. Thus, Fishback wondered, how could the Licking brethren see themselves as keepers of theological rectitude, seeing that their own leaders had framed the union they now found so objectionable?[81] "Your opinions and views in several respects must change before you get to heaven," he chided, "for the very same principles and dispositions which make you unhappy, when united with the children of God here, and which prompt you to disturb society, would dis- tress you there. You must have more charity."[82]

The Aftermath and Beyond

David Benedict, a Baptist historian at the time of the Early Republic, hap- pened to tour Kentucky during the Creath-Lewis controversy, and observed the carnage firsthand. He described Creath as "in the meridian of life, of popular talents, but not the most amiable in his manners, nor conciliating in his address. He evidently displayed too much of the air of triumph toward his aggrieved brethren."[83] As Benedict recalled, it was an unsettling trip. "I saw much to admire in my brethren on both sides, but I could not approve their treatment of each other. I was grieved to see a number of aged ministers, whom I had been taught to respect a thousand miles off, and who now ap- peared to be men of wisdom and men of God, so deeply engaged in a frivolous dispute. The majority party appeared more bent on conquest than reconcili- ation. On the whole, I was led to think there must be bad leaven somewhere, to produce such a sour fermentation."[84]

What began as a personal disagreement between two men exchanging slaves ended in associational schism. The personal animosities that each faction nursed occasionally erupted in shameful public displays. But locating what caused Benedict's "sour fermentation" may not be as difficult as one might assume. A comparison of the Licking Association's composition with Elkhorn reveals some interesting details, especially in average church membership. Licking organized with eleven churches totaling 764 members, for an average membership of just over 69 members per church. But, if one subtracts the three largest congregations that number falls to an average of about 45 members. The 1811 mintues for the Licking Association are equally instructive. In that year they claimed sixteen churches with a total membership of 802 members for an average membership of just over 50. By contrast, in 1810 Elkhorn claimed twenty churches with 1,800 members for an average membership of almost 90 members. The 1811 Elkhorn minutes claim a total membership of 2,880 with twenty-eight churches for an average membership of 102.[85] Statistically, Elkhorn's churches tended to be larger than Licking's churches.

Moreover, age may have been a contributing factor in forming the new association. The ministers most responsible for establishing the Licking Association numbered among Elkhorn's "elder statesmen," averaging sixty years old. By contrast, a sampling of Elkhorn ministers in 1810 suggests that the average age for its ministers was forty-one years.[86] One might suggest, therefore, that Licking's ministers were already settled men who did not stand to advance much further in society. They had made their fortune, so to speak, and their day was passing. By contrast, the bulk of the Elkhorn ministers were relatively young, and they still had many years ahead of them. They had more opportunities, and perhaps more significant, they were better attuned to those opportunities. This may have caused a certain amount of jealousy within the association. Since Elkhorn's churches tended to be larger, the opportunities must have seemed greater there.

Jacob Creath's acquittal was a slap in the face for Thomas Lewis on at least two fronts. On one hand the church's use of "rich" and "poor" to describe Creath and Lewis suggests a certain amount of class tension in TFBC. A majority of the church determined to show Lewis that his authority did not reign supreme in ecclesiastical affairs. On the other hand, family ties played a significant role in shaping the controversy. Ambrose Dudly's son, Jephthah, was married to Thomas Lewis's daughter, thus linking Lewis and Dudley through their children. Lewis's will confirmed the "gift of all the property" he had given his son-in-law, along with a gift of $1,000.00 for his grandson, Edmund Ambrose Dudley.[87] To further complicate matters, Thomas Lewis died in 1809. Consequently, Dudley may have been defending Lewis's honor even after his death.

By 1812 there was no shortage of ironies among Central Kentucky's Baptists. Elijah Craig, the man who more than anyone else precipitated the Elkhorn schism, died in 1808 and never saw his handiwork come to full fruition. Jacob Creath ultimately left Baptist ranks and became a Restorationist. Winney, Esther Boulware's slave who openly believed some white people would wallow in hell for their complicity in slavery, was restored to fellowship at the Forks of the Elkhorn Church. Finally, while neither was numbered among Kentucky's first Baptists, James Fishback and Henry Toler more than any of the state's original Baptists fought for the heart of the first Baptist association west of the Alleghenies. Toler was an older minister in the same generation as Dudley, Price, and Redding, while Fishback represented a new generation of ministers. Perhaps it goes without saying but Fishback was also a "settled preacher," the type against whom Craig railed in 1797.

By the early part of the second decade of the nineteenth century, the brethren of the Elkhorn Association probably missed the irony of their situation. Ties forged in battle could not bind them. The deep respect they held for ministers who were persecuted for the faith could not bind them. Not even the Christian love they professed for one another allowed them to lay aside their differences for the unity they said they desired. As Kentucky passed from a frontier state to a more settled, stable state, powerful personalities clashed over the application of basic Christian doctrine. Somehow, they needed to transcend personal agendas and petty squabbles. They needed to find a new consensus, but in their case, the new consensus found them.

6

A Story to Tell the Nations

The Missionary Impulse
and a New Consensus

On October 27, 1819, John Taylor celebrated his sixty-seventh birthday by penning the first few lines of *Thoughts on Missions*, his critique of the modern missionary movement.[1] Taylor was ill and did not expect to recover. As he ordered his affairs, he sensed that something was amiss in Baptist ranks and he felt duty-bound to alert others to certain dangers that were disrupting Baptist unity and harmony.

Taylor's disquietude began in 1812 while he lived on the Ohio River in Gallatin County, Kentucky. That November brought two unusual visitors. John F. Schermerhorn and Samuel J. Mills were conducting religious surveys of the Ohio and Mississippi Valleys on behalf of missionary societies in the northeast. Taylor remembered them as sincere young men, but they failed to make a favorable impression. They were appalled to learn that Taylor received practically no compensation for his preaching, a situation they assured him would change if he would only get his hearers to contribute toward missions.

Taylor understood that his guests were not Baptists, so he held his tongue. But, Mills and Schermerhorn had raised concerns in his mind about organized missions, missionaries, and mission societies. When he wrote *Thoughts on Missions*, Taylor vividly recalled the zealous but condescending missionaries and mused, "But surely it will not be thought uncharitable to say, that I did begin strongly to smell the *New England Rat*."[2]

At thirty-four pages, *Thoughts on Missions* was not Taylor's longest work, but it was arguably his most significant. This booklet earned Taylor a place alongside Daniel Parker and Alexander Campbell as one of the most outspoken critics of missionary societies in America's western territories. Missions bothered Taylor for sectional as well as theological reasons. Mission societies, he believed, were the brainchild of the same individuals who, not long ago, had persecuted his friends and fellow ministers. The missionary "scheme" they touted was merely their latest attempt to dictate religious practices to everyone else. Moreover, the mission movement raised questions about church

polity and religious authority that Taylor believed posed serious threats to the
nature of Baptist ministry itself. In voicing his concerns, he helped unleash
a firestorm of criticism against himself and those who shared his concerns.
John Taylor had no way to know it but the mission controversy of the early
nineteenth century was a test case for how Baptists would conceptualize their
own religious identity and practice in the new republic.[3]

Early Missionary Efforts

In America, mission work began soon after the Puritans arrived. Intent on
evangelizing Native Americans, John Eliot, David Brainerd, and others
preached to those Indians who would listen. They claimed relatively few converts but for some, rescuing Native Americans from savagery and paganism
ranked second behind survival in the grand scheme of things.[4]

Many accounts credit the rise of the so-called "modern" mission movement to William Carey and the formation of the Particular Baptist Society
for the Propagation of the Gospel Amongst the Heathen, or the more familiar
Baptist Missionary Society, in 1792. Among Baptists, however, George Liele,
an African American, actually antedated Carey by nearly ten years. Born a
slave in 1750, Liele professed conversion in 1773 at the age of twenty-three. He
soon began preaching, and in 1782 he left America for Jamaica where he soon
began his missionary work.[5]

As important as evangelizing Native Americans might have been, over
time some in the more settled eastern regions began fretting that primitive
conditions on the frontier could lead civilized folk into barbarism. They believed that near-savage North Americans needed civilization at least as much
as they needed the gospel. Writing at the behest of the Connecticut state
legislature, Yale's Timothy Dwight encouraged missionaries in the Western
Reserve to build Connecticut-style communities as quickly as possible. Familiar institutions like churches and schools, he reasoned, would shield locals
from dangers such as swearing, drunkenness, and Sabbath breaking, until
they could get themselves established. Dwight urged parents to watch their
children carefully and make certain that they were well taught in matters
both spiritual and secular, warning, "Religion and moral institutions are everything to a community. It is ruin, it is *death* to despise them."[6]

Thus, John F. Schermerhorn and Samuel J. Mills were on a scouting mission when they met John Taylor on that November day in 1812. They had
been tasked with surveying the west and determining its need for the gospel.
If Kentucky's earliest visitors and future settlers had gushed over Kentucky's
lush vegetation and rich, fertile soil, Mills and Schermerhorn scarcely noticed

the Commonwealth's flora and fauna. "The morals of the people are loose," groused Schermerhorn, "and many of the inhabitants are extremely ignorant, as well as very vicious."[7] Of course, the people were not entirely to blame for their condition. The poor quality of ministers likely contributed to the widespread degradation they encountered. He railed against Baptists for being "generally illiterate; few are possessed of good common English learning, and there are also some, that can neither read the Scriptures, nor write their names."[8] If Taylor's visitors indicated such prejudices in their initial meeting, there is little wonder that he looked askance at them both.

In Virginia, Taylor, his friends, and fellow ministers had faced opposition from hostile crowds. One of their fellow ministers, John Leland, appealed to the Virginia legislature to grant religious freedom to all who were unaffiliated with the Anglican Church. Originally from Massachusetts, Leland relocated to Virginia in the early 1770s and became widely known for his pulpit skills. He also established a reputation as a devout Jeffersonian and likely influenced Taylor's political and religious thinking in near-equal measures.[9]

Suspicious of centralized authority, Leland lent his voice to a growing chorus calling for the separation of church and state. He ranked among Virginia's most passionate proponents of religious liberty and his writings indicate a particular disdain for New England. For instance, in 1791 he scoffed at state-supported ministers by noting that with the exception of New England, states had lost their authority over religious groups, especially the power to levy taxes to support state-sanctioned ministers. "If religion cannot stand therefore without the aid of law," he chided, "it is likely to fall soon, in our nation, except in Connecticut and Massachusetts."[10] He also complained about Sabbath laws by noting that Christianity survived for the first three centuries without them, just as Pennsylvania, New York, and New Jersey survived without them in the eighteenth century. "They have no holy laws in those states," he argued, "and yet the Sabbath, so called, is not run out, but meeting-houses and public worship in those states are not inferior to those of New England."[11]

As for missionary societies, Leland denounced their New England origins, their regional support base, and their tendency to push human stratagems to unscriptural extremes. In 1818, one year before Taylor's birthday broadside, Leland noted that New Englanders handled large sums of money in the name of missions only to create occupations that the Bible did not sanction. The ancient "Galilean Society" knew only churches, and he saw no reason to augment the original structure of the church with modern inventions.[12]

Of course, neither Samuel J. Mills nor John F. Schermerhorn singlehandedly turned John Taylor against New England. Prior to their visit, Taylor already knew that folks from "back east" tended to look down their noses at

"Westerners." Travelers brave enough to venture west tended to be as horrified by what they had seen as they were eager to share their experiences. Some recounted gruesome tales of frontier hardship and privation. Others reported widespread drunkenness and an overall failure of moral government. Frontier entertainment, especially the "sport" of eye gouging, appeared barbaric. In their final reports, Mills and Schermerhorn informed their superiors they had encountered people whose savagery defied description. All told, western life amounted to a simple equation: hard conditions led to hard living; hard living led to hard people; hard people needed the gospel's civilizing effects.[13]

Taylor's opposition to organized missionary work did not stem from any aversion to calling sinners to repentance. On that subject, Taylor agreed with Mills and Schermerhorn. He supported revivals and by his own reckoning had preached in many of them. Neither did he oppose church growth or evangelism. In *A History of Ten Churches* Taylor notes church growth with great satisfaction. Rather, missions and the ministerial life that Mills and Schermerhorn described challenged Taylor's understanding of ministry at its very core, and threatened to redefine, if not destroy it.[14]

On the surface, Taylor saw two problems with New Englanders and their approach to American missions. First, they had the wrong view of people. Most Kentuckians earned their living by working the land, and notwithstanding negative frontier stereotypes, Thomas Jefferson deemed farmers as God's elect "if ever He had a chosen people. . . ."[15] Thus, Taylor saw himself and his friends as the epitome of Jeffersonian, agrarian self-sufficiency. Theirs was a "peculiar deposit" of "genuine virtue," not indescribable savagery; so said Jefferson. Even if early nineteenth-century Kentuckians did not live exactly like folk "up north," that was to their credit, not their detriment. In any case, virtuous yeomen were quickly transforming the "the dark and bloody ground" into a well-cultivated Commonwealth. The manners and affectations of the Bluegrass Region reflected refinement and civilization complete with its own crown jewel, Lexington, the self-styled "Athens of the West."[16]

Conflicting concepts of ministry posed a second, far more serious problem for Taylor. He understood Mills and Schermerhorn to say that missions loosened church purse strings, which meant better pay for ministers. Taylor had always seen himself as an itinerant minister, and as far as he was concerned, itinerancy was God's intended way to conduct ministry. Besides, itinerancy reflected republican virtue and self-sufficiency. It disgusted him to think that anyone claiming to be a God-called minister would expect compensation for doing God's work. In *A History of Ten Churches*, Taylor's ministerial memoir, he recounted how he had preached intermittently for the South River Church in Virginia for ten years without formal compensation. Finally, the church gave him $100.00 for past services. They offered the money with "readiness and pleasure," he recalled, and the Taylor family received it "with equal pleasure and gratitude."[17] Missionaries like Mills and Schermerhorn made missions sound like a scheme to civilize backwoods brutes while furnishing ministers with needless baubles. The whole thing smacked of a debate he had heard before, and the more Taylor thought about it, the more vexed he became.

Luther Rice

John Taylor targeted neither Mills nor Schermerhorn as he wrote *Thoughts on Missions*. In fact, most of *Thoughts on Missions* is a polemic against organized missionary activity in general and Luther Rice in particular. Inspired by British missionary work and fueled by early nineteenth-century religious revivalism, many young, idealistic Americans dedicated themselves to becoming missionaries and winning the world for Christ. Luther Rice, Adoniram Judson, and his wife, Ann Hasseltine Judson, numbered among the first Americans who dedicated their lives to international mission work.

In February 1812 Rice and the Judsons sailed for India as Congregationalist missionaries, duly commissioned by the American Board of Commissioners for Foreign Missions. But, after intensive study while at sea, the Judsons decided to become Baptists. Luther Rice followed suit, shortly after arriving in India. Upon resigning their commissions as Congregationalist missionaries, Adoniram and Ann Judson decided to stay on the mission field, while Rice returned to the United States to see if the nation's Baptists would support them as their missionaries.

The Judsons' story passed immediately into Baptist lore, but the decision to become a Baptist was not easy. Congregationalists had nurtured both Adoniram and Ann from their youth, educated them, and sent them to the mission field. Leaving Congregational life meant alienating nearly everyone that he knew, and Adoniram counted the cost. "Must I forfeit the good opinion of all my friends and native land," he mused, "occasioning grief to some, and provoking others to anger, and be regarded henceforth by all my former acquaintances as a weak, despicable Baptist, who had not sense enough to comprehend the connection between the Abrahamic and the Christian systems."[18] In the end, conviction won out, as Judson concluded, "It is better to guided by the opinion of Christ, who is truth, than by the opinions of men, however good, whom I know to be in error."[19]

As the Judsons struggled to establish themselves in the field, Luther Rice extolled the virtues of missions to his new spiritual kin. In 1814 he along with other interested parties formed the General Missionary Convention of the

Baptist Denomination in the United States for Foreign Missions. Its founders determined to meet every three years, hence the new organization became commonly known as the Triennial Convention. Recognizing their need both to marshal and manage financial resources for propagating the gospel, the convention's founders created a managing board to supervise denominational work. Since Luther Rice had raised their awareness of missions, they asked him to become their field agent. As such, he was responsible for raising missionary revenue support and educating his brethren on their missionary mandate. He accepted his responsibilities gladly.[20]

In 1815 Luther Rice came to Kentucky and pleaded with Elkhorn's Baptists to support those who would preach the gospel abroad. John Taylor was present that day and listened closely to Rice's presentation. When the meeting ended, he recalled, "For my own part I was more amused with his ingenuity than edified by his discourse, and more astonished at his art in the close, than at any other time."[21] Taylor watched in amazement as some twenty designated individuals collected between $150.00 and $200.00 for missionary causes.[22]

Taylor did not question Rice's sincerity, but he wondered if Luther Rice and his fellows had any appreciation for what he perceived to be correct Baptist doctrine and practice. After all, Rice and Judson had gone to India as Congregationalists, and their dramatic "conversion" to Baptist life raised questions that few seemed willing to address. Precisely who were these men? More important, what did they believe? Since none of Taylor's acquaintances had ever met Adoniram Judson, how could they be sure that he really was a Baptist? For that matter, how could they be sure that Rice was a Baptist? Who could say with certainty that Adoniram Judson ever received the funds Rice raised for him or if he preached Baptist doctrine? Taylor claimed that most of what anyone really knew about Judson they had gleaned from his wife's letters, and it was not a flattering picture. "If we attend to the long, celebrated letter of Mrs. Judson, in the first report of the Board of Foreign Missions, in page 34," quipped Taylor, "it would look as if her husband had the same taste for money as the horse leech has for blood."[23]

Of course, one could accept Luther Rice's testimony at face value, but Rice had credibility problems of his own that fueled continual skepticism. In Philadelphia, Rice came under fire soon after the Triennial Convention dispatched him as a missionary fundraiser. Henry Holcombe, pastor of the city's First Baptist Church claimed that Baptists had been hoodwinked in the name of missions. Holcombe charged Philadelphia-area ministers with high-handed trickery and arm twisting to co-opt other unsuspecting men into following their scheme. Worse, Holcombe questioned Rice's credentials both as a Baptist and as a minister of the gospel. Who, he wondered, had ordained this man to the ministry and where had it taken place? Even if he had submitted to baptism by immersion, for all anyone knew Rice may have harbored secret Congregationalist convictions. Further, if Rice really was a Baptist, where was his church membership? According to Holcombe, Rice had never bothered to join a church when he returned to America.[24]

Taylor may or may not have known about the fuss Rice had raised in Philadelphia. No matter. He had seen and heard enough to form an opinion and Missionary Rice did not pass muster. In his estimation, Luther Rice was a sham who came back to America as a fortune hunter. Unfortunately, he found scores who eagerly became the "half-witted" dupes that comprised Rice's missionary "machine."[25] Taylor must have wondered what the eastern brethren were thinking when they dispatched a New Englander they scarcely knew to raise money for another New Englander they had never seen, after both became Baptists in a land that no one on the board had ever visited. If Luther Rice represented their most gifted representative, John Taylor wanted nothing to do with him or the board.

Beside the fact that no one really knew Rice or Judson, Taylor denounced Rice and other "home missionaries" for what he believed to be unscrupulous behavior. Bad enough they were beggars, but Taylor also accused them of exaggerating, if not misrepresenting, the dearth of frontier churches in order to raise money. "When they write of the great space of country between St. Louis and Boon's Lick (KY), they state it to the board, as destitute and needing preaching as much as the Empire of Burmah; when in truth," Taylor insisted, "the same country, at the very time they wrote was overspread by two Baptist associations, of which they had full knowledge."[26] Without adequate measures for accountability, such deception would never be questioned. Further, he warned his fellow Baptists that education societies, corollaries to mission societies, threatened to create a de facto priesthood of Baptist ministers by accentuating the differences between formally trained ministers and their uneducated fellow ministers. If churches did not challenge Rice, the mission board, and other mission-related agencies, they were surrendering their own right of self-determination to organizations that the Bible did not sanction to men bent on robbing churches of their liberty. Hence, *Thoughts on Missions* sounded an alarm to Taylor's fellow Baptists that mission boards threatened local church autonomy because no one could hold them accountable for practices that might be deemed questionable.

So, as John Taylor approached what he thought was the end of his life, he sensed the presence and influence of "the New England Rat." To his way of thinking, the Rat had two striking features. On the one hand, the Rat disregarded local church autonomy, choosing rather to wield arbitrary power from its throne in New England. On the other hand, the same Rat had an insatiable appetite for money without accountability. Luther Rice was *not* the New England Rat. Rather, Rice stood as the one New Englander who defined all that was wrong with mission societies. Pompous, power hungry, greedy, unethical, and a theologically questionable Yankee to boot, Rice personified the Rat, and thanks to his influence Taylor feared that unwitting Baptists were embracing the mission movement without considering the ramifications.

Early nineteenth-century missionary activity raised serious issues for Baptists of all persuasions. Significantly, however, Taylor cast his opposition to missions more in anti-New England, anti-Rice terms than antimissionary terms. Taylor encouraged individuals to convert to Christianity, but he questioned the relative worth of missionary societies to convert nonbelievers. If Taylor saw accountability and authority as more than merely theological considerations, it seems likely that his political leanings and his cultural context played crucial roles in shaping his opposition to organized missionary work. They in turn raise broader interpretive issues that bear directly on early nineteenth-century Baptist identity.[27]

Politically, John Taylor's commitment to Jeffersonian Republicanism mirrored that of his friend and fellow preacher, John Leland. In fact, the early Elkhorn ministers who recorded their thoughts tended to express their Jeffersonian Republican sentiments freely.[28] There is no direct evidence that Taylor discussed this issue with his old friend Leland, but they tracked along similar lines. Leland once complained that Federalists were so anti-Jeffersonian that during the War of 1812 they had both undermined government authority and "triumphed in our disasters." Long after the war, Leland claimed the Federalists reasserted themselves and "became great and exercised all the authority of the first beast of 1797."[29]

Taylor extended Leland's biblical metaphor of a beast with political power to organized missionary work, and blasted everyone associated with it. He observed that the new mission board was a "young beast" like the "old beast" of Revelation and sought dominion over Baptists everywhere. "Power," Taylor intoned, "is acquired by connection with a hundred associations, a fine nest egg of gold to answer their future ambition."[30] The missionary enterprise, Taylor reasoned, rendered spiritually gifted, God-called ministers superfluous. One's ability to generate revenue amounted to a new form of giftedness. As he explained, "[I]t seems not so much the question, what is your character or preaching talents, as who will go for us—answer our purpose to hood wink the people, and get plenty of money?"[31] As a passionate advocate of equality and democratic principle, Taylor could not abide the sort of pragmatism that elevated money and power over all other concerns while claiming the salvation of sinners in foreign lands as the end that justified its means.

Likely, Taylor eyed New Englanders suspiciously because he associated the region and its inhabitants with Federalism. By 1820 Federalism at the national level had fallen on hard times, as Virginians with Jeffersonian sympathies enjoyed a remarkable run on the White House. But, state legislatures, especially in New England, had never been hospitable toward Baptists. Rice and Judson were native New Englanders. The new Baptist missionary agencies were headquartered in New England. Taylor feared that Baptist life as he knew it would be destroyed if these agencies styled themselves after Federalist politics and its centralizing tendencies. Had not Taylor's first whiff of the New England Rat come when he learned that Mills and Schermerhorn represented missionary societies in Connecticut and Massachusetts? They had, as Taylor noted, attended the same school as Rice and Judson. The former represented "home" missions, the latter "foreign" missions.

Taylor's suspicion of Rice and Judson went beyond their relative anonymity in Baptist ranks. "Their being baptized at Calcutta," he opined, "is no evidence of their religious or political principles being changed, only in the use of much water."[32] Even more telling, in another place Taylor labels Rice a "well taught Yankee"—in the same sentence where he equated him with Johann Tetzel, the infamous sixteenth-century indulgence seller whose name evoked images of papal corruption and unbiblical polity.[33]

Yet, the majority of Elkhorn's ministers *did* trust Rice, and they saw merit in organized missionary activity. Potential danger in certain aspects of missionary organizations aside, the nation's rapidly changing religious landscape presented both challenges and opportunities. Taylor had witnessed numerous frontier revivals that had shaken the foundations of Kentucky's Baptists, Methodists, and Presbyterians. As he witnessed the rise of the modern mission movement, Taylor had no way of knowing how efficiently or how quickly churches would rally around the missionary cause. Neither could he have foreseen how generously his fellow Americans would support a host of endeavors ranging from preaching and publication to education and social services—all under the missionary banner.[34] Since most of Elkhorn's older ministers had cast their lots with the Licking Association, mission work highlighted a generational divide between Elkhorn's older ministers and its younger ones, who seemed more willing to embrace missions.

If the Rat really was little more than Federalism in preacher's clothing, it surely wanted to spread its repugnant notions of "Holy Commonwealth" to the nation's hinterland. The Bill of Rights guaranteed religious freedom; but Taylor's was the first generation to grapple with what that entailed, and some, most notably in New England, were reluctant to grant this liberty. In the absence of clearly defined lines of religious authority, some thought that without proper vigilance popular religious practice might fall under the control of new structures as injurious to religious liberty as state establishment had once been. If Luther Rice raised money for missions through "sophistry and Yankee art," as Taylor claimed, should it surprise anyone if New England–style politics ultimately dominated America's religious world? Would New England influences corrupt the Baptist doctrine and polity that Taylor cherished? Taylor feared Baptists might unwittingly lay their hard-won freedom at the feet of New Englanders—whoever they may be—for the supposed "greater good" that missions promised. The "New England way" might become everyone else's way, not by coercion, but by volunteerism.[35]

Taylor feared the Rat would infiltrate Baptist ranks through their associations. He deemed local churches the "highest court" Christ ordained, as did nearly all early nineteenth-century American Baptists.[36] However, the Baptist churches that Taylor knew traditionally met together in associations. Such associations were usually shaped by local geographical boundaries. The Philadelphia Association, a notable exception to this general principle, maintained a friendly correspondence with churches all along the eastern seaboard.[37]

Rice advocated what amounted to a new form of ministry, and Taylor feared that his younger brethren would embrace it uncritically. Rice saw associational meetings as a venue to share his views on missions with ministers and church leaders who influenced congregations and made financial decisions. Taylor credited Rice with resourcefulness, but he believed he had discerned a vicious, self-propagating system at work that undermined the ministry culture that framed Baptist identity.[38] After creating the society, missionaries created a board to administrate the society's affairs, and "then they select the most vigorous and artful agent they can find, to create more societies of different grades, as Female Societies, Cent Societies, Mite Societies, Children Societies, and even Negro Societies, both free and bond; besides the sale of books of various kinds, and in some instances the sale of images."[39] These modern missionaries, Taylor said, were a far cry from "the ancient missionaries of the cross of Christ; for they went forth taking nothing from the Gentiles—and all for the name's sake of Jesus Christ—3d John, 7th verse."[40]

If missionary societies and their governing boards robbed churches of their autonomy, they might also eventually bypass associations, especially in practical matters. Taylor saw potential harm in creating agencies that could subordinate theological issues to pragmatic concerns, noting that boards were not likely to care about a minister's character—much less local doctrinal disputes—as long as they received sufficient funding for the missionary enterprise.[41] Taylor's first acquaintance with Rice made a lasting impression, one that left him with a sense of foreboding. Taylor recalled, "I consider these great men are verging close to an aristocracy, with an object to sap the foundation of Baptist republican government."[42]

By late 1820 it was clear that John Taylor would recover from the illness he thought would claim his life. It was equally clear that *Thoughts on Missions* had landed him in quite a stir. Taylor anticipated as much, and perhaps with good reason. Even before the missionary controversy erupted, he had earned a "mixed" reputation among his brethren. For some, he was a well-respected senior minister who had endured much for the faith. For others, especially certain young preachers, he could be encouraging and helpful. For others, however, John Taylor could be a crotchety old man. He was known to disrupt preachers mid sermon if he felt they were especially long-winded or boring. On other occasions, he simply waited for them to finish their sermon and then prayed publicly that God would instruct them on proper exposition and delivery.[43] When it came to missions he believed that he was fighting for a "proper" understanding of Baptist principles. He argued that missionaries were disingenuous in their methods and that "self-created" mission societies represented "an outrage in Baptist principles of republican government." He felt duty bound to warn others even if it meant incurring their wrath.

Regardless of Taylor's intent, *Thoughts on Missions* did not sit well with mission advocates. While the Elkhorn Association minutes do not register a formal rebuke or censure, critics outside the association lampooned Taylor without mercy. The *Baptist Monitor and Political Compiler*, a pro-missionary paper in Bloomfield, Kentucky, detailed an alleged encounter between Taylor and an unnamed adversary in its June 3, 1823, edition. By the paper's account, the issue arose at an associational meeting. As Taylor began defending his position, another person interrupted him and asked, "If, sir, it were in your power to take back the money that has been expended for the support of missionaries among the heathen, and undo all the good that has been effected by the labors of those missionaries, would you do it?" Taken aback and in an obvious bind, Taylor at last said no, to which his antagonist snapped, "[N]ever again let me hear another word from you against missions."[44]

Taylor's own testimony suggests that reactions to his work were mixed. Theophilus Gates, editor of a Philadelphia paper, *The Reformer*, and staunch critic of the mission movement, reprinted part of a letter Taylor sent to a friend in Philadelphia. The letter revealed that Taylor's friend wanted a hundred copies of *Thoughts* should he decide to reprint it, but as Taylor noted, republication was not likely. "After conversing with some of my friends, they think it not best for me to re-publish it," Taylor said, "for a dreadful tempest is already in Kentucky, on account of my homespun book. The most influential Baptists are the most set against it. This you know, brother, is enough to make a poor little fellow tremble, and especially if he should be a little cowardly."[45]

Taylor then recounted how Jacob Creath Sr. had disrupted an ordination service by refusing to sit on the same council with him. Taylor's home church at that time, Buck Run, asked Creath to explain himself in a public meeting. "He was two months preparing to come," Taylor explained, "and in place of the law of Jesus Christ in coming to me, he went to their Board of Missions, and solicited help, asking them if they meant to leave him to make the attack single handed at Buck Run, or if it was ever known for a general to go into the field without an army."[46] In the end, six men including two lawyers accompanied Creath to Taylor's hearing at Buck Run, but Creath refused to lay a charge against him. In the absence of either charge or evidence, Buck Run took no action against Taylor.[47]

Buck Run may not have taken action against John Taylor, but he still heard a chorus of negative criticism. Among the verbal brickbats hurled Taylor's way were some that said he had ruined himself by publishing *Thoughts on Missions*. Others "lament that I did not die more than a year ago, when it looked as if the dropsy would kill me." And even though some received him gladly, "many appear to think, that circulating such a book raises the fist against God himself. Indeed the clamour from some is so bad, and their displeasure is so great, that I fear they would rejoice to see me commit some penitentiary crime, so as to be punished for life."[48]

Ironically, John Taylor insisted that he was not opposed to all mission work. In fact, to deny his own missionary impulses "would contradict the actions of my life, for near half a century, for much of my poor little preaching has been in destitute places. . . ." Likely, he captured the sentiments of other itinerants when he styled himself as a missionary of sorts. He could indeed endorse the "missionary scheme," but he could not deny his life's work. Taylor was convinced that "under proper management and with well-chosen instruments" there was no higher calling than proclaiming the gospel.[49] By "well-chosen instruments," Taylor meant men who were either proving their ministerial mettle or those who had already been ordained; by "proper management," he meant supervision by a congregation. Even so, the well-defined limits that earmarked "proper management" in Taylor's thinking were not as clear to his opponents, who embraced the organizational mania reflected in missionary societies.

The Gospel Imperative as a Matter of Honor

When it came to choosing sides in the early phases of the mission controversy, large-scale organization marked the most pronounced dividing line between pro- and antimission forces. Mission societies and denominational bureaucratization quickly became abiding features of American religious life. Taylor watched as the modern mission movement launched one of the most far-reaching drives for organizational efficiency in the history of Christianity. He did not like what he saw, but he was powerless to stop it.

Generally, Christians enthusiastically embraced what they believed was a God-given mandate to evangelize the world. There were missionary initiatives among Baptists as early as 1772, when Rev. David Jones visited a number of Native American tribes for the purpose of making religious "first contact."[50] Jones's mission to the Indians was not successful, but the Philadelphia Association renewed their interest in evangelizing Native Americans in 1800. They also discussed partnering with Virginia's Baptists to form a missionary society in 1800.[51] As their interest in missions grew, at least one man, Rev. William Rogers, made his sentiments clear, and probably spoke for the majority. In the association's circular letter for 1806, Rogers said, "The object of missionary societies, beloved brethren, is great, greater indeed than the Reformation itself. *That* aimed at the overthrow of the beast; *this* at the destruction of the dragon, from whom the beast derived its power: 'For this purpose was the Son of god manifested, that he might destroy the works of the devil.'"[52]

Much like their sister association, Elkhorn expressed interest in evangelizing Native Americans from an early date. In 1801 the association heard a request from the South Elkhorn Church to send missionaries to the "Indian nations." They responded by forming a committee of five including, Ambrose Dudley, David Barrow, George S. Smith, Joseph Redding, Augustin Easton, and John Price—or any three of them—to search for a missionary and raise funds to support him.[53] Details are sketchy but apparently one month later, the committee ordained John Young as a missionary to American Indians. The Minutes for 1802 indicate that the committee continued its work but say little else.[54]

Taylor did not object to Elkhorn's attempts to evangelize Native Americans. Whereas the Baptist General Board had been created ex nihilo in Philadelphia, Elkhorn's work among the Indians had been initiated and conducted under the auspices of an established association, and he saw a marked difference between the two.[55] Mission work to the American Indians required locally initiated, cooperative effort. Elkhorn even sent a man they knew personally as their missionary. But it was anyone's guess who the board would send to evangelize the rest of the world, or how they would support them.

The Elkhorn Association engaged in missionary activity long before Luther Rice came calling. His visit, however, seems to have accelerated organized mission work. According to one writer, "There was some mission interest in the associations before the arrival of Luther Rice, but the Baptists of the state had never been brought to face the task of foreign missions until presented by this dynamic man, Luther Rice."[56] At least six missionary societies existed in

Kentucky as of 1816, including the Kentucky Baptist Society for Propagating the Gospel and five other societies affiliated with the Baptist Board of Foreign Missions.[57]

Information on these early missionary agencies is not easy to come by. In one of the few existing records, *Proceedings of the Board of Managers for the Baptist Missionary Society of Kentucky, 1818*, includes an amended constitution. Article 1 stipulates, "This society shall hereafter be known and called by the name of the Baptist Mission Society of Ky. for diffusing the *blessings of civilization and religion*."[58] Supporters dedicated themselves to Native American evangelism and cooperating "with the General Convention, in their several missionary enterprises, so far as may be compatible with the avowed object of this society."[59] The *Proceedings* is laced with references to Indian reform, and it leaves little doubt that the main object in educating Native Americans would be to first tame them and then convert them to the Baptist faith.

Existing sources suggest that the Kentucky Baptist Missionary Society prioritized education among Native American children. Their plan included erecting a school in Kentucky and bringing First Nation children from surrounding territories to be educated there. But, according to a report filed in the Proceedings back matter, Native Americans were reluctant to send their children to a boarding school in Kentucky. Rather, they wanted teachers to come to them.[60]

If mission schools were important for Indians, why not middling and poor whites? According to William Rogers's testimony, missionary societies existed for the purpose of destroying the dragon. What better way to do that than by building schools for whites, especially ministers? The *Proceedings* indicates that the society formed a committee "to take into consideration the propriety of making arrangement for a college, for the education of the Heathen and other persons, and to select a suitable spot to locate the same, and also to make enquiry as to some fit person to take charge of such institution, and make report to the next meeting of the Board."[61] Their work ultimately led to Georgetown College.[62]

Providing "proper" education to frontier learners proved especially challenging and frequently turned into something of a farce. Daniel Drake came to Kentucky as a child in the late 1780s. His parents tried to secure an education for him, but he recalled that his opportunities were meager and his teachers were frequently substandard, knowing little more than their pupils. He remembered one Daniel Beaden who had relocated to Kentucky from Maryland and served as "an ample exponent of the state of society in that benighted region." His job was to teach "spelling, reading, writing, and ciphering as far as the rule of three; beyond which he could not go. His attainments in that branch harmonized as to the quality and compass with his erudition in the others."[63]

While a minister's ordination did not hinge on a specified amount of formal education, ministers were still expected to demonstrate some degree of learning and ministerial know-how. The Philadelphia Baptist Association could look to Hopewell Academy or possibly Brown as places where ministers could study. Even so, preparation tended to be informal and many ministers in training could simply not afford tuition, board, and books.[64]

Kentucky in the late eighteenth and early nineteenth centuries fared no better. Ministers with some education might supplement their income by opening academies. David Barrow maintained a rudimentary school as early as 1801, but as one writer notes, "[N]o record remains of his success as a pioneering teacher on the Kentucky frontier."[65] Even before Barrow, John Gano taught ministers in his home in the 1790s. Education of a sort was available, but it would be decades before anyone discussed standardized curricula and even longer before Kentucky moved away from one-room schools.[66]

Kentucky's Presbyterians assumed a more structured stance toward education by establishing Transylvania University in 1780. Transylvania enhanced Lexington's reputation and served as the Bluegrass Region's intellectual epicenter until it was wracked by theological controversy bearing upon Unitarianism. Concerned parties shifted their attention to Centre College in Danville, Kentucky, as an alternative to Transylvania once the Kentucky Synod gained control of the institution in 1824.[67] Given the demands that congregations made of more settled ministers and the intellectual challenges of ideas such as Unitarianism, it soon became clear that ministers needed more formal training.

The Elkhorn Association had dealt with Unitarianism when it disfellowshipped Augustin Eastin and James Garrard in 1802; and Transylvania's Unitarian controversy doubtless fueled fears that heresy could surface at any time. The association's preachers needed to be prepared, and missions afforded them the perfect rationale to build schools that would prepare ministers to address all challenges to orthodoxy.

Framing a New Consensus

The rapid multiplication of missionary societies signaled a new day for the Elkhorn Association. Obviously, something beyond "church work" in its usual sense was taking place. Here a hypothesis by historian Donald G. Mathews may offer some insight. In "The Second Great Awakening as an Organizing Process," Mathews concedes that while it may be ill-defined, "the Second Great Awakening was characterized by unity as well as organization, and demonstrated the dynamism of a movement."[68] Of course, Mathews spoke of the ways in which the awakening "helped to give meaning and direction to people suffering in various degrees from the social stress of a nation on the move into new political, economic, and geographical areas."[69]

Since Mathews, other scholars have tried to make sense of America's rapidly changing cultural milieu from roughly 1790 to 1830 or so. Westward expansion and its resulting growth pangs led Jon Butler to conclude that religious institutions scrambled to maintain or impose order, while Nathan Hatch maintains that Americans were consumed with democratization and expanding personal liberty.[70] The Elkhorn Association fits somewhere between these positions, but they leaned heavily toward order.

Elkhorn's first forty-five to fifty years are instructive on a number of levels. Mathews is correct; the so-called Second Great Awakening marked a period of remarkable growth, expansion, and organization. The mission movement represents one way among many that the Second Great Awakening influenced the Elkhorn Baptists. John Taylor and others like him would likely testify that certain kinds of organization were as apt to divide as they were to unite. Nevertheless, in the wake of associational turmoil that precipitated schism, the "missionary enterprise" gave Elkhorn a new locus from which they framed a new, stable consensus that was part theological and part cultural.

Theologically, Elkhorn's constituency had weathered challenges from Unitarian impulses in the early nineteenth century by holding closely to the Philadelphia Confession of Faith. They did not compromise Trinitarian theology even for James Garrard and Augustin Eastin, two of their most respected ministers. But, their union with their Separate Baptist neighbors featured a concession by Elkhorn's more staunch Calvinists with respect to Christ's atonement and particular election. The Union of 1801 stipulated that "the teaching that Christ tasted death for every man shall not be a bar to communion," caused a minor flap in the association, but it moved Elkhorn away from an extreme form of predestinarianism. Once Baptists cleared the "free offer" hurdle, international mission work appeared to be a small, but eminently logical next step. Significantly, by embracing missions Elkhorn's ministers and messengers created a space for agreement in the face of disagreement. That is, ministers might disagree on certain doctrinal or theological tenets and yet maintain fellowship with one another, so long as they supported missions.[71] Briefly stated, the mission movement framed a new, theologically generic consensus for Baptists.

Socially, Elkhorn's Baptists simmered over slavery until 1805. By agreeing not to "meddle with emancipation" the association not only endorsed slavery, it also swore fealty to Kentucky's slaveholding Bluegrass barony and set an example that other associations followed. They shunned David Barrow, one of their own heroes, who taught that slavery was incompatible with scripture, republican government, and revolutionary principles. The erstwhile counter-cultural radicals from Virginia adjusted to their social position with relative ease, and rather than raising a prophetic, democratic voice against slavery, the majority embraced political and economic expediency and celebrated the cultural acceptance it brought.[72] They also consoled themselves by evangelizing their slaves and allowing them to participate in church life with white people, albeit within well-defined boundaries. And, if it came to pass that someone harbored reservations about slavery, he need not break fellowship with the majority as long as he supported the broader mission agenda.

Kentucky's African Americans were not the only ones to experience white paternalism. Missions on the home front called for the nation's benighted westerners, frontier folk, and Native Americans to be educated. Home missions provided a means of white uplift that resonated not only with the South's honor culture but also with what appeared to be a national interest in learning, especially reading.[73]

The missionary impulse also reshaped the ministry culture that the Elkhorn brethren had brought with them to Kentucky. Taylor had been offended by "well-schooled Yankees" in 1812, but the association heard Rice gladly in 1815. Taylor waited in vain for voices from the pews to come to his defense, but the groundswell never came. Elkhorn's preachers, some of Taylor's closest friends, played significant roles in directing their members toward organized missions, and ultimately a settled, salaried ministry.

The informal ministerial pecking order still existed in 1830. Organized mission work did nothing to change that. Certain elite ministers were still tapped to serve elite churches. Certain ministers were still called upon to mediate internal conflicts, write associational letters, and correspond with other Baptist associations. They may have been well-to-do or simply recognized for their giftedness and natural abilities, but local ministers understood who commanded the most respect.

Many of those gifted and popular ministers divided their attention between their church work and their support for organized mission work. They were insiders with their fellow ministers because they were ordained; they were insiders with certain laity because of wealth, position, or some other factor. In the transition from itinerant ministry to the more professional, "settled ministry" that Elijah Craig had so bitterly denounced, ministers began identifying with their increasingly settled congregants and their needs as well as the mission movement. This may help explain why Elkhorn's "older" ministers led the exodus that resulted in the Licking Association.

Elkhorn's ministers assumed a role in integrating religion in Kentucky's

Bluegrass Region with the South's emerging honor culture. Some claim that the American Revolution marked the end of deferential politics, but judging by Elkhorn's actions deference never really died.[74] Rather, it assumed new forms. Would-be aristocrats, ministers, and social climbers of all sorts faced the same problems; namely, how should one legitimize their wealth once they obtained it, especially if it came from slave labor? In Wyatt-Brown's analysis, even excessive wealth was acceptable as long as it represented a means to an end and not an end in itself.[75] Missionary work opened new avenues for believers of means to use their wealth properly, and all the while, ministers kept watch on the Commonwealth's spiritual climate.

Honor culture and ministry culture met at this juncture. At first glance, honor and religion might appear to work against one another. Ayers maintains that honor, a "*secular* system of values, clashed with the ideals of Christian virtue. Evangelical southerners deplored and denounced the violence and pride honor condoned. In their eyes, people who let their actions be dictated by honor allowed themselves to become mere slaves to public opinion."[76] But did honor culture and ministry culture really clash? Ayers may be correct at some level, but there was more to honor than violence.[77]

Southern ministers in general and Elkhorn's ministers in particular encouraged what they believed to be positive, morally grounded elements of the South's honor culture. It could scarcely be otherwise. As historian Edward R. Crowther argues, most southern planters and preachers shared too many common cultural artifacts with their well-to-do church members including a theistic worldview, similar challenges from a changing political economy, and a certain status anxiety in the face of those changes only to become alienated from their congregations.[78] Social elites and those aspiring to upward mobility needed common ground. Perhaps most important, Crowther notes that "many preachers and planters sprang from the same upwardly mobile ethos of the early nineteenth century South and carried with them the same moral values of self-reliance, common sense, and duty to God and family."[79] Crowther further contends that "evangelicalism infused and to a great degree transformed other values of the larger society."[80]

As mutually beneficial as the honor culture and the ministry culture may have been, it is important to note that they were not mutually dependent upon one another. That is, an honor culture could exist independent of ministry culture, and vice versa. However, when combined, they generated a cultural dynamism that neither could manage alone. On one hand, men of means, who were also considered "ministering brethren," were expected to reflect a certain *noblesse oblige* toward their neighbors and especially their slaves. In performing this duty, they used their wealth toward an end; and it was up to the public, or the association—or in some cases both—to determine if they were successful. Those found wanting might face church discipline and public humiliation. On the other hand, white uplift through measures like church planting and educational missions confirmed that one's wealth was being used for ennobling, even honorable ends. By investing in one's fellows, one lifted them to new cultural status and thereby set a good example for others to follow. If one should disagree on ethical or doctrinal matters, missions could always serve as common touchstone, a point of agreement, even if it did not solve difficulties. It was the very climate that paved the way for the emergence of what Brooks Holifield called the "gentlemen theologians" of the antebellum era.[81]

Moving Forward

The shift away from smaller scale, association-centered religious life to large-scale organization and denominationalism called for all Baptists to reassess their basic purpose and polity. The mission movement, or more precisely, the mission controversy, provided a "test case" for how Baptists would conceptualize religious freedom in the new republic. James R. Mathis observes that Baptists had both advocated religion's disestablishment and prospered in the nation's newly created religious free market.[82] Most early nineteenth-century Baptists followed the "eastern example" and supported the new boards and denominational agencies in some form. Their ecclesiology, or doctrine of the church, allowed for a polity flexible enough to accommodate the shift. By the middle of the nineteenth century the Baptist denomination—if that was ever a proper moniker—had become the Baptist denominations, as various groups exercised their right to worship God as they saw fit.[83]

The emerging mission consensus dovetailed nicely with America's political culture. John Taylor saw to that by pioneering a form of dissent in Baptist ranks that by 1820 was commonplace in American politics. Saul Cornell has demonstrated that the Federalist/Anti-Federalist debates over the Constitution's ratification established a culture of dissent in American politics. The Federalists won the battle over ratification, but the Anti-Federalists demonstrated that politics and the political process itself could be challenged peacefully in the "public sphere." These peaceful challenges could, in turn, lead to meaningful social and cultural change. They might even be conducted in an honorable way.[84]

According to Mathews, "The search for relevance is often interpreted as a conservative counteroffensive against a rising democracy, and some Federalist clerics may well have understood it as such—social movements are contrivable for such purposes even if not so conceived for such purposes. The Awakening may have been on the other hand a process whereby the conservative clergy became resigned to the democracy."[85] This may be true in certain circles, but among Elkhorn's Baptists, it was missions that allowed ministers to embrace a certain amount of democracy and even shape it to their own ends, at least in their churches and associations.[86]

Early nineteenth-century America's rapidly changing religious and cultural contexts raised serious issues regarding Baptist identity. Essentially, Baptists faced at least two dilemmas: The missionary impulse tapped the religious energy of a young nation and played a leading role in shaping Baptist denominationalism throughout the nineteenth century; but it also posed a serious problem for Baptists like Taylor. They had to acknowledge that evangelism and missions were closely related—if one believed in preaching the gospel at home, should they not also support preaching the gospel abroad?

Yet, the "missionary scheme" also called for unprecedented levels of organization, and that posed a second dilemma for Baptists. For many like John Taylor, large-scale organization smacked of Federalism and they believed such organization threatened local church autonomy. Moreover, in their minds organized missionary endeavors appeared to encourage self-aggrandizement. Thus, well-meaning Baptists could either endorse the organization necessary for far-ranging missionary endeavors and run headlong into a system fueled by ministerial pride, or they could refuse, and turn their backs on an apparent biblical mandate to evangelize the world.

Missionary societies posed issues other than questionable finances and accountability. Taylor and his like-minded brethren noted that if the Bible offered no direct authority for their existence, the new offices filled by these agencies were unbiblical. Taylor and his frontier brethren recognized two church offices, pastor-elder and deacon. They could not bring themselves to acknowledge field agents and board presidents as occupying bona fide, New Testament-affirmed offices in God's economy. Ultimately, denominational bureaucrats played crucial roles in framing the "business culture" of American denominations. In voicing their discontent, Taylor and other so-called antimissioners furnished emerging denominational leaders with "negative examples" by which they could fashion their programs. Ironically, so-called antimission Baptists like John Taylor inadvertently helped shape the sort of ministerial professionalization they detested.[87]

Conclusion

Crabgrass in the Bluegrass?

Change comes at a cost, a lesson the Elkhorn Association's founding generation of ministers learned all too well. John Taylor seemed especially sensitive to those changes. He left the Bluegrass Region in 1795 to search for opportunity in Northern Kentucky, only to return to Central Kentucky in 1815. Life had been difficult for him in Northern Kentucky and his labors in the Bullittsburg and Corn Creek churches had not been especially successful. In his more reflective moments, Taylor believed he had been a failure. "For some of the stings from Mount Byrd, and Corn Creek, would haunt me at times," he recalled, "as if all some way had not been right in my proceedings there; for I began to take notice, that from the time of the burning of my fine barn with fire from heaven, my substance in life, had been crumbling away."[1] Personal misfortunes aside, much of Taylor's unsettledness reflected changes in his religious world that he could not fathom.

Taylor hoped that by returning to friends and familiar surroundings he might salve his conscience and renew his spirit. That did not happen. Upon his return, Taylor and his wife, Elizabeth united with the Big Spring Church, not far from Frankfort. Big Spring was a small, relatively new church and Silas Noel was a relatively new pastor. Professing a fondness for "new things," the Taylors united with the church. At first, they fit in well and it seemed like a good place for the aging minister, but he soon found himself embroiled in controversy.

The church may have been small, but they boasted several prominent members. Henry Davidge, a local judge was a member at Big Spring. Additionally, the church had licensed him to preach soon after his baptism, a move Taylor believed to be ill-advised. Taylor believed Davidge was a moral man, "though much tinctured with Arminianism"; and that posed a problem, seeing that the Big Spring Church had been organized on Calvinistic tenets.[2] When Davidge published his theological views in a book, Taylor felt compelled to take action. He spoke to Noel about it, but he claimed his pastor ignored him. Soon, the church became irritated with him for broaching the subject in a business conference. Clearly taken aback, Taylor pondered three possibilities. Noel may have ignored his concerns because he was young in the ministry. On the other hand, since Noel and Davidge were both trained lawyers, it was possible that the church valued their status in the community and they would rather incur Taylor's ire than either Davidge or Noel. A third, more disturbing possibility would be that the two of them were bent on deliberately changing the kind of religious life he had known since the 1780s.[3]

Before long, the matter came before the Elkhorn Association for consideration. The association rejected Davidge's book and his theological Arminianism, but they did it without damaging the judge's position in the association. They left it to his church to deal with him and Big Spring chose to take no action. Consequently, if his church was satisfied, the association reasoned that they, too, were satisfied, and unlike the debacle at Town Fork, there would be no trial. If there were any lingering hard feelings, they belonged to Taylor. And, as if to prove that Davidge enjoyed the association's full confidence, they tapped him to write the circular letter for 1817.

Not content to leave the matter alone, Taylor saw to it that the Long Run and Salem Associations received copies of Davidge's work. These associations rejected it outright, and Taylor felt a measure of vindication. Still one can only imagine what he thought as he pondered it all. Less than one generation earlier the Elkhorn Association struggled to unite with the South Kentucky Association in part because some South Kentucky ministers preached that "Christ tasted death for every man." Now, less than two decades into the nineteenth century, the Elkhorn Association appeared willing to tolerate an entire theological system at odds with its founding principles.[4]

The Taylors felt at home at Big Spring Church, but the Davidge controversy soured many of their personal relationships. In early 1816 they moved their membership to Frankfort but that, too, proved troublesome. Among other issues, Taylor complained that "when I would set out from home, even at a monthly meeting, it was often unknown where it would be held, 'till we got to Frankfort; sometimes in the Assembly Hall, Senate Chamber, or Court-House; and sometimes neither of the places could be gotten."[5] The church also struggled to secure a pastor which ultimately led to an appalling spectacle. Silas Noel agreed to serve the Frankfort church, and when they met to install him as pastor, they ordained Porter Clay to the ministry as well.

In his horror and disgust, Taylor described the service as a "farce of the most outlandish kind that I ever knew played out in a Baptist church. . . ." The church had recruited six "ripe and orthodox" ministers for the ordination council, but Taylor was not among them. In his words, "I was not there myself for common men were not invited, but I had the honor afterward to see at least part of their records." Those records perplexed him because they focused on divinity almost to the exclusion of practical ministry. One question stood out: "'Do you recollect, brother, that you ever knew a sheep turned into a goat or a goat turned into a sheep?' After a long and solemn pause, the candidate replied, 'I do not recollect that I ever knew such a circumstance.'" In Taylor's assessment it was a question designed to see what the candidate believed about one's status prior to conversion, that is, were the elect "sheep" in Christ or "goats" who would ultimately be lost. Even so, it was an odd way to phrase the question, and it left Taylor wondering what spectators might have thought of such interrogation.[6]

After what Taylor described as a "pompous parade," the church installed the minister and ordained Clay to the ministry. This ordination, however, stood in stark contrast to Taylor's own ordination, or to numerous others in which he had participated. If this was the kind of theological acumen churches sought, he wanted nothing to do with it. Curiously, Porter Clay was Henry Clay's brother.[7] There was no escaping it; Kentucky's religious climate was indeed changing.

Taylor wanted out of Frankfort and he jumped at the chance to be part of a new church start at nearby Buck Run in 1818. He claimed that he never intended to stay long at Frankfort largely because did not see himself as a "town preacher." Besides, Buck Run offered John Taylor the opportunity to be part of a new church. His old friend and colleague William Hickman moderated the organizational meeting along with Silas Noel, James Sugget, John H. Ficklin, and the Boulware brothers, Mordecai and Theodrick. Buck Run was Taylor's tenth church—and his final one. But while at Buck Run, Taylor discovered just how much ministry was changing when he excited Kentucky's missionary controversy.

Opposition to organized missionary work had been gathering steam since 1820 and battle lines were being drawn. Some associations, like North Carolina's Kehukee Association, declared nonfellowship with missionary Baptists in 1826, but the Black Rock Address marked the major fault lines between pro- and antimissionary Baptists. The so-called antimissioners argued that the Bible gave no mandate for creating organizations beyond local churches to do God's work in the world. They claimed that the churches were not responsible for building schools, Bible societies, and the like.[8] But, missionary advocates countered with an eloquence that marginalized their opposition. So what if the so-called antimissioners were correct in observing that the New Testament never mandated missionary boards or any number of points? Who could argue against winning converts to the faith? Who could really argue against church-related schools? Missions gave Baptists entry into America's emerging religious mainstream. Missions afforded Baptists a measure of respect and the social status they had wanted all along—and the majority liked it.

By 1830 few of Elkhorn's original cadre remained. John Gano passed from this world in 1804, followed by Elijah Craig in 1808; John Tanner, 1812; Joseph Redding, 1815; David Barrow, 1819; Lewis Craig and Ambrose Dudley in 1824 and 1825, respectively. Perhaps it is only fitting that John Taylor was among the last of the "first ones" to pass in 1835. He had seen it all, and as de facto scribe for the Elkhorn Association, he had written about a good bit of it. Where would scholars of frontier Baptist life be without *A History of Ten Churches*? His booklet, *Thoughts on Missions*, challenged his generation to consider the missionary enterprise carefully before embracing it wholeheartedly. Most Baptists ignored his admonition, and by Taylor's reckoning even those who read *Thoughts*, did so to refute what he had written rather than understand what he meant. His last major work, *Campbellism Exposed,* was a blistering exposé of Alexander Campbell and the impact he was having on Kentucky Baptist churches. Some probably left their Baptist moorings because they were tired of posturing preachers and a haughtiness that seemed to permeate so much of Baptist life in early Kentucky. Few heeded his admonitions here either, as the Disciples claimed Baptist converts by the dozens.[9] Maybe Taylor had lost his credibility with *Thoughts on Missions*. Maybe Taylor did not resonate with the current generation. Silas Mercer Noel had emerged as Elkhorn's leading theological voice, but he was scarcely Taylor's friend. In fact, Noel had established himself as one of Kentucky's more eloquent spokesmen for missions and may have numbered among Taylor's foes.[10] Either way, Taylor had grown weary of it all.

One idealistic generation was almost gone, replaced by another. Advocates for the "old ways" who lived long enough could sense their time was passing if, indeed, it had not passed already. John Leland knew it. The ardent Jeffersonian who had been the voice for Virginia's persecuted Baptists remained a hero to early Elkhorn ministers even after he moved to Massachusetts in 1792.[11] Much like Taylor, Leland harbored deep ambivalence toward the mission movement, but he could never completely separate himself from it. "I do not wish to be a bigoted old man who always finds faults with new customs," he said, "but when I see the same measures pursued that were in the third century, I am afraid the same effect will follow."[12] And when it came to slavery, this once outspoken emancipationist even backpedaled on the issue in his final years.

John Taylor died on April 12, 1835. He was the last of Elkhorn's founding generation. No one wrote more on the Elkhorn Association than Taylor. Likely, no one thought more about the changes in religious life than he. Seasoned, well-established itinerant ministers like John Taylor had a difficult time relating to early nineteenth-century religious life, especially missionaries. New networks, new forms, and new expectations made stalwarts like Taylor more than a little nervous. In his analysis of *Thoughts on Missions*, historian Chester

Raymond Young found Taylor raising four main objections to organized mission work. First, the missionaries he met all wanted money, but from what Taylor gathered, there would never be enough money to satisfy all demands. Second, Taylor believed that missionaries were promoting a kind of aristocracy that undermined Baptist republicanism. Third, in touting formal education, missionaries encouraged strange doctrine and promoted concepts foreign to local folkways. Finally, Taylor could not stomach missionaries who complained about hardship and privation, for as Young aptly observed, "It never occurred to him that he had suffered unbearably for preaching the gospel."[13]

Some Baptists could never accept the mission movement or the changes that it demanded. Some claimed that field agents were really out to levy taxes on churches. Others declared nonfellowship with the missionary Baptists over Sunday Schools, mission, education, and publication societies. While not necessarily opposed to preaching, learning, or print media, per se, they saw such ventures as beyond their purview. Many such groups went their own way, styling themselves as Primitive Baptists.[14]

Baptist concepts of ministry had changed. It was part of the price for a "settled," professional ministry with interests that spanned the globe. Taylor had no way of knowing what large-scale organization would do to Baptists, but he was certain of one thing: itinerant ministries like the one to which he and his friends had been ordained were not needed in settled areas. He was right to argue that mission work was expensive, but the concept initiated an organizational revolution for Baptists. The tangible benefits of mission work seemed worth any "tweaking" in Baptist thought that might be necessary. Taylor even admitted, albeit grudgingly, that he would not take back monies spent on missions if it meant losing the "good" that missionary work had accomplished.

Taylor continued to attend associational meetings, even into his twilight years. In 1830 he attended a meeting of the Long Run Association in Kentucky where he encountered James Welch, one of the missionaries he had criticized by name in *Thoughts on Missions*. Welch confronted Taylor about his accusations and, after a brief exchange, Taylor replied, "Oh, never mind, let it sleep in silence."[15]

In that moment Taylor may have thought about denominational politics and the perils of going against the majority. He may have thought about the Elkhorn-Licking schism and the friends he had lost along the way. He may even have thought about the changes he had seen, some good, some bad, but all coming at a cost. Regardless, Welch took Taylor's comment to mean that he was sorry he had created such a stir. Who knows? Perhaps he was.

Appendix 1

Virginia Term of Union 1787

From Robert Baylor Semple, *History of the Baptists in Virginia*, p. 101

To prevent the confession of faith from usurping a tyrannical power over the conscience of any, we do not mean that every person is bound to the strict observance of everything therein contained; yet that it holds forth the essential truths of the Gospel, and that the doctrine of salvation by Christ and free, unmerited grace alone ought to be believed by every Christian and maintained by every minister of the Gospel. Upon these terms we are united; and desire hereafter that the names *Regular* and *Separate* be buried in oblivion, and that, from henceforth, we shall be known by the name of the *United Baptist Churches in Virginia*.

Appendix 2

Proposed Terms of Union for Tates Creek and South Elkhorn

Minutes of the Elkhorn Association, 1793

We do agree to receive the regular Baptist Confession of Faith but to prevent its usurping a tiranical power over the Consciences of any, we do not mean that every person is to be bound to the strict observance of every thing therein Contained, Yet that it holds forth the essential truths of the Gospel, and that the Doctrines of Salvation by Christ and free and unmerited grace alone ought to be believed by every Christian, and maintained by every minister of the Gospel and that we do believe in those Doctrines relative to the Trinity the Divinity of Christ, the sacred authority of the Scriptures the universal depravity of human nature; the total inability of men to help themselves withot the aid of divine grace; the necessity of repentance towards, God, and faith in the Lord Jesus Christ, the justification of our persons entirely by the righteousness of Christ imputed; Believers Baptism by immersion only and self-denial. And that the supreme Judge by which all controversies of religion are to be determined, and, all decrees of Councils opinions of ancient writers doctrins of men and private spirits are to be examioned and in whose sentance we are to rest, can be no other than the Holy Scriptures, delivered by the Spirit, into which scriptures so delivered our faith is finally resolved.

Appendix 3

Term of Union between
Tates Creek and Elkhorn

Minutes of the Elkhorn Association, 1797

Received a report from the Committee appointed to visit the united Baptist respecting an union They reported that they conferred with a committee appointed by the united Baptist association on the following principals.

> 1st Respecting man and his utter inability to recover him-Self on which they were agreed,
>
> 2dly How and by what means he is recovered (there they agreed)
>
> 3dly on regeneration. (in this they agreed)
>
> 4thly. On Justification. (on this they agreed)
>
> 5thly. On the perseveance of the Saints (here they agreed)
>
> 6th. On Church disciplin. (here they agreed)
>
> 7th.Whether any of our members holding the doctrine of general provision would be a bar of union? This was not answered.

The Association approved of the conduct of this Committee and the following proposition was made. Shall we unite with said united Baptists agreeably to the report of the Committee, and acceded to by them which was agreed to and the right hand of fellowship interchangeably given by the moderator and messengers of said united Baptist association.

Appendix 4

Terms of Union between the Elkhorn and South Kentucky, or Separate Associations

We, the committees of Elkhorn and South Kentucky Associations, do agree to unite on the following plan:

1st. That the Scriptures of the Old and New Testament are the infallible word of God, and the only rule of faith and practice.

2d. That there is only one true God, and in the Godhead or divine essence, there are Father, Son and Holy Ghost.

3d. That by nature we are fallen and depraved creatures.

4th. That salvation, regeneration, sanctification, and justification are by the life, death, resurrection, and ascension of Jesus Christ.

5th. That the saints will finally persevere through grace to glory.

6th. That believer's baptism by immersion is necessary to receiving the Lord's supper.

7th. That the salvation of the righteous and punishment of the wicked will be eternal.

8th. That it is our duty to be tender and affectionate to each other, and study the happiness of the children of God in general; to be engaged singly to promote the honor of God.

9th. And that the preaching Christ tasted death for every man, shall be no bar to communion.

10th. And that each may keep up their associational and church government as to them may seem best.

11th. That a free correspondence and communion be kept up between the churches thus united.

Unanimously agreed to by the joint committee:

Ambrose Dudley,	Robert Elkin,
John Price,	Thos. J. Chilton,
Joseph Redding,	Daniel Ramey,
David Barrow,	Moses Bledsoe,
	Samuel Johnson.

Appendix 5

Elkhorn Association Growth, 1799–1805

Year	Churches	Baptisms	Rec'd	Dis'ed	Excluded	Total
1799	31	83	66	66	22	1,718[a]
1800	27	82	96	101	12	1,642
1801	36	3011	318	318	47	4,853
1802	48	488	275	994	143	5,223[b]
1803	39	64	194	215	138	4,319[c]
1804	40	22	163	180	165	4,220
1805	35	23	147	150	137	3,550

[a]Elkhorn's minutes show Mount Sterling's membership to be 214 but this number is almost certainly wrong. Combining the figures for 1798 with the total for 1799 yields 43, not 214.

[b]Elkhorn's minutes indicate a total membership of 5310, but this number is likely an error. The total should be 5,223.

[c]Elkhorn's minutes indicate a total membership of 2442, but this number is likely an error. The total should be 4,319.

Notes

Introduction

1. See John Gano, *Biographical Memoirs of the Late John Gano, of Frankfort (Kentucky) formerly of the City of New York* (New York: Southwick and Hardcastle, 1806). See also Terry Wolever, *The Life of John Gano, 1727–1804: Pastor-Evangelist of the Philadelphia Association* (Springfield, MO: Particular Baptist Press, 2012); J. H. Spencer, *A History of Kentucky Baptists from 1769–1885,* revised and corrected by Mrs. Burrilla B. Spencer (Cincinnati: J. R. Baumes, 1885; repr., Gallatin, TN: Church History Research and Archives, 1984), 1: 116–27; David Benedict, *A General History of the Baptist Denomination in America, and Other Parts of the World* (Boston: Lincoln & Edmands, 1813; repr., Gallatin, TN: Church History Research and Archives, 1985), 1: 485, 532–45, 562–89; and *The Baptist Encyclopedia,* rev. ed., ed. William Cathcart (Philadelphia: Louis H. Everts, 1883), s.v. "Gano, Rev. John."

2. John Gano, *Biographical Memoirs,* 118–20. See also the essays in Craig Thompson Friend, ed., *The Buzzel About Kentuck: Settling the Promised Land* (Lexington, KY: Univ. Press of Kentucky, 1999).

3. See George W. Ranck, "'The Travelling Church': An Account of the Baptist Exodus from Virginia to Kentucky in 1781 Under the Leadership of Rev. Lewis Craig and Capt. William Ellis," (n.p., 1910; repr., *Register of the Kentucky Historical Society,* 79 [1910]: 240–65).

4. Felix Walker, "Narrative," in George W. Ranck, *Boonesborough,* (Louisville, KY: Filson Club First Publication Series, no. 16), 164.

5. Spencer, *History of Kentucky Baptists*, and Frank M. Masters, *A History of Baptists in Kentucky* (Louisville: Kentucky Baptist Historical Society, no. 5, 1953) are indispensable to students of Kentucky Baptist history, and both will be used extensively in this inquiry. For the Elkhorn Association see Ira (Jack) Birdwhistell, *The Baptists of the Bluegrass: A History of Elkhorn Baptist Association, 1785–1985* (Berea, KY: Berea College Press, 1985). Birdwhistell's account is brief but extremely valuable for setting Elkhorn's early chronology. Richard C. Traylor's *Born of Water and Spirit: The Baptist Impulse in Kentucky, 1776–1860* (Knoxville: Univ. of Tennessee Press, 2015) attests to Elkhorn's enduring fascination to scholars.

6. See Stephen Aron, *How the West Was Lost: The Transformation of Kentucky from Daniel Boone to Henry Clay* (Baltimore and London: Johns Hopkins Univ.

Press, 1996). According to Aron, "Evangelical ways defied cultural hegemony, if not the political economy of the Bluegrass System. The selfless spirit of evangelicalism starkly contrasted with the gentry's self-assertive spirit of gain" (171). This assessment cannot be applied to the Elkhorn Association.

7. For accounts of Baptist persecution see Wesley M. Gewehr, *The Great Awakening in Virginia, 1740–1790* (Durham, NC: Duke Univ. Press, 1930); Lewis Peyton Little, *Imprisoned Preachers and Religious Liberty in Virginia* (Lynchburg, VA: J. P. Bell, 1938); and William Taylor Thom, *The Struggle for Religious Freedom in Virginia: the Baptists,* ser. 18 (Baltimore: Johns Hopkins Univ. Press, Oct.–Dec. 1900). Equally important, one might consult Robert Baylor Semple, *History of the Baptists in Virginia,* revised and extended by G. W. Beale, 1894. (1810; repr., Gallatin, TN: Church History and Archives, 1976); James B. Taylor, *Lives of Virginia Baptist Ministers* (Richmond, VA: Yale and Wyatt, 1837); and *Lives of Virginia Baptist Ministers,* 2nd rev. ed. (Richmond, VA: Yale and Wyatt, 1838). Whenever possible these works emphasize positive character traits in their subjects. Taylor also notes Revolutionary War service for Baptist veterans. They may have been persecuted in certain quarters, but both Semple and Taylor contend that Baptists had been good citizens of the Republic all along. Moreover, in each of the first two editions of *Lives,* Taylor lists revivalistic Separate Baptist Shubel Stearns first, even though Stearns spent little time in Virginia. This suggests that in addition to certifying his entries as "good citizens" he also wanted to tie them to Stearns.

8. Compare Jon Butler's *Awash in a Sea of Faith: Christianizing the American People* (Cambridge, MA, and London: Harvard Univ. Press, 1990), 272, and his *Power, Authority, and the Origins of American Denominational Order: The English Churches in the Delaware Valley, 1680–1730* (Philadelphia: American Philosophical Society, 1978); with Nathan O. Hatch, *The Democratization of American Christianity* (New Haven, CT, and London: Yale Univ. Press, 1989). Whereas Hatch sees the Early Republic as a time of religious "democratization," Butler sees it as a time where religious leaders imposed order via the structures they created.

9. D. W. Bebbington, *Evangelicalism in Modern Britain: A History from the 1730s to the 1980s* (London: Unwin Hyman, 1989), 1–19. For a brief review of Bebbington's critics, see "Roundtable: Re-examining David Bebbington's "Quadrilateral Thesis," *Fides et Historia* 47 (Winter/Spring 2015): 44–98. Some contend that "evangelicalism" has become so far-ranging that it is too amorphous to be very useful to scholars. See Alan Wolfe, *The Transformation of American Religion: How We Actually Live Our Faith* (New York: Free Press, 2003); and D. G. Hart, *Deconstructing Evangelicalism: Conservative Protestantism in the Age of Billy Graham* (Grand Rapids: Baker Book House, 2004).

10. Anon., *Gospel News, Or a Brief Account of the Revival of Religion in Kentucky and Several Other Parts of the United States* (Baltimore, 1801), 5.

11. Daniel T. Rogers, "Republicanism: The Career of a Concept," *Journal of American History,* 79 (June 1992): 11–38. See also Robert E. Shalhope, "Toward a Republican Synthesis: The Emergence of an Understanding of Republican-

ism in American Historiography," *William and Mary Quarterly*, 29 (Jan. 1972): 49–80. Standard works on Republicanism include Bernard Bailyn, *The Ideological Origins of the American Revolution* (Cambridge, MA: Harvard Univ. Press, 1967); and Gordon S. Wood, *The Creation of the American Republic, 1776–1787* (Chapel Hill: Univ. of North Carolina Press, 1969). For this study, Lance Banning, *The Jeffersonian Persuasion: Evolution of a Party Ideology* (Ithaca and London: Cornell Univ. Press, 1978) is also helpful. Finally, Rhys Isaac, *The Transformation of Virginia, 1740–1790* (1982; repr., New York: W. W. Norton, 1988), may not specifically address republicanism, but one can scarcely discuss Virginia's eighteenth-century Baptists and politics without referencing it.

12. Jewell Spangler, "Salvation Was Not Liberty: Baptists and Slavery in Revolutionary Virginia," *American Baptist Quarterly* 13 (Sept. 1994): 221–36. See also Spangler, *Virginians Reborn: Anglican Monopoly, Evangelical Dissent, and the Rise of the Baptists in the Late Eighteenth Century* (Charlottesville and London: Univ. of Virginia Press, 2008); Monica Najar, *Evangelizing the South: A Social History of Church and State in Early America* (Oxford and New York: Oxford Univ. Press, 2008); and Charles F. Irons, *The Origins of Proslavery Christianity: White and Black Evangelicals in Colonial and Antebellum Virginia* (Chapel Hill: Univ. of North Carolina Press, 2008).

13. Bertram Wyatt-Brown, *Southern Honor: Ethics and Behavior in the Old South* (Oxford and New York: Oxford Univ. Press, 1982), 14. See also Bertram Wyatt-Brown, *The Shaping of Southern Culture: Honor, Grace, and War, 1760s–1880s* (Chapel Hill and London: Univ. of North Carolina Press, 2001).

14. Wyatt-Brown, *Southern Honor*, 14. See also Joanne B. Freeman, *Affairs of Honor: National Politics in the New Republic* (New Haven and London: Yale Univ. Press, 2002).

15. As Charles F. Irons perceptively observes, "Virginia's evangelicals faltered in part because they found it difficult to recalibrate their rhetorical postures from that of dissenters to that of insiders. As ecclesiastical outsiders, white evangelicals had very publicly reached out to black Virginians as part of their protest against Anglican authority. True, they universally disavowed antislavery ambitions, but they nonetheless earned a reputation as the loudest advocates for those ambitions." See Irons, *Origins of Proslavery Christianity*, 55.

16. Aron, *How the West Was Lost*, 183. Again, the present study's findings differ in several respects from Aron's assessment.

17. Traylor, *Born of Water and Spirit*, 1–9.

18. Daniel Blake Smith, "'This Idea of Heaven': Image and Reality on the Kentucky Frontier," in Friend, *Buzzel About Kentuck*, 83–84.

19. See Edmund S. Morgan, *American Slavery, American Freedom: The Ordeal of Colonial Virginia* (New York: W. W. Norton, 1975). Equally important for this study are Irons, *Origins of Proslavery Christianity*; Najar, *Evangelizing the South*; and Spangler, *Virginians Reborn*.

1. A Vortex of Baptist Preachers

1. Ranck, "The Travelling Church," 1–37.

2. Ibid., 30.

3. Semple, *History of the Baptists in Virginia*, 226.

4. William A. Withington, "Bluegrass Region," in John E. Kleber, editor in chief, *The Kentucky Encyclopedia* (Lexington: Univ. Press of Kentucky, 1992), 91.

5. Smith, "This Idea in Heaven," in Friend, *Buzzel About Kentuck*, 77.

6. There are a number of impressive works on the Great Awakening. For example, see Thomas D. Kidd, *The Great Awakening: The Roots of Evangelical Christianity in Colonial America* (New Haven and London: Yale Univ. Press, 2007); and Frank Lambert, *Inventing the "Great Awakening"* (Princeton: Princeton Univ. Press, 1999). For the rise of Separate Baptists, see C. C. Goen, *Revivalism and Separatism in New England, 1740–1800: Strict Congregationalists and Separate Baptists in the Great Awakening* (Middletown, Ct.: Wesleyan Univ. Press, 1987). For an alternative to traditional understandings of the Great Awakening, see Jon Butler, "Enthusiasm Described and Decried: The Great Awakening as Interpretive Fiction," *Journal of American History* 69 (September 1982): 305–25.

7. See Goen, *Revivalism and Separatism in New England, 1740–1800*, 258–295.

8. See William Lumpkin, *Baptist Foundations in the South: Tracing through the Separates the Influence of the Great Awakening* (Nashville: Broadman Press, 1961), 28. Lumpkin identifies the original sixteen members as Shubal Stearns, Daniel Marshall, Peter Stearns, Ebinezer Stearns, Shubel Stearns Jr., Enos Stinson, Joseph Breed, Jonathan Polk, and their wives. See also J. Allen Easley, "Stearns, Shubal" in the *Encyclopedia of Southern Baptists* (Nashville: Broadman Press, 1958), 2:1298.

9. See A. D. Gillette, ed., *Minutes of the Philadelphia Association, 1707–1807* (Philadelphia: American Baptist Publication Society, 1851), for examples of how the association used the confession.

10. See Semple, *History of the Baptists in Virginia*, 62–93; Benedict, *General History of the Baptist Denomination*, 2:61. Benedict observes that the Separates tended to look askance at how Regulars dressed.

11. John Leland, *The Virginia Chronicle* (Fredericksburg, VA: T. Green, 1790), 22. Although it is much shorter and far more concerned with religious matters, *The Virginia Chronicle* is reminiscent of Thomas Jefferson's *Notes on Virginia* (1785; first English edition, 1787).

12. Leland, *The Virginia Chronicle*, 22–23.

13. For the remarkable story of James Ireland's life and testimony, see Keith Harper and C. Martin Jacumin, eds., *Esteemed Reproach: The Lives of Reverend James Ireland and Reverend Joseph Craig* (Macon, GA: Mercer Univ. Press, 2005). The quote regarding Separate and Regular Baptists is on page 104.

14. Ibid., 105.

15. John Taylor as quoted in Spencer, *History of Kentucky Baptists*, 1:161–62.

16. William Hickman, *A Short Account of my Life and Travels. For more than fifty years, A Professed Servant of Jesus Christ* (1828; repr., Louisville: Kentucky Baptist Historical Commission, 1969), 1.

17. Ibid.

18. Ibid., 2.

19. See Taylor, *Lives of Virginia Baptist Ministers*, 221; and John Taylor, *A History of Ten Baptist Churches, of Which the Author Has Been Alternately a Member.* (1827; repr., New York: Arno Press, 1980), 48.

20. Taylor, *A History of Ten Baptist Churches*, 11.

21. Ibid., 211–24. Taylor does not offer specific dates for hearing William Marshall preach or publicizing his conversion. He says he was "about 17" when he heard Marshall and "about 20" when he was baptized. If Taylor was born in 1752, he was converted some time in 1772.

22. Ibid., 222.

23. Ibid., 44. For a thorough discussion of Taylor's life and how he accrued his wealth, see John Taylor, *Baptists on the American Frontier: A History of Ten Churches of Which the Author Has Been Alternately a Member by John Taylor*, 3rd ed., ed. Chester Raymond Young (Macon, GA: Mercer Univ. Press, 1995), 1–84. Hereafter cited as Young, *Baptists on the American Frontier.*

24. Ibid., 44.

25. Isaac, *Transformation of Virginia.*

26. Merrill D. Peterson, *Thomas Jefferson: A Biography* (London and New York: Oxford Univ. Press, 1970), 722.

27. See Thomas S. Kidd, *God of Liberty: A Religious History of the American Revolution* (New York: Basic Books, 2010).

28. Charles F. Irons, "Believing in America: Faith and Politics in Early National Virginia," *American Baptist Quarterly* 21 (2002): 409n. The quote is found in note 3. See also Robert G. Gardner, "The Statistics of Early American Baptists: A Second Look," *Baptist History and Heritage* 24 (Oct. 1989): 29–44.

29. Spangler, *Virginians Reborn*, 207. Virginia Baptists were not alone in flooding their legislature with petitions for justice. The literature on Virginia during the Revolutionary War is extensive, but Spangler's work remains the best starting place for Baptists in Virginia's Revolutionary War Era. See also Irons, *Origins of Proslavery Christianity.* While Irons does not address Baptists exclusively, this work is nonetheless extremely valuable in understanding the interconnections between religion, slavery, and politics in Virginia's Revolutionary Era.

30. David Thomas, *The Virginian Baptist* (Baltimore: Enoch Story, 1774), 32–33.

31. Ibid., 16, 20.

32. Ibid., 33. Curiously, by the mid-nineteenth century David Thomas was being remembered as a warm-hearted advocate of religious freedom. The entry for David Thomas in the 1859 edition of Taylor's *Lives of Virginia Baptist Ministers*, 43–48, featured a poem not found in the earlier editions. The poem is on page 48.

> "'Tis all one voice, they all agree,
> God made us, and we must be free.
> Freedom we crave, with every breath,
> An equal freedom, or a death.
> The heav'nly blessing freely give,
> Or make an act we shall not live.
> Tax all things: water, air, and light,
> If need there be; yea, tax the night;
> But let our brave, heroic minds
> Move freely as celestial winds.
> Make vice and folly feel your rod,
> But leave our consciences to God."

33. Little, *Imprisoned Preachers*, 516–20. In Little's narrative persecution began in earnest in the 1760s.

34. Ibid. The Craigs had another brother, Benjamin, but he never attracted attention like his more famous brothers.

35. Taylor, *History of Ten Baptist Churches*, 280.

36. Taylor, *Lives of Virginia Baptist Ministers*, 84.

37. Ibid.

38. Ibid. 85–86.

39. Ibid. See also Little, *Imprisoned Preachers*, 53–58.

40. Taylor, *Lives of Virginia Baptist Ministers*, 87.

41. See Little, *Imprisoned Preachers*, 516–17. By Little's reckoning Lewis Craig appears to have been confronted for preaching no fewer than five times.

42. Taylor, *Lives of Virginia Baptist Preachers*, 84.

43. Ibid.

44. Ibid. See also Jon Butler, "James Ireland, John Leland, John 'Swearing Jack' Waller, and the Baptist Campaign for Religious Freedom in Revolutionary Virginia," in *Revolutionary Founders: Rebels, Radicals, and Reformers in the Making of the Nation*, ed. Alfred E. Young, Gary B. Nash, and Ray Raphael (New York: Alfred A. Knopf, 2011), 169–84.

45. If the existing records are accurate, Waller was as bold in his preaching as he had been in his depravity. See Taylor, *Lives of Virginia Baptist Preachers*, 83–85.

46. Robert B. Semple as quoted in Taylor, *Lives of Virginia Baptist Ministers*, 63.

47. John Taylor, as quoted in J. H. Spencer's *History of Kentucky Baptists*, 1: 89.

48. Compare Spencer, *History of Kentucky Baptists*, 1:28–32 and 1:87–89.

49. Little, *Imprisoned Preachers*, 132–36. Elijah Craig was jailed at least twice and perhaps as many as four times for preaching; see Little's chart, 516. Little is relying on Semple's *History of the Virginia Baptists* for this account.

50. Spencer, *History of Kentucky Baptists*, 1:83.

51. Ibid.

52. Little, *Imprisoned Preachers*, 127.

53. See 1 Samuel 21:10–15. King David pretended to be out of his mind before Achish of Gath. See also Spencer, *History of Kentucky Baptists*, 1:82. By all accounts, Joseph Craig had no difficulty in appearing to be out of his mind.

54. Taylor, "The Author's Conversion and Call to Ministry," in *History of Ten Baptist Churches*, 222. Precisely what Craig meant by "the Ass colt" is anyone's guess. He may have been referencing Matthew 21:5, where Jesus triumphantly entered Jerusalem "sitting upon an ass, and a colt, the foal of an ass." As such, Craig may have seen Taylor's preaching as "bearing Christ" to the congregation, but this is only conjecture.

55. William G. McLoughlin, "Patriotism and Pietism. The Dissenting Dilemma: Massachusetts Rural Baptists and the American Revolution," *Foundations* 19 (1976): 130.

56. See Nathan O. Hatch, *The Sacred Cause of Liberty: Republican Thought and the Millennium in Revolutionary New England* (New Haven, CT: Yale Univ. Press, 1977); Lance Banning, *The Sacred Fire of Liberty: James Madison and the Founding of the Federal Republic* (Ithaca, NY: Cornell Univ. Press, 1995); and Kidd, *God of Liberty*.

57. For biographical information on John Gano, see Cathcart, *Baptist Encyclopedia*, s.v. "Gano, John"; *Encyclopedia of Southern Baptists*, s.v. "Gano, John"; and William H. Brackney, *Historical Dictionary of the Baptists*, 2nd ed., Historical Dictionaries of Religions, Philosophies, and Movements No. 94 (Lanham, Md., Toronto, and Plymouth, UK: Scarecrow Press, 2009), s.v. "Gano, John." See also Semple, *History of the Baptists in Virginia*, 66.

58. Taylor, *Lives of Virginia Baptist Ministers*, 214.

59. Ibid.

60. James E. Welsh as quoted in William B. Sprague, *Annals of the American Pulpit; or Commemorative Notices of Distinguished American Clergymen of Various Denominations*, vol. 6, The Baptists (New York: Robert Carter & Brothers, 1865), 204.

61. Taylor, *Lives of Virginia Baptist Ministers*, 155.

62. Ibid. 157–59.

63. See Little, *Imprisoned Preachers*, 461–64.

64. David Barrow, Diary, July 16, 18. This "diary" chronicles Barrow's early exploration of Kentucky and is not an account of his entire life. Available at the Kentucky Historical Society, Frankfort, KY.

65. David Barrow, circular letter, February 14, 1798, reprinted in "David Barrow's Circular Letter of 1798," ed. Carlos R. Allen Jr., *William and Mary Quarterly*, 3rd ser., 20 (July 1963): 444.

66. Ibid., 445.

67. Ibid. 445–46.

68. Ibid. 447–48.

69. Ibid. 449.

70. Ibid. (emphasis in the original).

71. John Asplund, *The Annual Register of the Baptist Denomination in North*

America (n.p.: 1791; repr., *Baptist Banner*, Goodlettsville, TN, Church History Research and Archives, Lafayette, TN, 1979), 47. Asplund distinguished between ordained ministers and licensed ministers. Here, I am combining the numbers. Thus, by Asplund's reckoning in 1790, Kentucky claimed 40 ordained Baptist ministers and 21 licentiates for a total of 61 preachers. As people streamed into the Commonwealth, however, that number was probably inaccurate by year's end.

72. By the same token, several ministers served more than one church.

73. Spangler, *Virginians Reborn*, 222.

74. McLoughlin, "Patriotism and Pietism," 131.

75. See William Fristoe, *A Concise History of the Ketoctin Association, 1766–1808* (Staunton: William Gilman Lyford, 1808), 62–95. See Also Irons, "Believing in America."

2. Between Backwoods Brethren and Bluegrass Barons

1. I am borrowing the phrase "Barons of the Bluegrass" for this chapter title from Thomas Perkins Abernethy, *Three Virginia Frontiers*, Walter Linwood Fleming Lectures in Southern History (Baton Rouge: Louisiana State Univ. Press, 1940), 67. Paul W. Gates found the phrase "fetching." See Gates, *Landlords and Tenants on the Prairie Frontier: Studies in American Land Policy* (Ithaca and London: Cornell Univ. Press, 1973), 17. Thomas Jefferson, *Notes on the State of Virginia*, with an introduction by Thomas Perkins Abernethy (New York: Harper Torchbooks, 1964), 157.

2. Ibid.

3. For Thomas Jefferson's religious views, see Edwin S. Gaustad, *Sworn on the Altar of God: A Religious Biography of Thomas Jefferson* (Grand Rapids, MI: Wm. B. Eerdmans, 1996), and David L. Holmes, *The Faiths of the Founding Fathers* (Oxford: Oxford Univ. Press, 2006).

4. Samuel Meredith Jr. to John Breckinridge, March 2, 1791. Breckinridge Family Papers, Manuscript Division, Library of Congress, Washington, DC. Meredith used Craig's words to describe Kentucky's beauty to Breckinridge. See also Lowell H. Harrison, *Kentucky's Road to Statehood* (Lexington: Univ. Press of Kentucky, 1992), 5.

5. Gaining an understanding of land policy in early Kentucky history is a daunting task. Interested parties would be well-advised to consult Harrison, *Kentucky's Road to Statehood*; Thomas Perkins Abernethy, *Western Lands and the American Revolution* (New York: Russell and Russell, 1959); Patricia Watlington, *The Partisan Spirit: Kentucky Politics, 1779–1792* (New York: Atheneum, 1972); Roy M. Robbins, *Our Landed Heritage: the Public Domain, 1776–1936* (Princeton, NJ: Princeton Univ. Press, 1950); Joan Wells Coward, *Kentucky in the New Republic: The Process of Constitution Making* (Lexington: Univ. Press of Kentucky, 1979); and of course, Gates, *Landlords and Tenants*.

6. Gilbert Imlay, *A Topographical Description of the Western Territory of North America*, 3d ed. (1797; New York: August M. Kelley, 1969), 28–29. Imlay was also a notorious rogue. For more on Imlay see Wil Verhoeven, *Gilbert Imlay: Citizen of the World* (London and New York: Routledge, 2008).

7. Daniel Drake, *Pioneer Life in Kentucky, 1785–1800*, ed. Emmet Field Horine (New York: Henry Schuman, 1948), 7–11. Limestone is present-day Maysville. See also Ellen Eslinger, "The Shape of Slavery on the Kentucky Frontier," *Register of the Kentucky Historical Society* 92 (Winter 1994): 4.

8. Hickman, *A Short Account of My Life and Travels. For More than Fifty Years; A Professed Servant of Jesus Christ*, (np., 1828), 20–22. It is possible that Hickman had his dates confused. In his memoir he says he and his family left on August 16. He also said that he tried to preach on the day he left, but according to a calendar for 1784, Sunday fell on August 15, not 16. Nonetheless, he may have tried to preach a farewell sermon for his friends. Perhaps more questionable, Hickman claimed that he arrived at the Smith cabin on November 9 and he and his family worshiped the next day because it was Sunday. Yet, according to a 1784 calendar, November 9 fell on a Tuesday. It is possible that Hickman meant to say that he arrived on November 6, 1784. Hickman's wife gave birth to a daughter, Mary, on January 11, 1785.

Hickman's *A Short Account of My Life* was originally published in 1828 and republished in 1873. The Kentucky Baptist Historical Society reissued the work in 1969, but this edition was type scripted from an earlier edition and the page numbers do not match the earlier editions. This work relies on the 1828 edition.

9. Taylor, *History of Ten Baptist Churches*, 44.

10. Drake, *Pioneer Life In Kentucky*, 25.

11. Ibid., 26–27.

12. Moses Austin as quoted by Daniel Blake Smith, "This Idea in Heaven," 87.

13. James Thomas Flexner, *Washington: The Indispensable Man* (Boston and Toronto: Little, Brown, 1974), 54–55.

14. George Washington as quoted by Flexner, *Washington*, 55.

15. Gates, *Landlords and Tenants*, 16.

16. Abernethy, *Western Lands*, 12. According to Abernethy the Loyal Company received some 800,000 acres and the Ohio Company received 200,000 acres. See also "Loyal Company" and "Ohio Company," in Kleber, *Kentucky Encyclopedia*, 585 and 689, respectively.

17. "Proclamation of 1763," in Kleber, *Kentucky Encyclopedia*, 743–44.

18. Peterson, *Thomas Jefferson*, 43–44.

19. Ibid., 117–18

20. Daniel Blake Smith, "This Idea in Heaven," in Friend, *Buzzel About Kentuck*, 82.

21. "Transylvania Company," in Kleber, *Kentucky Encyclopedia*, 894. This land that North Carolina claimed would ultimately comprise most of north-central Tennessee. See also Paul H. Bergeron, Stephen V. Ash, and Jeanette Keith, *Tennesseans and Their History* (Knoxville: Univ. of Tennessee Press, 1999), 27.

22. "Transylvania Company," in Kleber, *Kentucky Encyclopedia*, 894. See also Kenneth C. Carstens, "Clark, George Rogers," in Kleber, *Kentucky Encyclopedia*, 195–96.

23. Hickman, *My Life and Travels*, 7. Before they reached the Cumberland River, they encountered a small dispirited party returning from Kentucky. One

of the men joined Hickman's group and went back to Kentucky with them. Hickman identifies him only as Harrod and notes, "We thought him much of a coward, though he boasted very much. . . ."

24. Ibid., 8.

25. Ibid., 9.

26. "Transylvania Company," in Kleber, *Kentucky Encyclopedia*, 894. See also "Kentucky County," in Kleber, *Kentucky Encyclopedia*, 495.

27. Peterson, *Thomas Jefferson*, 121.

28. Temple Bodley, Introduction, in *Reprints of Littell's Political Transactions in and concerning Kentucky and Letter of George Nicholas to His Friend in Virginia, also General Wilkinson's Memorial*, Filson Club Publications, no. 31 (Louisville, KY: John P. Morton, 1926), viii.

29. John Brown, Benjamin Sebastian, Harry Innes, and Caleb Wallace are usually numbered among Wilkinson's supporters.

30. Jeffrey Scott Suchanek, "Spanish Conspiracy," *Kentucky Encyclopedia*, 839.

31. Patricia Watlington, *The Partisan Spirit: Kentucky Politics, 1779–1792* (New York: Atheneum, 1972), 202.

32. Wilkinson to Innes, as quoted by Watlington, *Partisan Spirit*, 202.

33. Abernethy, *Three Virginia Frontiers*, 65.

34. Abernethy, *Three Virginia Frontiers*, 65.

35. Cynthia Lynn Lyerly, *Methodism and the Southern Mind, 1770–1810* (New York and Oxford: Oxford Univ. Press, 1998), 27–46. See also Isaac, *Transformation of Virginia*, and Christine Leigh Heyrman, *Southern Cross: The Beginnings of the Bible Belt* (New York: Alfred A. Knopf, 1997).

36. Scripture references abound but Philippians 2:5–9 expresses the thought well.

37. Robert Elder, *A Sacred Mirror: Evangelicalism, Honor, and Identity in the Deep South, 1790–1860* (Chapel Hill: Univ. of North Carolina Press, 2016). Although Elder finds honor in South Carolina as early as the 1790s the bulk of his analysis focuses on the period between the 1820s and 1860. See also Charity Carney, *Ministers and Masters: Methodism, Manhood, and Honor in the Old South* (Baton Rouge: Louisiana State Univ. Press, 2011); and Ted Ownby, *Subduing Satan: Religion, Recreation, and Manhood in the Rural South, 1865–1920* (Chapel Hill: Univ. of North Carolina Press, 1990).

38. Edward Ayers, "Honor," in *Encyclopedia of Southern Culture*, ed. Charles Reagan Wilson and William Farris et al. (Chapel Hill: Univ. of North Carolina Press, 1989), 1482.

39. Ibid. See also Edward R. Crowther, "Iron Chests: Honor and Manhood in Southern Evangelicalism," in John Mayfield and Todd Hagstette, eds., *The Fields of Honor: Essays on Southern Character and American Identity* (Columbia: Univ. of South Carolina Press, 2017) 276–291.

40. Gates, *Landlords and Tenants*, 17.

41. Mary K. Bonsteel Tachau, "Marshall, Humphrey," in Kleber, *Kentucky Encyclopedia*, 609–10.

42. Humphrey Marshall, *History of Kentucky*, vol. 1 (Frankfort, KY: Geo. S. Robinson 1824), 149–50.

43. Ibid. See also Abernethy, *Western Lands and the American Revolution*, 302–337.

44. Marshall, *History of Kentucky*, vol. 1, 150.

45. Ibid.

46. Ibid., 150–51. It is hard to say with certainty, but Marshall may be referring to George Stokes Smith, another Baptist minister and friend of Lewis Craig.

47. Ibid., 150. Of course, Marshall appears to be one of those fortunate individuals whose land claims were solid.

48. Gates, *Landlords and Tenants*, 16. Gates adds that in such cases, individuals were paying not only for their own land, but the improvements they had made on their own property.

49. Ibid., 16–17.

50. Minutes, 27 August 1791, Elkhorn Association.

51. See Minutes, September and December 1791, Elkhorn Association.

52. See Minutes, 1785–1790, Elkhorn Association.

53. Of the three, only Ambrose Dudley was still affiliated with the Elkhorn Association when the Craig/Creath controversy erupted. Garrard became a Unitarian before he became governor, and Eastin soon followed suit. Eastin even wrote a theological treatise on Unitarianism titled "Essays on the Divine Unity."

54. See Hatch, *Sacred Cause of Liberty*. See also Banning, *Sacred Fire of Liberty*. Both Hatch and Banning point to the overtly religious overtones that shaped the conversation over freedom both before and after the American Revolution.

55. Compare Charles B. Heinemann and Gaius Marcus Brumbaugh, *"First Census" of Kentucky, 1790* (Washington, DC: G. M. Brumbaugh, 1940); and G. Glenn Clift, *"Second Census" of Kentucky, 1800* (1954; Baltimore: Genealogical Publishing, 1976).

56. Robert M. Ireland, *The Kentucky State Constitution* (Oxford and New York: Oxford Univ. Press, 2011), 6.

57. Gary R. Matthews, *More American than Southern: Kentucky, Slavery, and the War for an American Ideology, 1828–1861* (Knoxville: Univ. of Tennessee Press, 2014), 38–40.

58. Harrison, *Kentucky's Road to Statehood*, 103–8.

59. Ibid., 108–9.

60. Rev. Vernon P. Martin, "Father Rice, the Preacher Who Followed the Frontier," *Filson Club History Quarterly* 29 (October 1955): 324–30.

61. David Rice, *Slavery Inconsistent with Justice and Good Policy* (1792; London: M. Gurney, 1793), 3, 5.

62. Ibid., 9.

63. Ibid., 24.

64. "Nicholas, George," in Kleber, *Kentucky Encyclopedia*, 680–81.

65. Hugh Blair Grigsby, *The History of the Virginia Federal Convention of 1788*, vol. 1 (Richmond: Virginia Historical Society, 1890), 79.

66. Grigsby, *History of the Virginia Federal Convention*, 79n96. The note reads in part: "I have alluded to the fatness of Nicholas. As he continued a prominent politician to his death in Kentucky in 1799, and as it was hard to meet his argument, his opponents resorted to caricature, and pictured him as broad as he was long. A friend told me that he once saw Mr. Madison laugh till the tears came to his eyes at a caricature of George Nicholas which represented him 'as a plum pudding with legs to it.' He was probably one of the fattest lawyers since the days of his namesake Sir Nicholas Bacon, the lord keeper, who was so blown by the mere effort of taking his seat in the court of chancery that it was understood that no lawyer should address him until he had signified the recovery of his wind by three taps of his cane on the floor." See also Harrison, *Kentucky's Road to Statehood*, 74.

67. Matthews, *More American than Southern*, 39–40. As Matthews puts it, "Nicholas reasoned that any law that permitted emancipation without just compensation threatened all property rights and would make Kentucky a less attractive destination for new settlers."

68. See chapter 5, "Ties That Would Not Bind," especially the sections on David Barrow and William Hickman.

69. For instance, see Elizabeth Fortson Arroyo, "Poor Whites, Slaves, and Free Blacks in Tennessee, 1796–1861," in *Tennessee History: The Land, the People, and the Culture*, ed. Carroll Van West (Knoxville: Univ. of Tennessee Press, 1998) 101–12. Arroyo maintains that interrelations between blacks and whites posed significant challenges long before Tennesseans thought of statehood. As early as 1741 North Carolina had even taken repressive measures to limit interaction between blacks and whites.

70. Bergeron, Ash, and Keith, *Tennesseans and Their History*, 47. Settlers in the region that would become Tennessee wanted federal supervision of the territory rather than North Carolina. Apparently, a certain amount of animosity existed between the territory and state, except on property rights and slavery.

71. Larry Tice, "'Taking Up' Quaker Slaves: The Origins of America's Slavery Imperative," in Regina D. Sullivan and Monte Harrell Moore, eds., *Varieties of Southern Religious History: Essays in Honor of Donald G. Mathews* (Columbia: Univ. of South Carolina Press, 2015), 35–50.

72. Ibid., 36–38.

73. Ibid., 48. Tice further concludes that Revolutionary Era Quakers in North Carolina were more interested in cleansing themselves from the sin of slavery than they were in advancing rights for free persons of color.

74. Harrison, *Kentucky's Road to Statehood*, 110–11.

75. See A Constitution or Form of Government for the State of Kentucky, 1792, Article 9, Kentucky Historical Society, http://www.kyhistory.com/cdm/ref /collection/MS/id/9918. Last accessed 21 June 2016.

76. Harry S. Laver, "'Chimney Corner Constitutions': Democratization and Its Limits in Frontier Kentucky," *Register of the Kentucky Historical Society* 95 (Autumn 1997): 338–39 (emphasis Laver).

77. George Nicholas to Madison, May 2, 1792, in *The Papers of James Madison*, vol. 14, 6 April – 16 March 1793, ed. Robert Rutland, et al. (Charlottesville: Univ. of Virginia Press, 1983).

78. Nicholas to Madison, May 2, 1792. Nicholas does not identify the "N. brethren" by name, and given his attitude toward slavery, it is doubtful that he would refer to African Americans as "brethren." In *Kentucky's Road to Statehood*, Lowell Harrison claims "N. brethren" is a reference to unnamed Northerners. See Harrison, 125.

79. Nicholas to Madison, May 2, 1792, 297. See also Harrison, *Kentucky's Road to Statehood*, 125.

80. According to Harrison, seven delegates were ministers; three Presbyterians, three Baptists, and one Methodist.

81. Ireland, *The Kentucky State Constitution*, 6.

82. Abernethy, *Three Virginia Frontiers*, 72.

83. Abernethy, *Western Lands*, 368.

84. Everett Dick, *The Lure of the Land: A Social History of the Public Lands f rom the Articles of Confederation to the New Deal* (Lincoln: Univ. of Nebraska Press, 1970), 1.

3. Good Old Virginia Doctrine

1. Hickman, *My Life and Travels*, 20–22.

2. Ibid., 21. See also Masters, *History of Baptists in Kentucky*, 12–13.

3. Thomas Bender, *Community and Social Change in America* (Baltimore and London: Johns Hopkins Univ. Press, 1978), 11.

4. There are numerous works that discuss church discipline among Baptists. For two helpful examples see Gregory A. Wills, *Democratic Religion: Freedom, Authority, and Church Discipline in the Baptist South, 1795–1900* (New York: Oxford Univ.Press, 1996) and Jessica Madison, *In Subjection: Church Discipline in the Early American South, 1760–1830* (Macon, GA: Mercer Univ. Press, 2014).

5. Alistair McGrath, *The Genesis of Doctrine: A Study in the Foundation of Doctrinal Criticism* (Grand Rapids, MI, and Cambridge, UK: Wm. B. Eerdmans), 11.

6. Ibid., 12, 46.

7. Ibid., 79. The Latin phrases are "man is sinner" and "man is just or righteous." Italics McGrath.

8. Walter B. Shurden, "The Associational Principle, 1707–1814: Its Rationale," *Foundations*, 21 (July–September, 1978): 222. See also Shurden's longer work, *Associationalism among Baptists in America, 1707–1814* (New York: Arno Press, 1980), which remains the most thorough discussion of Baptist associationalism.

9. Semple, *History of the Baptists in Virginia*, 19.

10. For example, see E. Brooks Holifield, *A History of Pastoral Care in America: From Salvation to Self-Realization* (Nashville: Abingdon Press, 1983); and *God's Ambassadors: A History of Clergy in America*, (Grand Rapids, MI, and Cambridge, UK: Wm. B. Eerdmans, 2007). See also Richard L. Bushman, *From Puritan to*

Yankee: Character and the Social Order in Connecticut, 1690–1765 (Cambridge, MA: Harvard Univ. Press, 1967).

11. Minutes, 25 June 1785, Elkhorn Association. The four churches were Clear Creek, South Elkhorn, Big Crossing, and Gilbert's Creek. At their next meeting the association drafted a constitution that claimed the Philadelphia Association had been organized under a "Baptist confession of faith first put forth in the name of the seven even congregations met together in London in the year 1643. . . ." This confession was actually the First London Confession. The Philadelphia Association was organized under the Second London Confession (1689), and the Philadelphia Confession (1742) upon which the Elkhorn Association was founded represented an amended version of Second London.

12. Jon Butler, *Power, Authority, and the Origins of American Denominational Order: The English Churches in the Delaware Valley, 1680–1730* (Tuscaloosa: Univ. of Alabama Press, 2009), 75–93. The best sources for the Philadelphia Association are Gillette, *Minutes of the Philadelphia Association* and Francis W. Sacks, *The Philadelphia Baptist Tradition of Church Authority: An Ecumenical Analysis and Theological Interpretation*, Studies in American Religion, vol. 48 (Lewiston, NY: Edwin Mellen Press, 1989). On the Philadelphia Confession of Faith, see William Lumpkin, *Baptist Confessions of Faith* (1959; rev. ed., Valley Forge, PA: Judson Press, 1969), 235–295, especially 285–290.

13. The Second London Confession, Article One, "Of the Holy Scriptures." See Lumpkin, *Baptist Confessions of Faith*, 248–252.

14. See Lumpkin, *Baptist Confessions of Faith*, 348–52.

15. Cathcart, *Baptist Encyclopedia*, s.v. "Griffith, Rev. Benjamin." Jenkin Jones's name is never mentioned in conjunction with the treatise. Originally, the PBA petitioned Jones to solicit funding for the printing and distribution of the revised confession. The association may have wanted him to help raise funds for producing and disseminating the new discipline rather than offering any editorial assistance.

16. Benjamin Griffith, *A Short Treatise Concerning a True and Orderly Gospel Church*, 1743, reprinted in *Polity: Biblical Arguments on How to Conduct Church Life*, ed. Mark Dever (Washington, DC: Center for Church Reform, 2001), 96–97.

17. Griffith, *Short Treatise*, in Dever, *Polity*, 97.

18. Ibid., 98.

19. Ibid.

20. Ibid.

21. Ibid., 111.

22. Ibid., 112. Griffith also referenced the *Confession*, ch. 26, subpoints 14 and 15. Likely, he referred to the Second London Confession. The Philadelphia Confession discussed ecclesiology in ch. 27.

23. Gillette, *Minutes of the Philadelphia Association*, 55.

24. Gillette, *Minutes of the Philadelphia Association*, 63. See also Shurden, *Associationalism among Baptists in America* and Brackney, *Historical Dictionary*, s.v. "Associations, Baptist."

25. Butler, *Origins of American Denominational Order*, 91–92. Butler explains that Nathan Jenkins, pastor of the Cape May church exposed Loveall/Baker as a fraud in a letter to the Piscataway church dated December 30, 1730. Butler adds that "details about Baker's offences were omitted from the printed version (of John Comer's Diary) but can be found in the manuscript diary at the Rhode Island Historical Society, Providence Rhode Island," (172n64).

26. Brackney, *Historical Dictionary*, s.v. "Palmer, Paul." See also Benedict, *General History of the Baptist Denomination*, 2:13, 24, 96.

27. Holifield, *History of Pastoral Care in America*, 67–106.

28. Baptists were not the only ones struggling to define the limits of religious power and authority. See Holifield, *God's Ambassadors*.

29. Edwards, *Customs of the Primitive Churches*; Or A Set of Propositions, (Philadelphia: Andrew Steuart, 1768), Article 6.

30. Ibid., Article 7. Edwards maintained that the outward call consisted in three parts, namely, election to the pastorate, ordination, and installment.

31. Morgan Edwards, "Sermon, Preached in the College of Philadelphia, at the Ordination of the Rev'd Samuel Jones, A. B.," (Philadelphia: Andrew Steuart, 1763).

32. Ibid., 26–27.

33. Harper and Jacumin, *Esteemed Reproach*, 106–15.

34. Ibid., 118.

35. Taylor, *History of Ten Baptist Churches*, 29.

36. Ibid. Craig and Redding later played instrumental roles in shaping the Elkhorn Association.

37. Minutes of Bryan Station Baptist Church, Third Saturday in April 1790, Kentucky Historical Society, Frankfort, Kentucky. It seems likely that Boswell himself raised the issue.

38. Ibid., 15 May 1790, 28.

39. Ibid., September 1791, 41–42.

40. Ibid., September 1792, 49.

41. The Committee, *A Brief History of David's Fork Baptist Church, Fayette County, Ky.* (Louisville: Western Recorder Print, 1876), 7. See also Spencer, *History of Kentucky Baptists*, 1:142.

42. Taylor, *History of Ten Baptist Churches*, 54.

43. Ibid., 64–65 (emphasis mine).

44. Ibid., 65–88.

45. Minutes, 1744–1807, Philadelphia Association, 54–448.

46. Ibid. Associational Minutes are an excellent source for changing concepts of ministry. For Taylor's work at Clear Creek see *A History of Ten Churches*, 54–127.

47. Minutes, 1774, Philadelphia Association, 141.

48. Associations of Separate Baptists usually disdained confessions of faith and refused to adopt them. Rather, Separate Baptist churches tended to have church covenants that specified doctrinal conviction.

49. Minutes, 1774, Philadelphia Association, 140–147.

50. Ibid., 20–21.

51. Ibid., 37.

52. This is clearly evident among Baptists when one compares the Griffith polity with an earlier statement, Elias Keach, *The Glory and Ornament of a True Gospel-Constituted Church,* (London: 1697) and a later work by Samuel Jones, *A Treatise on Church Discipline* (Philadelphia: S. C. Ustick, 1798).

53. Theodrick Boulware, *A Second Enlarged Edition of A Sketch of the Life of Theodrick Boulware* (Saint Louis: Sherman Spencer, 1859), 9. Boulware published his life story in 2 separate editions and while they are similar, the 1859 edition contains information not found in the first edition.

54. Of course, pastors had always been subject to disciplinary actions if they engaged in openly sinful behavior or taught heresy. However, Jones was the first to address the issue of ministerial transition.

55. Gano, *Biographical Memoirs,* 118.

56. Ibid., 119.

57. See Minutes, 1787–1807, Elkhorn Association.

58. Ministerial training among Baptists in the eighteenth century is a topic that deserves extended treatment. See Robert G. Torbet, *A Social History of the Philadelphia Association, 1707–1940* (Philadelphia: Westbrook, 1944), 64–76.

59. Rhode Island College later became Brown University. Cathcart, *Baptist Encyclopedia,* s.v. "Brown University." See also F. Perko, "Brown University," in *Dictionary of Baptists in America,* ed. Bill J. Leonard (Downers Grove, Ill.: Inter-Varsity Press, 1994). Although Cathcart's encyclopedia was first published in 1880, his biographical data for individual entries lists education wherever possible. See also Edward C. Starr, "William Staughton: Baptist Educator and Founder of the First Theological School in Philadelphia," in *The Chronicle: A Baptist Historical Quarterly* 12 (October 1949): 166–77.

60. Boulware, *Sketch of the Life,* 12–13. Boulware lists his mentors as J. Hayon, D. Peak, and T. Hicklin.

61. Ibid., 13. It is possible that the society met at Town Fork Church where Gano served as pastor.

62. William E. Ellis, *A History of Education in Kentucky* (Lexington: Univ. Press of Kentucky, 2011), 3–36.

63. Asa C. Barrow, "David Barrow and His Lulbegrud School, 1801," in *Filson Club History Quarterly* 7 (April 1933): 89–90.

64. Ibid., 90.

65. J. N. Bradley, *History of Great Crossing Church* (n.p., 1876), 18–20.

66. Spencer, *History of Kentucky Baptists,* 1:86–87.

67. Elijah Craig, *A Few Remarks on the Errors That are Maintained in the Christian Churches of the Present Day; and Also, On the Movements of Divine Providence Respecting Them* (Lexington, KY: James H. Stewart, 1801), 2. Craig did not identify his mentor by name, but he likely meant Samuel Harris. Converted in 1758, Harris was well-educated, and he quickly became a leader of Virginia's revivalistic Baptists. Early in his ministry Harris decried a paid ministry but later changed

his mind on the subject. Most likely, Craig did not know Harris had changed his position on a paid ministry when he wrote *A Few Remarks*. See "Samuel Harris," in Taylor, *Lives of Virginia Baptist Ministers*, 28–37.

68. Craig, *A Few Remarks*, 17–18.

69. Ibid., 29. Prior to disestablishment, Virginia's Episcopal church was supported by income generated from tobacco sales. Craig's statement, "worried the tobacco from under the church" refers to the loss of income the Episcopalian church suffered as a result of disestablishment.

70. Ibid., 9–10.

71. Ibid., 8.

72. Ibid., 14.

73. P. Donan, *Memoir of Jacob Creath, Jr. to Which Is Appended the Biography of Elder Jacob Creath, Sr.* (Cincinnati: Chase and Hall, 1877), 201. According to Donan, Samuel Creath was imprisoned by the British upon declaring his sympathies for the revolutionaries. His property was confiscated, and he spent seven years in prison. Creath moved his family to the states in 1784.

74. Spencer, *History of Kentucky Baptists*, 1:310. Part of Spencer's text appears in quotation marks and it is difficult to say if he is quoting someone else on this point.

75. Donan, *Memoir of Jacob Creath, Jr.*, 205.

76. Theodrick Boulware, *A Sketch of the Life of Theodrick Boulware* (Fulton, MO, 1858), 6.

77. Ibid.

78. Ibid.

79. Ibid. Boulware would have been about twenty-six when this incident occurred.

80. Spencer, *History of Kentucky Baptists*, 1:309. See also Elkhorn's minutes for the period.

81. See Minutes of Stamping Ground Baptist Church, 1806–1807, Kentucky Historical Society, Frankfort, Kentucky, and J. W. Singer, *A History of the Baptist Church at Stamping Ground, Kentucky, 1795 –* (n.p., 1971). On p. 21 Singer says that the church voted 45 to 6 to call Creath as pastor.

82. Singer, *Baptist Church at Stamping Ground*, 24.

4. Revive Us Again

1. Portions of this chapter come from a previously published essay titled, "'And All the Baptists in Kentucky Took the Name *United Baptists*': The Union of Kentucky's Separate and Regular Baptists," *Register of the Kentucky Historical Society* 110 (Winter 2012): 3–32.

2. See Paul K. Conkin, *Cane Ridge: America's Pentecost* (Madison: Univ. of Wisconsin Press, 1990).

3. See David C. McCullom, "A Study of Evangelicals and Revival Exercises from 1730–1805: Tracing the Development of Exercise Tradition through the First

Great Awakening Period to the Southern Great Revival" (PhD diss., Southeastern Baptist Theological Seminary, 2009).

4. John Boles, *The Great Revival, 1787–1805: The Origins of the Southern Evangelical Mind* (Lexington: Univ. Press of Kentucky, 1972) remains the best treatment of the Great Revival's southern phase. See also Ellen Eslinger, *Citizens of Zion: The Social Origins of Camp Meeting Revivalism* (Knoxville: Univ. of Tennessee Press, 1999); George M. Thomas, *Revivalism and Cultural Change: Christianity, Nation Building, and the Market in the Nineteenth-Century United States* (Chicago and London: Univ. of Chicago Press, 1989); and Ann Taves, *Fits, Trances, and Visions: Experiencing Religion and Explaining Experience from Wesley to James* (Princeton: Princeton Univ. Press, 1999).

5. See Najar, *Evangelizing the South*; and Spangler, *Virginians Reborn*.

6. Semple, *History of the Baptists in Virginia*, 100.

7. Ibid., 101.

8. Ibid.

9. Taylor, *History of Ten Baptist Churches*, 55.

10. Minutes, 25 June 1785, Elkhorn Association.

11. The First London Confession (1644) and the Second London Confession (1689) share a number of similarities but they are substantially different confessions. The Philadelphia Confession is almost identical to the Second London Confession with the exception of two articles, one addressing hymn singing and one addressing the imposition of hands. In *History of Ten Baptist Churches*, John Taylor stipulates that Regular Baptists use the Philadelphia Confession (10).

12. Minutes, 30 September 1785, Elkhorn Association. The meeting began on September 30 and continued into early October.

13. Minutes of the South Kentucky Association, October 1787, transcribed by George F. Doyle, Filson Historical Society, Louisville, Kentucky. These minutes exist in transcription form only and should be used with due caution. All quotations come from the transcription and are cited as they appear in the text, with respect to spelling and capitalization.

14. Ibid., 4.

15. Ibid. The South Kentucky Association minutes do not specify that the Separate Baptist congregation used the meetinghouse formerly occupied by the Regular Baptists, but it is easy to see how the name alone might annoy the Elkhorn Association. The South Kentucky minutes do not offer a yearly, specific listing of affiliated churches but a comparative reading of the South Kentucky and Elkhorn minutes suggests that the both associations claimed Boones Creek and Tates Creek.

16. Gano, *Biographical Memoirs*, 116–25.

17. For the Regulator Movement, see Carole Watterson Troxler, *Forming Dissenters: The Regulator Movement in Piedmont North Carolina* (Raleigh: North Carolina Office of Archives and History, 2016); and Marjoleine Kars, *Breaking Loose Together: The Regulator Rebellion in Pre-Revolutionary North Carolina* (Chapel Hill and London: Univ. of North Carolina Press, 2002).

18. Morgan Edwards, *Materials Towards a History of the Baptists* (Danielsville, GA: Heritage Papers, 1984), 2:100–101. See also George W. Purefoy, *A History of the Sandy Creek Association, from its Organization in A.D. 1758 to A.D. 1858* (New York: Sheldon & Co., 1858), 65–73; and Howard R. Stewart, *A Dazzling Enigma: The Story of Morgan Edwards* (Lanham, MD: Univ. Press of America, 1995).

19. John Taylor and J. H. Spencer, two of Kentucky's earliest chroniclers, relied heavily on biography to tell the Baptist story in early Kentucky. While they are both quick to point out a minister's political persuasion, if known, neither of them says much about the politics of South Kentucky's ministers.

20. In the footnote on p. 34 of *The Virginia Chronicle*, John Leland reflected on Virginia's union and mused, "[B]ut had they united without any confession of faith, as they did in *Georgia*, perhaps it would have been better" (emphasis Leland).

21. Letter dated 2 October 1788, Minutes, 1792, South Kentucky Association, 6–7. Curiously, the letter appears after the associational minutes for 1792.

22. Ibid., 7–8. The Elkhorn Association's minutes dated May 30, 1789, mention correspondence with "United Baptists," doubtless a reference to the South Kentucky Association.

23. Compare Minutes, 1789, South Kentucky Association, 4 and Minutes, 1789, Elkhorn Association.

24. Benedict, *General History of the Baptist Denomination*, 2:236–37.

25. Spencer, *History of Kentucky Baptists*, 1:482.

26. Minutes, 1792, South Kentucky Association, 5.

27. Minutes, 20 May 1793, Elkhorn Association.

28. Minutes, 1793, South Kentucky Association, 9.

29. Ibid., 10.

30. Semple, *History of the Baptists in Virginia*, 101.

31. Minutes, 14 October 1793, Elkhorn Association.

32. Ibid.

33. Ibid. For a discussion of religion and Revolutionary rhetoric, see Hatch, *Sacred Cause of Liberty*; and Ruth Bloch, *Visionary Republic: Millennial Themes in American Thought, 1756–1800* (New York: Cambridge Univ. Press, 1985).

34. Minutes, 9 August 1794, Elkhorn Association. The minutes specify neither which churches complained about the union nor their specific concerns.

35. Ibid., 30 September 1785.

36. Ibid., 20 May 1793.

37. Ibid., 10 August 1795.

38. Ibid., 15 August 1796. The Marble Creek church withdrew their former query, perhaps because John Price was their pastor.

39. Ibid., 14 August 1797.

40. Compare Taylor, *History of Ten Baptist Churches*, 54–66; and Spencer, *History of Kentucky Baptists*, 1:174.

41. Compare the minutes of the Elkhorn Association for 1791, 1792, and 1793. Unfortunately, the minutes for the South Kentucky Association do not provide the sort of statistical data found in the Elkhorn minutes.

42. See appendix 4; see also Spencer, *History of Kentucky Baptists*, 1:546.

43. Spencer, *History of Kentucky Baptists*, 1:546.

44. Ibid.

45. Ibid., 547.

46. See the minutes of the Elkhorn Association from 1788 onward. In 1791 the association added a column for "Restored" members, but dropped it for 1792. The designation "Restored" does not reappear until 1810.

47. See Minutes, 1800–1802, Elkhorn Association. See also appendix 5.

48. There are a number of excellent works bearing on church order and discipline, especially Wills, *Democratic Religion*; and Madison, *In Subjection*. See also Najar, *Evangelizing the South*.

49. See Minutes, 1802–1807, Elkhorn Association.

50. Minutes, 1788, South Kentucky Association, 6–8. The quote is from p. 8.

51. Taylor, *Lives of Virginia Baptist Ministers*. By way of contrast, few South Kentucky ministers appear in Taylor's work.

52. See appendix 2. John Gano did not represent Elkhorn on this occasion due to age and declining health.

53. Compare appendixes 1, 2, and 3.

54. John Leland, "The Virginia Chronicle," in *The Writings of the Late Elder John Leland with Additional Sketches, & Etc. by Miss L. F. Greene* (New York: G. W. Wood, 1845), 114n.

55. Coward, *Kentucky in the New Republic*, 97–99. See also Harrison, *Kentucky's Road to Statehood*, 124–30.

56. Clift, *"Second Census" of Kentucky*, iii–xiv. According to Clift, in 1800 there were 4,225 slaves in Fayette County, 2,163 slaves in Bourbon County, and 2,107 slaves in Woodford County for a total of 8,493. If one includes Jessamine (1561), Garrard (1259), and Franklin (1369) counties, the number swells from 8,493 to 12,684. As of 1800 approximately 31 percent of Kentucky's slave population was concentrated in six central Kentucky counties.

57. Coward, *Kentucky in the New Republic*, 118.

58. Minutes of the Marble Creek Baptist Church, April 6, 1799.

59. Coward, *Kentucky in the New Republic*, 125–27.

60. See appendix 4.

61. Spencer, *History of Kentucky Baptists*, 1:547.

62. Arianism maintains, contrary to Trinitarianism, that Jesus was God's first creation and therefore neither co-equal nor co-eternal with God the Father. As such, Jesus was God's greatest of all creations, but a creation nonetheless. For a discussion of American Universalism, see Ann Lee Bressler, *The Universalist Movement in America, 1770 –1880* (Oxford, New York: Oxford Univ. Press, 2001). See also Howard Dorgan, *In the Hands of a Happy God: The "No-Hellers" of Central*

Appalachia (Knoxville: Univ. of Tennessee Press, 1997) for the story of the Primitive Baptist Universalists.

63. Spencer, *History of Kentucky Baptists,* 1:547.

64. See appendix 4 for a list of the doctrines that formed the basis for the union of Kentucky's Separates and Regulars.

65. Spencer, *History of Kentucky Baptists,* 1:548.

66. Leland, *Virginia Chronicle,* 29–30 (emphasis Leland).

67. Spencer, *History of Kentucky Baptists,* 1:548 (emphasis Spencer).

68. Ibid., 1:79–81; 2:138–39. The Elkhorn Association refused fellowship with the South Kentucky Association of Separate Baptists.

69. See Monica Najar, "'Meddling with Emancipation': Baptists, Authority, and the Rift over Slavery in the Upper South," *Journal of the Early Republic* 25 (Summer 2005); as well as David Barrow, *Involuntary, Unmerited, Perpetual, Absolute, Heredity Slavery, Examined; on the Principles of Nature, Reason, Justice, Policy, and Scripture* (Lexington: D. & C. Bradford, 1808); and Barrow's diary (see ch.1, note 64).

70. Semple, *History of the Baptists in Virginia,* 59.

71. Ibid., 60.

72. Ibid., 56.

5: Ties That Would Not Bind

1. Minutes, 1786, Elkhorn Association.

2. Ibid., 1787.

3. Ibid., 1789.

4. Brackney, *Historical Dictionary,* s.v. "Barrow, David." For the tension between religious dissenters and the established church, see Isaac, *Transformation of Virginia.* See also Little, *Imprisoned Preachers,* 461–63; and Taylor, *Lives of Virginia Baptist Ministers,* 155–61.

5. Spencer, *History of Kentucky Baptists,* 1:192–95.

6. David Barrow, "Circular Letter. Southampton County, Virginia, February 14, 1798" (Norfolk, Va.: Willett & O'Connor, 1798). David Barrow, "David Barrow's Circular Letter of 1798," ed. Carlos R. Allen Jr., in *William and Mary Quarterly,* 3rd ser., 20 (July 1963): 444–51. See also Vivien Sandlund, "'A Devilish and Unnatural Usurpation': Baptist Evangelical Ministers and Antislavery in the Early Nineteenth Century, A Study of the Ideas and Activism of David Barrow," *American Baptist Quarterly* 13 (September 1994): 262–77.

7. Barrow, "Circular Letter," 449–50.

8. Ibid.

9. Ibid., 450 (emphasis Barrow).

10. Ibid., 449.

11. Spencer, *History of Kentucky Baptists,* 1:185.

12. Minutes, 1805, Elkhorn Association.

13. Spencer, *History of Kentucky Baptists,* 1:192–97. Originally affiliated with

the Elkhorn Association, the Mt. Sterling church united with the North District
Association in 1804. This association was formed shortly after the South Kentucky
Association dissolved and the Separate Baptists united with the Regular Baptists
to become United Baptists.

14. Ibid. See also Masters, *History of Baptists in Kentucky*, 167–68; and Carter
Tarrant, *History of the Baptised Ministers and Churches in Kentucky, and Friends to
Humanity* (Frankfort, KY: William Hunter, 1808). The association's constitution
noted that the official name for the association would be The Baptized Church
of Christ; Friends to Humanity. Members and affiliates usually styled themselves
"Friends to Humanity."

15. Barrow, *Involuntary, Unmerited*.

16. Tarrant, *History of the Baptised Ministers*, 8–48.

17. Compare the minutes of the Forks of the Elkhorn Baptist Church for May
1806 and June 1806 (Kentucky Historical Society, Frankfort, Kentucky).

18. Minutes, December 1806, Forks of the Elkhorn Baptist Church. Presum-
ably, the "M" stands for moderator. Standard practice for these minutes has the
moderator identifying himself at the end of each session. Since charges had been
brought against William Hickman, it appears that Mordecai Boulware assumed
the role of moderator for this business session.

19. Minutes, January 1807, Forks of the Elkhorn Baptist Church.

20. Minutes, February 1807, Forks of the Elkhorn Baptist Church.

21. Taylor, *History of Ten Baptist Churches*, 202.

22. Boulware, *Sketch of the Life*, 5. According to Boulware's recollection, Hickman resigned in 1805. The "abusive letter" to the church apparently has not survived, but assuming there was in fact a letter, Hickman may have been responding
at least in part to the church's censure for inviting Carter Tarrant to preach at his
house. Likely, Hickman did not believe the church had any authority over who
spoke at his residence.

23. Tarrant, *History of the Baptised Ministers*, iii.

24. Ibid, 6.

25. Tarrant also mentions a circular letter that was too lengthy to include in
his brief history. The work is likely David Barrow's *Involuntary, Unmerited, Perpetual, Absolute, Hereditary, Slavery Examined on the Principles of Nature, Reason,
Justice, Policy, and Scripture*.

26. Tarrant, *History of the Baptised Ministers*, 38.

27. Minutes, October 1808, Forks of the Elkhorn Baptist Church.

28. Compare the minutes of the Forks of the Elkhorn Baptist Church for
December 1808 and January 1809.

29. Minutes, January 1809, Forks of the Elkhorn Baptist Church.

30. Boulware, *A Sketch of the Life of Theodrick Boulware* (St. Louis: Sherman
Spencer, 1859) 14. On a curious note, Boulware published his autobiography in
two editions in consecutive years. The accounts are similar but not identical. In
the first edition, Boulware wrote, "The Church called Elder John Shackleford

as its minister for one year. Before Elder W. Hickman delivered his sermon his large and very extravagant family were bountifully and comfortably supported; but now all communications were withheld. In less than one year Elder Hickman returned to the Church, finding that his conscientious, emancipating principles were not as strong as his appetite for meat, bread, &c., &c." (p. 5). In his second edition Boulware also claimed that the church had kept Hickman's letter on record at Boulware's behest. Apparently, this letter no longer exists. See also Minutes, November 1809, Forks of the Elkhorn Baptist Church.

31. Boulware, *Sketch of the Life*, 14.

32. Compare Minutes, January 1807, Forks of the Elkhorn Baptist Church, with Spencer, *History of Kentucky Baptists*, 1:314.

33. Ermina Jett Darnell, *Forks of the Elkhorn* (Louisville: Standard Printing, 1946), 20–21.

34. Ibid., 30.

35. Ibid.

36. Compare the Kentucky tax rolls for 1800 and 1810. Specifically, the 1810 tax record lists two men named William Hickman. One owned 75 acres on the Elkhorn Creek with an additional 552 additional acres in Shelby County, 4 horses, and 1 black male over sixteen. The other Hickman owned 150 acres and a total of 4 blacks. The William Hickman who owned property on Elkhorn Creek seemed the most likely to be pastor of Forks of the Elkhorn Baptist Church. Both William Hickmans, however, apparently owned slaves. Franklin County Tax Records, 1810, Kentucky Department of Library and Archives, microfilm, 007977, pp. 17 and 19.

37. Franklin County Tax Records, 1800 and 1810.

38. Spencer, *History of Kentucky Baptists*, 1:311. Spencer gives a fairly detailed account of the Craig/Creath agitation, as does Masters, *History of Baptists in Kentucky*, 178–80. For a biographical discussion of Creath, see ch. 3 under "Ministers, Ministry, and the 'Elkhorn Way.'"

39. Spencer, *History of Kentucky Baptists*, 1:311.

40. J. H. Spencer references this pamphlet, as does nearly every early history of Kentucky Baptists, but it apparently does not exist in any cataloged collection.

41. J. H. Spencer devotes eleven pages to Gano. See Spencer, *History of Kentucky Baptists*, 1:116–27.

42. Harrison, *Kentucky's Road to Statehood*, 138. See also Joan E. Brooks-Smith, comp., *Master Index, Virginia Surveys and Grants, 1774–1791* (Frankfort: Kentucky Historical Society, 1976), 118.

43. Benjamin Franklin Van Meter, *Genealogies and Sketches of Some Old Families Who Have Taken Prominent Part in the Development of Virginia and Kentucky Especially, and Later of Many Other States of this Union* (Louisville: John P. Morton, 1901), 20.

44. Minutes, 1806, Elkhorn Association.

45. Spencer, *History of Kentucky Baptists*, 1:311.

46. Compare Spencer, *History of Kentucky Baptists*, 1:311, and Masters, *History of Baptists in Kentucky*, 178.

47. "Report of the Committee on Helps, Called by the Town Fork Church, to enquire into Sundry Charges against the Religious and Moral Character of JACOB CREATH, Exhibited in a Pamphlet, Published by ELIJAH Craig," July 31, 1807. E1–5, Pamphlet file, Southern Baptist Theological Seminary, Louisville KY.

48. Ibid. See the statement at the end of the report.

49. Minutes, 1807, Elkhorn Association.

50. Ibid. Each of these churches would eventually leave Elkhorn and become founding members of the Licking Association.

51. Ibid.

52. Minutes, 7 October 1807, Bryan Station Baptist Church (emphasis mine).

53. See Minutes, 1807–1808, Bryan Station Baptist Church.

54. Peruse, Esquire, "A Caution to the Churches Composing the Elkhorn Association, to Avoid the Snare Which Four or Five Jealous Priests Have Laid to Involve You In, by Calling the Association, under the Pretense of Trying Their Friend E. Craig," (n.p.: n.d.). The four or five "disappointed priests" were probably the main leaders in the formation of the Licking Association; namely, Ambrose Dudley, John Price, Joseph Redding, Lewis Corbin, and Absalom Bainbridge.

55. Ibid. Peruse is invoking Matthew 1–2.

56. Peruse, Esquire, "Caution to the Churches."

57. Minutes of the Marble Creek Baptist Church, 2nd Saturday in February 1807, Kentucky Historical Society, Frankfort, Kentucky. Marble Creek Baptist Church became East Hickman Baptist Church in 1802.

58. Minutes, May 1807, Marble Creek Baptist Church.

59. Benedict, *General History of the Baptist Denomination*, 2:233.

60. Minutes, 1810, Bryan Station Baptist Church.

61. Spencer, *History of Kentucky Baptists*, 1:551–52.

62. Minutes, 1810, Elkhorn Association.

63. Ibid.

64. Ibid.

65. Ibid.

66. Minutes, 1810, Elkhorn Association.

67. See "Elder H. Ranking, 1872—Circular Licking Association of Particular Baptists of Kentucky," in *Thomas P. Dudley and the Golden Age of the Particular Baptists in America, 1792–1886*, comp. and ed. Stanley Philips (Quitman, MS: Predestinarian, 2010) 2:635–45.

68. Spencer, *History of Kentucky Baptists*, 2:27–28. Of Henry Toler, Spencer writes, "With all his fine abilities, his unspotted character and his former success, it is probable that he did more harm than good, in Kentucky."

69. See Keith Harper, "'And All the Baptists in Kentucky Took the Name *United Baptists*': The Union of Kentucky's Separate and Regular Baptists," *Register of the Kentucky Historical Society* 110 (Winter 2012), 3–31.

70. Henry Toler, "Union – No Union" (Lexington, KY: Joseph Ficklin, 1821), 5.

71. Ibid.

72. Ibid.

73. See appendix 1.

74. The 1801 Plan of Union was never intended to be a full confession of faith. As its framers stipulated, the plan of union offered general statements on select points so that the "united" Baptists might reach consensus.

75. Ibid., 12.

76. James Fishback, *A Defence of the Elkhorn Association; in Sixteen Letters Addressed to Elder Henry Toler, Pastor of Grier's Creek Particular Baptist Church; in Answer to His Publication, Entitled "Union – No Union"* (Lexington, KY: Thomas T. Skillman, 1822).

77. Whereas Toler's pamphlet amounted to a little over 15 pages, Fishback's *Defence* numbered 185 pages.

78. Fishback, Preface, *Defence of the Elkhorn Association*.

79. Ibid.

80. Ibid., 30.

81. Ibid., 43–50.

82. Ibid., 50.

83. Benedict, *General History of the Baptist Denomination*, 2:234.

84. Ibid., 235.

85. Compare Minutes of the Licking Association, 1810–1811, Kentucky Historical Society, Frankfort, Kentucky, and Minutes, 1810–1811, Elkhorn Association. Between 1810 and 1811 the Licking Association added 5 churches but netted a total of 38 additional members. This statistic seems strange, but it probably reflects adjusted numbers from churches whose minority party left to form new congregations and united with the Elkhorn Association.

86. Assuming the biographical information in J. H. Spencer's *A History of the Kentucky Baptists* is accurate, these ages should be close. For this study, I calculated ages for Elkhorn's ministers by comparing respective birth and death dates.

87. See Thomas Lewis's will, Fayette County Will Book B, Kentucky Department of Library and Archives, microfilm, 008966, pp. 57–58. Lewis did not specify how much land he had given to Jephthah Dudley.

6. A Story to Tell the Nations

1. Portions of this essay have appeared under the title, "Downwind from the New England Rat: John Taylor, Organized Missions, and the Regionalization of Religious Identity on the American Frontier," in *Ohio Valley History* (Fall 2009), 25–41. Used by permission.

2. John Taylor, *Thoughts on Missions* (Franklin County, KY, 1820), 6 (emphasis Taylor). See also Young, *Baptists on the American Frontier*, 1–81. According to Young, Taylor amassed a sufficiently large estate to be considered a small planter. Moreover, Taylor did not see himself as a "money preacher," and he was not interested in preaching for a salary.

3. A second printing of *Thoughts on Missions* included nine biographical

sketches of Taylor's fellow preachers and totaled 72 pages. Daniel Parker's opposition to missions and mission societies initially stemmed from his suspicion of centralized authority and later from his peculiar understanding of human nature, i.e., Two Seedism, a kind of Baptist Manichaeism. Alexander Campbell, much like Taylor, saw no biblical precedent for mission societies and opposed them on the ground that that they were unbiblical. Standard Baptist history textbooks usually have broad overviews of the antimission movement. See H. Leon McBeth, *The Baptist Heritage: Four Centuries of Baptist Witness* (Nashville: Broadman Press, 1987); and Robert G. Torbet, *A History of the Baptists*, 3rd ed., with a foreword by Kenneth Scott Latourette (Valley Forge: Judson Press, 1968) as examples. See also Richard Hughes, *Reviving the Ancient Faith: The Story of the Churches of Christ in America* (Grand Rapids: Wm. B. Eerdmans, 1996).

4. James Axtell, *The Invasion Within: The Contest of Cultures in Colonial North America* (New York and Oxford: Oxford Univ. Press, 1986); and Neal Salisbury, *Manitou and Providence: Indians, Europeans, and the Making of New England, 1500–1643* (New York and Oxford: Oxford Univ. Press, 1982) are both thorough studies of Indian and white interaction.

5. Daniel L. Akin, *Ten Who Changed the World* (Nashville: B & H Publishing Group, 2012), 85–101. Akin uses an alternative spelling, "Leile." See also Clement Gayle, *George Liele, Pioneer Missionary to Jamaica* (Kingston: Jamaica Baptist Union, 1982); and David T. Shannon Sr., sr. ed., with Julia Frazier White and Deborah Van Broekhoven, eds., *George Liele's Life and Legacy: An Unsung Hero* (Macon, GA: Mercer Univ. Press, 2012). For African American contributions to early missionary work, see Christopher Brent Ballew, *The Impact of African-American Antecedents on the Baptist Foreign Missionary Movement, 1783–1825*, Toronto Studies in Theology 96 (Lewiston, New York: Edwin Mellen Press, 2004).

6. Timothy Dwight, *Address to the Emigrants from Connecticut, and from New England Generally, in the New Settlements in the United States* (Hartford: Peter Gleason & Co. 1817), 9 (emphasis Dwight). See also Amy DeRogatis, *Moral Geography: Maps, Missionaries, and the American Frontier*, Religion and American Culture Series, edited by Randall Balmer (New York: Columbia Univ. Press, 2003).

7. John Freeman Schermerhorn and Samuel J. Mills, *A Correct View of That Part of the United States Which Lies West of the Allegany Mountains, with Regard to Religion and Morals* (Hartford, CT.: Peter B. Gleeson and Co. Printers, 1814), 20.

8. Ibid., 38.

9. Jack Manly, "Leland, John," *Encyclopedia of Southern Baptists*, 2:783.

10. Leland, "The Rights of Conscience, & c.," in *Writings of the Late Elder John Leland*, 182. Leland baptized Taylor's wife, Betsy, and the Lelands and Taylors maintained a lifelong friendship. For more information on this relationship, see Young, *Baptists on the American Frontier*, 18 and 152. For information on Leland and James Madison, see Banning, *Sacred Fire of Liberty*, 271, 478n10.

11. Leland, "On Sabbatical Laws," in *Writings of the Late Elder John Leland*, 442.

12. Leland, "Correspondent in Palestine," in *Writings of the Late Elder John Leland*, 471–72. Missionary critics frequently decried titles like "field agent."

13. It was a rare visitor to the American frontier who did not come away with a strong opinion of its living conditions. For a good summary, see Thomas P. Slaughter's aptly titled chapter, "Lice, Labor, and Landscape," in *The Whiskey Rebellion: Frontier Epilogue to the American Revolution* (New York and Oxford: Oxford Univ. Press, 1986), 61–74. Of course, the accounts depicting frontier savagery usually came from visitors who were returning to homes in settled areas.

14. Eighteenth-century Calvinistic Baptists, especially in England, fought over whether or not a minister should extend the offer of salvation to the non-elect. Much of this debate ended with Andrew Fuller's treatise, *The Gospel Worthy of All Acceptation.*

15. Jefferson, *Notes on the State of Virginia,* 157.

16. Lexington had been dubbed "Athens of the West" as early as 1811. See J. Winston Coleman, *Lexington, the Athens of the West* (Lexington, KY: Winburn Press, 1981), 13. By 1837 a certain P. Doyle described Lexington as the Athens of the West in a poem on the front page of the December 21, 1837, edition of the *Kentucky Gazette.* See also James C. Klotter and Daniel Rowland, eds., *Bluegrass Renaissance: The History and Culture of Central Kentucky, 1792–1852* (Lexington: Univ. Press of Kentucky, 2012).

17. Young, *Baptists on the American Frontier,* 111.

18. Adoniram Judson as quoted in Francis Wayland, *Pulling the Eye Tooth from a Live Tiger: A Memoir of the Life and Labor of Adinoram Judson* (Boston: Phillips, Sampson; London: Nisbet, 1853), 1:102. See also Torbet, *History of the Baptists,* 300–301. For an excellent treatment of Ann Hasseltine Judson and her role in shaping early missionary practice, see Laura Rodgers Levens, "Leaving Home and Finding Home: Theology and Practice of Ann Hasseltine Judson and the American Baptist Mission to Burma, 1812–1826," (ThD diss., Duke Divinity School, 2015).

19. Judson as quoted in Wayland, *Pulling the Eye Tooth,* 1:102.

20. Most Baptist history textbooks deal with organized mission work and the Triennial Convention in some detail. See McBeth, *The Baptist Heritage,* 343–57.

21. Taylor, *Thoughts on Missions,* 9–10.

22. Ibid. Although Taylor claims that the donations totaled $200.00, Elkhorn's minutes are much less specific, indicating that the offering totaled between $150.00 and $200.00. See Minutes, 1815, Elkhorn Association, 2–3. Rice later spoke in glowing terms of his visit to Kentucky. He claimed that he visited ten associations and collected "a sum not much short of $2,000." By his reckoning only Massachusetts had given more to missions. See *Second Annual Report of the Baptist Board of Foreign Missions for the United States* (Philadelphia: Anderson and Meehan, 1816), 68–76. The quote is on page 71.

23. Taylor, *Thoughts on Missions,* 7.

24. Henry Holcombe laid out his grievances in an extended treatise titled, *The Whole Truth Relative to the Controversy Betwixt the American Baptists* (Philadelphia: J. H. Cunningham, 1820). See also John B. Boles, "Henry Holcombe, A Southern Baptist Reformer in the Age of Jefferson," *Georgia Historical Quarterly* 54, no. 3 (Fall 1970), 381–407.

25. Taylor, *Thoughts on Missions*, 8–9.

26. Ibid., 14.

27. Opposition to organized mission work, or antimissionism, is a complicated phenomenon. Some characterize antimissionism as a movement led by
quasi-literate, jealous, ultra-Calvinists; others see it as a movement that featured
numerous theological positions with adherents from all social classes. In defense
of Taylor, Larry Douglas Smith maintains that the caricature of western preachers
as poorly educated, backwoods ranters obscures the arguments of men who challenged modern missions on a practical and theological level. Specifically, *Thoughts
on Missions* is more than a diatribe against international evangelism. Rather it
was a warning to Taylor's fellow Baptists to beware of Luther Rice, a field agent
for the Baptist Board of Foreign Missions, and others like him. Smith argues that
Taylor was not antimissionary, per se. Rather, he opposed the means by which the
Baptist missionary movement chose to structure and organize itself, effectively
developing a theological understanding of missions to suit its own prejudices.
Larry Douglas Smith, "The Rise of the Missionary Spirit Among the Kentucky
Baptists," *The Quarterly Review* 40 (April-June 1980) 74–79; and "John Taylor and
Missions: A New Interpretation," *The Quarterly Review* 42 (April-June 1982), 54–
61. See also William Warren Sweet, *Religion on the American Frontier: The Baptists,
1783–1830*, with a general introduction by Shirley Jackson Case (New York: Henry
Holt, 1931) 58–76; Byron Cecil Lambert, "The Rise of the Anti-Mission Baptists:
Sources and Leaders, 1800–1840" (PhD diss., Univ. of Chicago, 1957; repr., Arno
Press, 1980, Baptist Tradition series, edited by Edwin Scott Gaustad).

28. For example, see the Minutes, 1785–1800 Elkhorn Association, and Craig,
A Few Remarks, 1–37.

29. Leland, "Address, Delivered at Dalton, Massachusetts, January 8, 1831," in
Writings of the Late Elder John Leland, 606.

30. Taylor, *Thoughts on Missions*, 10.

31. Ibid., 11.

32. Ibid., 6.

33. Ibid., 9.

34. Boles, *Great Revival*. See also Eslinger, *Citizens of Zion*; and Conkin,
Cane Ridge.

35. Taylor, *Thoughts on Missions*, 9–10.

36. Taylor's Elkhorn Association followed the Philadelphia Confession of
Faith as a summary statement of its theological underpinning. They may also
have looked to Benjamin Griffith's *A Short Treatise Concerning a True and
Orderly Gospel Church*, which was written in 1743 and appended to the Philadelphia confession.

37. For Baptists and associationalism, see Sacks, *Philadelphia Baptist Tradition*;
and Shurden, *Associationalism among Baptists in America*.

38. See Butler, *Origins of American Denominational Order*, 43–51. See also Gillette, *Minutes of the Philadelphia Association*; and "Minutes of the Elkhorn Baptist
Association, Kentucky, 1785–1805," in Sweet, *Religion on the American Frontier*,

417–509, for examples of how associations conducted meetings and addressed their particular issues. As for meeting times, most associations met annually, but some met more often. All associations would convene for special business. When possible, associations scheduled their meetings so they would not conflict with neighboring associations.

39. Taylor, *Thoughts on Missions*, 12.

40. Ibid., 11–12.

41. Ibid.

42. Ibid., 10.

43. Young, *Baptists on the American Frontier*, 48–49.

44. Anonymous blurb, *Baptist Monitor and Political Compiler*, June 3, 1823, p. 4, cols. 1–2.

45. "Intelligence from Kentucky," *The Reformer*, September 1, 1821, vol. 2, no. 21, 192. Taylor did not mention him by name but his stance on missions put him at odds Silas Mercer Noel, a rising Kentucky preacher-aristocrat and Taylor's own pastor.

46. Ibid., 193.

47. Ibid., 194.

48. Ibid., 195.

49. Ibid., 199.

50. Minutes, 1772, Philadelphia Association, 124.

51. Minutes, 1800, Philadelphia Association, 350.

52. Minutes, 1806, Philadelphia Association, 432. See also Hatch, *Sacred Cause of Liberty*; Bloch, *Visionary Republic*; and James West Davidson, *The Logic of Millennial Thought: Eighteenth-Century New England*, Yale Historical Publications, Miscellany 112 (New Haven and London: Yale Univ. Press, 1977).

53. Minutes, 1801, Elkhorn Association. The minutes identify Smith only as "G Smith."

54. Compare Minutes, 1802, Elkhorn Association, and Spencer, *History of Kentucky Baptists*, 2:548. After the Elkhorn and Licking Associations parted ways, a question arose about this missionary venture. According to Spencer, Young wrote the following note to clarify his status: "I, John Young, certify that I was ordained and sent as a missionary to the Indians, by Ambrose Dudley, David Barrow, George S. Smith, Joseph Redding, Austin Easton, John Price, and Lewis Craig, in the month of September, 1801. Given under my hand, this 2nd day of November, 1842. (Signed) John Young."

55. See Young, *Baptists on the American Frontier*, 52.

56. Masters, *History of Baptists in Kentucky*, 190.

57. Spencer, *History of Kentucky Baptists*, 1:578. The five societies affiliated with the Baptist Board of Foreign Missions were the Green River Country Society, the Bardstown Society, the Mt. Sterling Society, the Shelbyville Society, and the Washington Kentucky Missionary Society.

58. *Proceedings of the Board of Managers for the Baptist Mission Society of Kentucky, 1818*, 4 (emphasis mine), Archives, Southern Baptist Theological Seminary.

These proceedings also stemmed from their fifth annual meeting, thus dating the society's origin to 1813.

59. Ibid.

60. Ibid., 16.

61. Ibid., 12–13.

62. Spencer, *History of Kentucky Baptists*, 1:599–603. See also Ellis, *History of Education in Kentucky*, 37–64; and Robert Snyder, *A History of Georgetown College* (Georgetown, KY: Georgetown College, 1979).

63. Drake, *Pioneer Life in Kentucky*, 144.

64. Torbet, *A Social History*, 66–69. For later developments in church-related higher education, see James Tunstead Burtchaell, *The Dying of the Light: The Disengagement of Colleges and Universities from Their Christian Churches* (Grand Rapids, MI: Wm. B. Eerdmans, 1998).

65. Ellis, *History of Education in Kentucky*, 5.

66. For one-room schools, see William Lynwood Montell, *Tales from Kentucky One-Room School Teachers* (Lexington: Univ. Press of Kentucky, 2011).

67. Niels Henry Sonne, *Liberal Kentucky, 1780–1820* (New York: Columbia Univ. Press, 1939; repr., Lexington: Univ. of Kentucky Press, 1968). See also John D. Wright Jr. and Eric Christianson, "Transylvania University," in Kleber, *Kentucky Encyclopedia*, 894–96.

68. Donald G. Mathews, "The Second Great Awakening as an Organizing Process: An Hypothesis" *American Quarterly* 21, no. 1 (1969); reprinted in John M. Mulder and John F. Wilson, eds., *Religion in American History: Interpretive Essays* (Englewood Cliffs, NJ: Prentice-Hall, 1978), 203. Mathews refers to the Second Great Awakening as a "happily vague generalization."

69. Ibid.

70. Compare Jon Butler, *Awash in a Sea of Faith: Christianizing the American People* (Cambridge, MA and London: Harvard Univ. Press, 1990); and Nathan O. Hatch, *The Democratization of American Christianity* (New Haven and London: Yale Univ. Press, 1991).

71. For a discussion of the significance of missionary consensus, see Bill J. Leonard, *God's Last and Only Hope: The Fragmentation of the Southern Baptist Convention* (Grand Rapids, MI: Wm. B. Eerdmans, 1990). Leonard uses the term with respect to missions as a binding agent in Southern Baptist life, but it was also a binding agent for many Baptists in the Early National period.

72. Barrow, *Involuntary, Unmerited*, passim. See also Najar, "Meddling with Emancipation," 157–186.

73. See Beth Barton Schweiger, *The Gospel Working Up: Progress and the Pulpit in Nineteenth-Century Virginia*, Religion in America Series, edited by Harry S. Stout (New York and Oxford: Oxford Univ. Press, 2000); and Schweiger, "A Social History of English Grammar in the United States," *Journal of the Early Republic* 30, no. 4 (Winter 2010): 533–55.

74. Gordon Wood observes, "In the end the disintegration of the traditional

eighteenth-century monarchial society of paternal and dependent relationships prepared the way for the emergence of the liberal, democratic, capitalistic world of the early nineteenth century." See Wood, *The Radicalism of the American Revolution* (New York: Vintage Books, 1993), 95.

75. Wyatt-Brown, *Southern Honor*, 21.

76. Ayers, "Honor," in *Encyclopedia of Southern Culture*, 1483–84 (emphasis mine).

77. For example, see James C. Klotter, *Kentucky Justice, Southern Honor, and American Manhood: Understanding the Life and Death of Richard Reid*, Southern Biography Series, ed. Bertram Wyatt-Brown (Baton Rouge: Louisiana State Univ. Press, 2003).

78. Edward R. Crowther, "Holy Honor: Sacred and Secular in the Old South," *Journal of Southern History* 62 (November 1992): 622.

79. Ibid.

80. Ibid., 618.

81. See E. Brooks Holifield, *The Gentlemen Theologians: American Theology in Southern Culture, 1795–1860* (Durham, NC: Duke Univ. Press, 1978).

82. James R. Mathis, *The Making of the Primitive Baptists: A Cultural and Intellectual History of the Anti-Mission Movement, 1800–1840*, Studies in American Popular History and Culture (New York: Routledge, 2004).

83. See Donald G. Mathews, *Religion in the Old South* (Chicago and London: Univ. of Chicago Press, 1977).

84. Saul Cornell, *The Other Founders: Anti-Federalism and the Dissenting Tradition in America, 1788–1828* (Chapel Hill and London: Univ. of North Carolina Press, 1999).

85. Mathews, "Second Great Awakening as an Organizing Process," 213–14.

86. See Najar, *Evangelizing the South*, 157–186.

87. Compare and contrast Daniel Parker, *A Public Address to the Baptist Society* (Vincennes, IN: Stout & Osborn, 1820); with Schweiger, *The Gospel Working Up*. In *The Democratization of American Christianity*, Nathan Hatch observes, "The rollicking irony of the attack of grassroots Baptist leaders John Taylor and Daniel Parker upon the pretensions of moderate Calvinism was that it was done in the name of extreme predestinarian or 'Hard shell' Calvinism" (178). That the moderate Calvinism of mission-society proponents, particularly in the Baptist ranks, was open to multiple interpretations is beyond dispute. However, Calvinism was not the real issue. Taylor scarcely mentions theology in *Thoughts on Missions* except to note that mission boards are not mentioned in the Bible or to question Rice's commitment to biblical ethics.

Conclusion

1. Taylor, *History of Ten Baptist Churches*, 183.

2. Ibid.

3. Ibid., 183–84.

4. According to Taylor, Henry Davidge ceased preaching soon after this episode for some unexplained reason and left church life altogether. See *History of Ten Baptist Churches*, 182–88.

5. Taylor, *History of Ten Baptist Churches*, 189.

6. Ibid., 192.

7. Spencer, *History of Kentucky Baptists*, 2:298.

8. Mathis, *Making of the Primitive Baptists*, 90–92. Some may date the Kehukee Declaration from 1827. According to Mathis, the association officially took its stand against missions in 1826 and reaffirmed its stance unanimously in the following year. See also Elder Cushing Biggs Hassell, *History of the Church of God from the Creation to A.D. 1885*, revised and completed by Elder Sylvester Hassell (Middletown, Orange County, New York: Gilbert Beebe's Sons, 1886), 719–46.

9. See also Hughes, *Reviving the Ancient Faith*; and Elder John Sparks, *Raccoon John Smith: Frontier Kentucky's Most Famous Preacher* (Lexington: Univ. Press of Kentucky, 2005). See also Spencer, *History of Kentucky Baptists*, 1:581–99; and Masters, *History of Baptists in Kentucky*, 198–223.

10. Kentucky Baptist historian J. H. Spencer observes that Taylor changed churches three times between 1815 and 1818 when he finally joined Buck Run Church, not far from Frankfort. He was a member of Big Spring Church in Woodford County for about ten months (1815) under Silas Noel's leadership. One wonders if Taylor left Big Spring at least in part because of Noel's commitment to missions. See Spencer, *History of Kentucky Baptists*, 1:62.

11. Jack Manly, "Leland, John," in *Encyclopedia of Southern Baptists*, 783.

12. Leland, *Writings of Elder John Leland*, 602.

13. Young, *Baptists on the American Frontier*, 55.

14. For church taxation, see "The Autobiography of Jacob Bower: A Frontier Baptist Preacher and Missionary," in Sweet, *Religion on the American Frontier*, 185–230. For the best scholarship on Primitive Baptists, see John Crowley, *Primitive Baptists of the Wiregrass South: 1815 to Present* (Gainesville: Univ. Press of Florida, 1999); and Mathis, *Making of the Primitive Baptists*.

15. James E. Welch, "John Taylor, 1772–1833," in *Annals of the American Pulpit* 6, edited by William B. Sprague (New York: Robert Carter & Brothers, 1860), 158.

Bibliography

Primary Material

Associational Minutes

Minutes of the Bracken Association
Minutes of the Elkhorn Association
Minutes of the Licking Association
Minutes of the North District Association
Minutes of the Philadelphia Association
Minutes of the South Kentucky Association
The Minutes of the Elkhorn Association (1785–1805) and the Philadelphia Association (1707–1801) are available in print. The South Kentucky Association Minutes (1787–1803) and the North District Association Minutes (1803–1823) are housed at the Filson Historical Society, Louisville, Kentucky. The other Minutes listed are housed at the Kentucky Historical Society, Frankfort, Kentucky.

Church Minutes

Minutes of the Bryan Station Church
Minutes of David's Fork Church
Minutes of the Forks of the Elkhorn Church
Minutes of the Great Crossing Church
Minutes of the Marble Creek Church
Minutes of Stamping Ground Baptist Church
These church records are all housed at the Kentucky Historical Society, Frankfort, Kentucky.

Books, Pamphlets, Etc.

Anon., *Gospel News, Or a Brief Account of the Revival of Religion in Kentucky and Several Other Parts of the United States.* Baltimore, 1801.

Asplund, John. *Universal Register of the Baptist Denomination in North America for the Years 1790, 1791, 1792, 1793, and part of 1794.* Reprinted by *Baptist Banner*, H. C. Vanderpool, ed. and Church History Research and Archives, Lafayette, TN. 1979.

Barrow, David. *The Diary of David Barrow*. Typescript. Frankfort: Kentucky Historical Society.

———. Circular Letter, February 14, 1798. In Carlos R. Allen Jr., "David Barrow's Circular Letter of 1798." *William and Mary Quarterly*, 20, no. 3 (July 1963): 444–51.

———. *Involuntary, Unmerited, Perpetual, Absolute, Heredity Slavery, Examined; on the Principles of Nature, Reason, Justice, Policy, and Scripture*. Lexington: D. & C. Bradford, 1808.

Boulware, Theodrick. *A Sketch of the Life of Theodrick Boulware*. Fulton: np, 1858. Available at the Southern Baptist Historical Library and Archives, Nashville, TN.

———. *A Second Enlarged Edition of A Sketch of the Life of Theodrick Boulware*. St. Louis: Sherman Spencer, 1859. Available at the Southern Baptist Historical Library and Archives, Nashville, TN.

Craig, Elijah. *A Few Remarks on the Errors That Are Maintained in the Christian Churches of the Present Day; and Also, On the Movements of Divine Providence Respecting Them*. Lexington, KY: James H. Stewart, 1801.

Dwight, Timothy. *Address to the Emigrants from Connecticut, and from New England Generally, in the New Settlements in the United States*. Hartford, CT: Peter Gleason, 1817.

Edwards, Morgan. *Materials Towards a History of the Baptists*. 2 vols. Prepared for publication by Eve B. Weeks and Mary B. Warren. Danielsville, GA: Heritage Papers, 1984.

———. Customs of the Primitive Churches; Or A Set of Propositions. Philadelphia: Andrew Steuart, 1768.

Gano, John. *Biographical Memoirs of the Late John Gano, of Frankfort (Kentucky), Formerly of the City of New York*. New York: Southwick and Hardcastle, 1806.

Hickman, William. *A Short Account of My Life and Travels. For More than Fifty Years; A Professed Servant of Jesus Christ*. 1828. Louisville: Kentucky Baptist Historical Commission and Kentucky Baptist Historical Society, 1969.

Holcombe, Henry. *The Whole Truth Relative to the Controversy Betwixt the American Baptists*. Philadelphia: J. H. Cunningham, 1820.

Jones, Samuel. *A Treatise on Church Discipline*. Philadelphia: S. C. Ustick, 1798.

Keach, Elias. *The Glory and Ornament of a True Gospel-Constituted Church*. London: n.p., 1697.

Leland, John. *The Writings of the Late Elder John Leland, with Additional Sketches, &c. by Miss L. F. Green*. New York: G. W. Wood, 1845. Reprint, Church History Research and Archives, 1986.

Parker, Daniel. *An Address to the Baptist Society Address*. Vincennes, IN: Stout and Osborn, 1820.

Rice, David. "Slavery Inconsistent with Justice and Good Policy; Proved by a Speech Delivered in the Convention Held at Danville, Kentucky." Philadelphia, 1792.

Schermerhorn, John Freeman, and Samuel J. Mills. *A Correct View of That Part of the United States Which Lies West of the Allegany Mountains, with Regard to Religion and Morals.* Hartford, CT: Peter B. Gleeson, 1814.

Second Annual Report of the Baptist Board of Foreign Missions for the United States. Philadelphia: Anderson and Meehan, 1816.

Taylor, John. *A History of Ten Baptist Churches, of Which the Author Has Been Alternately a Member.* 1827. Reprint, New York: Arno Press, 1980.

———. *Baptists on the American Frontier: A History of Ten Baptist Churches, of Which the Author has been Alternately a Member by John Taylor.* 1827. 3rd ed. Edited and annotated by Chester Raymond Young. Macon, GA: Mercer Univ. Press, 1995.

———. *Thoughts on Missions.* Franklin County, KY, 1820.

Baptist Histories

Benedict, David. *A General History of the Baptist Denomination in America, and Other Parts of the World.* 2 vols. Boston: Lincoln & Edmands, 1813. Reprint, Gallatin, TN: Church History Research and Archives, 1985.

Birdwhistell, Ira (Jack). *The Baptists of the Bluegrass: A History of the Elkhorn Association, 1785–1985.* Berea, KY: Berea College Press, 1985.

Hassell, Elder Cushing Biggs. *History of the Church of God, from the Creation to A. D. 1885, Including Especially the History of the Kehukee Primitive Baptist Association.* Revised by Elder Sylvester Biggs. Middletown, NY: Gilbert Beebe's Sons, 1886.

Little, Lewis Peyton. *Imprisoned Preachers and Religious Liberty in Virginia.* Lynchburg, VA: J. P. Bell, 1938.

Masters, Frank M. *A History of Baptists in Kentucky.* Louisville: Kentucky Baptist Historical Society, no. 5, 1953.

Nowlin, William Dudley. *Kentucky Baptist History, 1770–1922.* Louisville, KY: Baptist Book Concern, 1922.

Semple, Robert Baylor. *History of the Baptists in Virginia.* 1810. Revised and extended by G. W. Beale, 1894. Lafayette, TN: Church History Research and Archives, 1976.

Spencer, J. H. *A History of Kentucky Baptists.* 2 vols. Revised and corrected by Mrs. Burilla B. Spencer, 1885. Reprint, Gallatin, TN: Church History Research and Archives, 1984.

Secondary Sources

Abernethy, Thomas Perkins. *Western Lands and the American Revolution.* New York: Russell & Russell, 1959.

———. *Three Virginia Frontiers.* Baton Rouge: Louisiana State Univ. Press, 1940.

Akin, Daniel L. *Ten Who Changed the World.* Nashville: B & H Publishing Group, 2012.

Aron, Stephen. *How the West Was Lost: The Transformation of Kentucky from Daniel Boone to Henry Clay*. Baltimore and London: Johns Hopkins Univ. Press, 1996.

Ayers, Edward L. "Honor." In *Encyclopedia of Southern Culture*, edited by Charles Reagan Wilson and William Ferris, et al. Chapel Hill and London: Univ. of North Carolina Press, 1989, 1483—84.

Ballew, Christopher Brent. *The Impact of African-American Antecedents on the Baptist Foreign Missionary Movement, 1782–1825*. Toronto Studies in Theology 96. Lewiston, New York: Edwin Mellen Press, 2004.

Banning, Lance. *The Jeffersonian Persuasion: Evolution of a Party Ideology*. Ithaca, NY, and London: Cornell Univ. Press, 1978.

———. *The Sacred Fire of Liberty: James Madison and the Founding of the Federal Republic*. Ithaca, NY, and London: Cornell Univ. Press, 1995.

Bebbington, D. W. *Evangelicalism in Modern Britain: A History from the 1730s to the 1980s*. London: Unwin Hyman, 1989.

Beeman, Richard R. "Deference, Republicanism, and the Emergence of Popular Politics in Eighteenth-Century America." *William and Mary Quarterly*, 3rd ser., 49 (July 1992): 401–30.

Belue, Ted Franklin. *The Hunters of Kentucky: A Narrative History of America's First Far West*. Mechanicsburg, PA: Stackpole Books, 2003.

Bergeron, Paul H., Stephen V. Ash, and Jeanette Keith. *Tennesseans and Their History*. Knoxville: Univ. of Tennessee Press, 1999.

Bloch, Ruth. *Visionary Republic: Millennial Themes in American Thought, 1756–1800*. Cambridge: Cambridge Univ. Press, 1985.

Bodley, Temple, ed. *Reprints of Littell's Political Transactions in and Concerning Kentucky and Letter of George Nicholas to His Friend in Virginia, also General Wilkinson's Memorial*. Louisville, KY: John P. Morton, 1926.

Boles, John. "Henry Holcombe, A Southern Baptist Reformer in the Age of Jefferson." *Georgia Historical Quarterly* 54 (Fall 1970): 381–407.

———. *The Great Revival, 1787–1805: The Origins of the Southern Evangelical Mind*. Lexington: Univ. Press of Kentucky, 1972.

Bressler, Ann Lee. *The Universalist Movement in America, 1770–1880*. Oxford and New York: Oxford Univ. Press, 2001.

Brooks-Smith, Joan E., comp. *Master Index, Virginia Surveys and Grants, 1774–1791*. Frankfort: Kentucky Historical Society, 1976.

Buckley, Thomas E. "Evangelicals Triumphant: The Baptists' Assault on the Virginia Glebes, 1786–1801." *William and Mary Quarterly*, 3rd. ser., 45 (January 1988): 33–69.

Burtchaell, James Tunstead. *The Dying of the Light: The Disengagement of Colleges and Universities from Their Christian Churches*. Grand Rapids, MI: Wm. B. Eerdmans, 1998.

Bushman, Richard L. *From Puritan to Yankee: Character and the Social Order in Connecticut, 1690–1765*. Cambridge, MA: Harvard Univ. Press, 1967.

Butler, Jon. *Power. Authority, and the Origins of American Denominational Order: The English Churches in the Delaware Valley, 1680–1730.* Philadelphia: American Philosophical Society, 1978.

———. *Awash in a Sea of Faith: Christianizing the American People.* Cambridge, MA, and London: Harvard Univ. Press, 1990.

Carney, Charity R. *Ministers and Masters: Methodism, Manhood, and Honor in the Old South.* Baton Rouge: Louisiana State Univ. Press, 2011.

Clark, Thomas D. *A History of Kentucky.* Ashland, KY: Jesse Stuart Foundation, 1988.

Coleman, J. Winston., Jr. *Lexington, the Athens of the West.* Lexington, KY: Winburn Press, 1981.

Collins, Lewis, and Richard H. Collins. *History of Kentucky.* 1874. Louisville, KY: John P. Morton, 1924.

Cornell, Sean. *The Other Founders: Anti-Federalism and the Dissenting Tradition in America, 1788–1828.* Chapel Hill and London: Univ. of North Carolina Press, 1999.

Coward, Joan Wells. *Kentucky in the New Republic: The Process of Constitution Making.* Lexington: Univ. Press of Kentucky, 1979.

Crowther, Edward R. *Southern Evangelicals and the Coming of the Civil War.* Lewiston, NY: Edwin Mellen Press, 2000.

———. "Holy Honor: Sacred and Secular in the Old South." *Journal of Southern History* 62 (November 1992): 619–36.

———. "Honor and Literature." In *Encyclopedia of the Bible and its Reception,* edited by Dale C. Allison, Jr., Christine Helmer, Steven L. McKenzie, Thomas Römer, Jens Schröter, Choon-Leong Seow, Barry Dov Walfish, Eric J. Ziolkowski. Vol. 12. Berlin: DeGruyter, 2015.

———. "Iron Chests: Honor and Manhood in Southern Evangelicalism," in *The Field of Honor: Essays on Southern Character and American Identity,* edited by John Mayfield and Todd Hagstette. Columbia: Univ. of South Carolina Press, 2017.

Davidson, James West. *The Logic of Millennial Thought: Eighteenth-Century New England.* Yale Historical Publications, Miscellany, 112. New Haven and London: Yale Univ. Press, 1977.

DeRogatis, Amy. *Moral Geography: Maps, Missionaries, and the American Frontier.* Religion and American Culture Series, edited by Randall Balmer. New York: Columbia Univ. Press, 2003.

Dick, Everett. *The Lure of the Land: A Social History of the Public Lands from the Articles of Confederation to the New Deal.* Lincoln: Univ. of Nebraska Press, 1970.

Donan, P. *Memoir of Jacob Creath, Jr. to Which Is Appended the Biography of Jacob Creath, Sr.* Cincinnati: Chase and Hall, 1877.

Drake, Daniel. *Pioneer Life in Kentucky, 1785–1800.* Edited by Emmet Field Horine. New York: Henry Schuman, 1948.

Draper, Lyman C. *The Life of Daniel Boone*. Edited by Ted Franklin Belue. Mechanicsburg, MD: Stackpole Books, 1998.

Elder, Robert. *The Sacred Mirror: Evangelicalism, Honor, and Identity in the Deep South, 1790–1860*. Chapel Hill: Univ. of North Carolina Press, 2016.

Ellis, William E. *A History of Education in Kentucky*. Lexington: Univ. Press of Kentucky, 2011.

Eslinger, Ellen. *Citizens of Zion: The Social Origins of Camp Meeting Revivalism*. Knoxville: Univ. of Tennessee Press, 1999.

———. "The Shape of Slavery on the Kentucky Frontier." *Register of the Kentucky Historical Society* 92 (Winter 1994): 1–23.

Everman, H. E. *Governor James Garrard*. United States: Cooper's Run Press, 1981.

Faragher, John Mack. *Daniel Boone: The Life and Legend of an American Pioneer*. New York: Henry Holt, 1992.

Flexner, James Thomas. *Washington: The Indispensable Man*. Boston and Toronto: Little, Brown, 1969.

Freeberg III, Ernest A. "Why David Barrow Moved to Kentucky." *Virginia Baptist Register* 32 (1993): 1617–27.

Friend, Craig Thompson, ed. *The Buzzel About Kentuck: Settling the Promised Land*. Lexington: Univ. Press of Kentucky, 1999.

———. *Along the Maysville Road: The Early American Republic in the Trans-Appalachian West*. Knoxville: Univ. of Tennessee Press, 2005.

———. *Kentucke's Frontiers*. Bloomington and Indianapolis: Indiana Univ. Press, 2010.

Gardner, Robert G. "The Statistics of Early American Baptists: A Second Look," *Baptist History and Heritage* 24 (October 1989): 29–44.

Gates, Paul W. *Landlords and Tenants on the Prairie Frontier: Studies in American Land Policy*. Ithaca and London: Cornell Univ. Press, 1973.

Gaustad, Edwin S. *Sworn on the Altar of God: A Religious Biography of Thomas Jefferson*. Grand Rapids, MI: Wm. B. Eerdmans, 1996.

Gayle, Clement. *George Liele, Pioneer Missionary to Jamaica*. Kingston: Jamaica Baptist Union, 1982.

Gewehr, Wesley M. *The Great Awakening in Virginia, 1740–1790*. Durham, NC: Duke Univ. Press, 1930.

Gray, Kathryn N. *John Eliot and the Praying Indians of Massachusetts Bay: Communities and Connections in Puritan New England*. Lanham, MD: Bucknell Univ. Press; Roman and Littlefield Publishing Group, 2013.

Greene, Jack P. "Society, Ideology, and Politics: An Analysis of the Political Culture of Mid-Eighteenth Century Virginia." In *Society, Freedom, and Conscience: The American Revolution in Virginia, Massachusetts, and New York*, edited by Richard M. Jellison, New York: W. W. Norton, 1976: 14–76.

Griffiths, Olive M. *Religion and Learning: A Study in English Presbyterian Thought from the Bartholomew Ejections (1662) to the Foundations of the Unitarian Movement*. London: Cambridge Univ. Press, 1935.

Hall, David D. *The Faithful Shepherd: A History of the New England Ministry in the Seventeenth Century.* Chapel Hill: Univ. of North Carolina Press, 1972.

Hammon, Neal O. *Early Kentucky Land Records, 1773–1780.* Louisville, KY: Filson Club, 1992.

Hammon, Neal O., and Richard Taylor. *Virginia's Western War, 1775–1786.* Mechanicsburg, PA: Stackpole Books, 2002.

Harper, Keith. "Downwind from the New England Rat: John Taylor, Organized Missions and the Regionalization of Religious Identity on the American Frontier." *Ohio Valley History* 9 (Fall 2009): 25–42.

———. "'And All the Baptists in Kentucky Took the Name *United Baptists*': The Union of Kentucky's Separate and Regular Baptists." *Register of the Kentucky Historical Society*, 110 (Winter 2012): 3–32.

———. "Decently and in Order: The Philadelphia Association and the Search for a Usable Polity." *American Baptist Quarterly* 32 (Fall-Winter 2013): 395–413.

Harper, Keith, and C. Martin Jacumin. *Esteemed Reproach: The Lives of Reverend James Ireland and Reverend Joseph Craig.* Macon, GA: Mercer Univ. Press, 2005.

Harrison, Lowell H. *Kentucky's Road to Statehood.* Lexington: Univ. Press of Kentucky, 1992.

———. *John Breckinridge: Jeffersonian Republican.* Louisville, KY: Filson Club, 1969.

Hart, D. G. *Deconstructing Evangelicalism: Conservative Protestantism in the Age of Billy Graham.* Grand Rapids: Baker Book House, 2004.

Hatch, Nathan O. *The Sacred Cause of Liberty: Republican Thought and the Millennial Revolution in New England.* New Haven, CT: Yale Univ. Press, 1977.

———. *The Democratization of American Christianity.* New Haven and London: Yale Univ. Press, 1991.

Heyrman, Christine Leigh. *Southern Cross: The Beginnings of the Bible Belt.* New York: Alfred A. Knopf, 1997.

Hibbard, Benjamin Horace. *A History of Public Land Policies.* Madison and Milwaukee: Univ. of Wisconsin Press, 1965.

Hill, Samuel S. *Southern Churches in Crisis.* New York: Holt, Rinehart, and Winston, 1967.

Holifield, E. Brooks. *The Gentlemen Theologians: American Theology in Southern Culture, 1795–1860.* Durham, NC: Duke Univ. Press, 1978.

———. *God's Ambassadors: A History of Pastoral Ministry in America.* Grand Rapids, MI, and Cambridge, UK: Wm. B. Eerdmans, 2007.

———. *A History of Pastoral Care in America: From Salvation to Self-Realization.* Nashville: Abingdon Press, 1983.

———. *Theology in America: Christian Thought from the Age of the Puritans to the Civil War.* New Haven and London: Yale Univ. Press, 2003.

Holmes, David L. *The Faiths of Our Founding Fathers.* Oxford: Oxford Univ. Press, 2006.

Houston, Peter. *A Sketch of the Life and Character of Daniel Boone*, edited by Ted Franklin Belue. Mechanicsburg, PA: Stackpole Books, 1997.

Hughes, Richard. *Reviving the Ancient Faith: The Story of the Churches of Christ in America*. Grand Rapids: Wm. B. Eerdmans, 1996.

Irons, Charles F. *The Origins of Proslavery Christianity: White and Black Evangelicals in Colonial and Antebellum Virginia*. Chapel Hill: Univ. of North Carolina Press, 2008.

———. "Believing in America: Faith and Politics in Early America." *American Baptist Quarterly* 21 (2002): 396–412.

———. "The Spiritual Fruits of the American Revolution: Disestablishment and the Rise of the Virginia Baptists." *Virginia Magazine of History and Biography* 109 (2001):159–86.

Isaac, Rhys. *The Transformation of Virginia, 1740–1790*. 1982. Reprint, New York: W. W. Norton, 1988.

Jefferson, Thomas. *Notes on the State of Virginia*. With an introduction by Thomas Perkins Abernethy. New York: Harper Torchbooks, 1964.

Jillson, William Rouse. *The Kentucky Land Grants: A Systematic Index to All of the Land Grants Recorded in the State Land Office At Frankfort, Kentucky, 1782–1924*. Filson Club Publications, no. 33. Louisville, KY: Standard Printing, 1925.

———. *Old Kentucky Entries and Deeds: A Complete Index to the Earliest Land Entries, Military Warrants, Deeds, and Wills of the Commonwealth of Kentucky*. Filson Club Publications, no. 34. Louisville, KY: Standard Printing, 1926.

Jordan, Winthrop D. *The White Man's Burden: Historical Origins of Racism in America*. London and New York: Oxford Univ. Press, 1974.

Kars, Marjoleine. *Breaking Loose Together: The Regulator Rebellion in Pre-Revolutionary North Carolina*. Chapel Hill and London: Univ. of North Carolina Press, 2002.

Kidd, Thomas S. *The Great Awakening: The Roots of Evangelical Christianity in Colonial America*. New Haven and London: Yale Univ. Press, 2007.

———. *God of Liberty: A Religious History of the American Revolution*. New York: Basic Books, 2010.

Klotter, James C. *The Breckinridges of Kentucky, 1760–1981*. Lexington: Univ. Press of Kentucky, 1986.

———. *Kentucky Justice, Southern Honor, and American Manhood*. Baton Rouge: Louisiana State Univ. Press, 2003.

Klotter, James C., and Craig Thompson Friend. *A New History of Kentucky*, 2nd ed. Lexington: Univ. Press of Kentucky, 2018.

Klotter, James C., and Daniel Rowland, eds. *Bluegrass Renaissance: The History and Culture of Central Kentucky, 1792–1852*. Lexington: Univ. Press of Kentucky, 2012.

Kurtz, Stephen G., and James H. Hutson, eds. *Essays on the American Revolution*. Chapel Hill: Univ. of North Carolina Press; New York: W. W. Norton, 1973.

Lambert, Byron Cecil. "The Rise of the Anti-Mission Baptists: Sources and Leaders, 1800–1840." PhD diss., Univ. of Chicago, 1957. Reprint, Arno Press, 1980.

Laver, Harry S. "'Chimney Corner Constitutions': Democratization and Its

Limits in Frontier Kentucky." *Register of the Kentucky Historical Society* 95 (Autumn 1997): 337–67.

Lester, William Stewart. *The Transylvania Colony*. Spencer, IN: Samuel R. Guard, 1935.

Lindman, Janet Moore. *Bodies of Belief: Baptist Community in Early America*. Philadelphia: Univ. of Pennsylvania Press, 2008.

Littell, William, George Nicholas, and James Wilkinson. *Reprints of Littell's Political Transactions in and Concerning Kentucky and Letter of George Nicholas to His Friend in Virginia, also General Wilkinson's Memorial*. With an introduction by Temple Bodley. Louisville, KY: J. P. Morton, 1926.

Lucas, Marion B. *A History of Blacks in Kentucky from Slavery to Segregation, 1760–1891*. Frankfort: Kentucky Historical Society, 2003.

Lyerly, Cynthia Lynn. *Methodism and the Southern Mind, 1770–1810*. New York and Oxford: Oxford Univ. Press, 1998.

Macaulay, John Allen. *Unitarianism in the Antebellum South: The Other Invisible Institution*. Tuscaloosa and London: Univ. of Alabama Press, 2001.

Maddex, Jack P., Jr. "Proslavery Millennialism: Social Eschatology in Antebellum Southern Calvinism." *American Quarterly* 31 (Spring, 1979): 46–62.

Madison, Jessica. *In Subjection: Church Discipline in the Early American South, 1760–1830*. Macon, GA: Mercer Univ. Press, 2014.

Martin, Vernon P. "Father Rice, The Preacher Who Followed the Frontier." Paper read before the Filson Club, June 6, 1955.

Mathews, Donald G. *Religion in the Old South*. Chicago and London: Univ. of Chicago Press, 1977.

———. "The Second Great Awakening as an Organizing Process, 1780–1830: An Hypothesis." *American Quarterly* 21 (1969): 23–43.

Mathis, James R. The *Making of the Primitive Baptists: A Cultural and Intellectual History of the Antimission Movement, 1800–1840*. New York and London: Routledge, 2004.

Matthews, Gary R. *More American than Southern: Kentucky, Slavery, and the War for an American Ideology, 1828–1861*. Knoxville: Univ. of Tennessee Press, 2014.

McBeth, H. Leon. *The Baptist Heritage: Four Centuries of Baptist Witness*. Nashville: Broadman Press, 1987.

McLoughlin, William G. "Patriotism and Pietism. The Dissenting Dilemma: Massachusetts Rural Baptists and the American Revolution." *Foundations* 19 (April–June, 1976): 121–41.

———. "The Role of Religion in the Revolution: Liberty of Conscience and Cultural Cohesion in the New Nation." In *Essays on the American Revolution*, edited by Stephen G. Kurtz and James H. Hutson. Chapel Hill: Univ. of North Carolina Press; New York: W. W. Norton 1973.

Mulder, John M. and John F. Wilson, eds. *Religion in American History: Interpretive Essays*. Englewood Cliffs, NJ: Prentice-Hall, 1978.

Najar, Monica. "'Meddling with Emancipation,' Baptists, Authority, and the Rift

Over Slavery in the Upper South." *Journal of the Early Republic* 25 (Summer 2005): 157–86.

———. *Evangelizing the South: A Social History of Church and State in Early America.* Oxford and New York: Oxford Univ. Press, 2008.

Noll, Mark A. *America's God: From Jonathan Edwards to Abraham Lincoln.* Oxford and New York: Oxford Univ. Press, 2002.

Ownby, Ted. *Subduing Satan: Religion, Recreation, and Manhood in the Rural South, 1865–1920.* Chapel Hill: Univ. of North Carolina Press, 1990.

Parrish, Rev. C. A., ed. *Golden Jubilee of the General Association of Colored Baptists in Kentucky: the Story of 50 Years' Work from 1865–1915.* Louisville, KY: Mayes Printing, 1915.

Peterson, Merrill D. *Thomas Jefferson and the New Nation: A Biography.* London and New York: Oxford Univ. Press, 1970.

———. *The Jefferson Image in the American Mind.* Charlottesville and London: Thomas Jefferson Memorial Foundation and Univ. of Virginia Press, 1998. Originally published New York: Oxford Univ. Press, 1960.

Purefoy, George W. *A History of the Sandy Creek Association, from its Organization in A.D. 1758 to A.D. 1858.* New York: Sheldon & Co., 1858.

Ranck, George W. "'The Travelling Church:' An Account of the Baptist Exodus from Virginia to Kentucky in 1781 Under the Leadership of Rev. Lewis Craig and Capt. William Ellis." N.p., 1910.

Robbins, Roy M. *Our Landed Heritage: The Public Domain, 1776–1936.* Princeton, NJ: Princeton Univ. Press, 1942.

Rohrbaugh, Malcolm. *The Land Office Business: the Settlement and Administration of American Public Lands, 1789–1837.* New York: Oxford Univ. Press, 1968.

Rutland, Thomas A., Thomas A. Mason, Robert J. Brugger, Jeanne K. Sisson, Fredrika J. Teute, eds. *The Papers of James Madison, Vol. 14, 6 April 1791–16 March 1793.* Charlottesville: Univ. of Virginia Press, 1983.

Rutman, Darrett B. *American Puritanism: Faith and Practice.* Philadelphia: J. B. Lippincott, 1970.

Sachs, Honor. *Home Rule: Households, Manhood, and National Expansion on the Eighteenth-Century Kentucky Frontier.* New Haven & London: Yale Univ. Press, 2015.

Sacks, Francis. *The Philadelphia Baptist Tradition of Church Authority: An Ecumenical Analysis and Interpretation.* Studies in American Religion 48. Lewiston, NY: Edwin Mellen, 1989.

Schweiger, Beth Barton. *The Gospel Working Up: Progress and the Pulpit in Nineteenth-Century Virginia.* Religion in America Series, edited by Harry S. Stout. New York and Oxford: Oxford Univ. Press, 2000.

———. "A Social History of English Grammar in the United States." *Journal of the Early Republic* 30 (Winter 2010): 533–55.

Shannon, David T., Sr., sr. ed., with Julia Frazier White and Deborah Van Broekhoven, eds. *George Liele's Life and Legacy: An Unsung Hero.* Macon, GA: Mercer Univ. Press, 2012.

Shurden, Walter B. *Associationalism among Baptists in America, 1707–1814.* New York: Arno Press, 1980.

Smith, Larry Douglas. "The Rise of the Missionary Spirit Among the Kentucky Baptists." *The Quarterly Review* 40 (April–June 1980): 74–79.

———. "John Taylor and Missions: A New Interpretation." *Quarterly Review* 42 (April–June 1982): 54–61.

Snyder, Robert. *A History of Georgetown College.* Georgetown, KY: Georgetown College, 1979.

Sonne, Niels Henry. *Liberal Kentucky, 1780–1828.* New York: Columbia Univ. Press, 1939; Kentucky Paperbacks ed., Lexington: Univ. of Kentucky Press, 1968.

Spangler, Jewell L. *Virginians Reborn: Anglican Monopoly, Evangelical Dissent, and the Rise of the Baptists in the Late Nineteenth Century.* Charlottesville and London: Univ. of Virginia Press, 2008.

———. "Salvation Was Not Liberty: Baptists and Slavery in Revolutionary Virginia." *American Baptist Quarterly* 13 (September 1994): 221–36.

Spencer, J. H. *A History of Kentucky Baptists from 1769 to 1885.* Revised by Mrs. Burrilla B. Spencer. 2 vols. Cincinnati: J. R. Baumes, 1885.

Sprague, William B., ed. *Annals of the American Pulpit* 6 (New York: Robert Carter & Brothers, 1860): 158.

Stewart, Howard R. *A Dazzling Enigma: The Story of Morgan Edward.* Lanham, MD: Univ. Press of America, 1995.

Sundlund, Vivien. "'A Devilish and Unnatural Usurpation:' Baptist Evangelical Ministers and Antislavery in the Early Nineteenth Century, A Study of the Ideas and Activism of David Barrow." *American Baptist Quarterly* 13 (September 1994): 262–77.

Sweet, William Warren. *Religion on the American Frontier: The Baptists, 1783–1830.* With a general introduction by Shirley Jackson Case. New York: Henry Holt, 1931.

Tallant, Harold D. *Evil Necessity: Slavery and Political Culture in Antebellum Kentucky.* Lexington: Univ. Press of Kentucky, 2003.

Tarrants, Charles. "Carter Tarrant (1765–1816): Baptist and Emancipationist." *Register of the Kentucky Historical Society* 88, mo. 2 (Spring 1990): 121–47.

Taves, Ann. *Fits, Trances, and Visions: Experiencing Religion and Explaining Experience from Wesley to James.* Princeton: Princeton Univ. Press, 1999.

Taylor, James B. *Lives of Virginia Baptist Ministers.* Richmond, VA: Yale and Wyatt, 1837.

Thom, William Taylor. *The Struggle for Religious Freedom in Virginia: The Baptists.* Baltimore: Johns Hopkins Univ. Press, 1900.

Thomas, George M. *Revivalism and Cultural Change: Christianity, Nation Building, and the Market in the Nineteenth-Century United States.* Chicago and London: Univ. of Chicago Press, 1989.

Thompson, Wilson. *The Autobiography of Elder Wilson Thompson: His Life, Travels, and Ministerial Labors.* Cincinnati, OH: Moore, Wilstach, and Baldwin,

Printers, 1867. Republished by Elder Edgar T. Aleshire and Elder Lasserre Bradley, Jr., 1962.

Torbet, Robert G. *A Social History of the Philadelphia Baptist Association, 1707–1940*. Philadelphia: Westbrook, 1944.

———. *A History of the Baptists*. 3rd ed. With a foreword by Kenneth Scott Latourette. Valley Forge: Judson Press, 1968.

Treat, Payson Jackson. *The National Land System, 1785–1820*. New York: E. B. Treat, 1910.

Troxler, Carole Watterson. *Forming Dissenters: The Regulator Movement in Piedmont North Carolina*. Raleigh: North Carolina Office of Archives and History, 2011. Reprint, 2016.

Van Meter, Benjamin Franklin. *Genealogies and Sketches of Some Old Families Who Have Taken Prominent Part in the Development of Virginia and Kentucky Especially, and Later of Many Other States of this Union*. Louisville: John P. Morton, 1901.

Watlington, Patricia. *The Partisan Spirit: Kentucky Politics, 1779–1792*. New York: Atheneum, 1972.

Wayland, Francis. *Pulling the Eye Tooth from a Live Tiger: A Memoir of the Life and Labor of Adinoram Judson*. 2 vols. Boston: Phillips, Sampson; London: Nisbet, 1853.

———. *Notes on the Principles and Practices of Baptist Churches*. New York: Sheldon, Blakeman, 1857.

Weaver, C. Douglas. "David Thomas and the Regular Baptists in Colonial Virginia." *Baptist History and Heritage* 18 (October 1983): 3–19.

Welch, James E. "John Taylor, 1772–1833." In *Annals of the American Pulpit* 6 (New York: Robert Carter & Brothers, 1860).

West, Carroll Van, ed. *Tennessee History: The Land, the People, and the Culture*. Knoxville: Univ. of Tennessee Press, 1998.

Wills, Gregory A. Democratic Religion: *Freedom, Authority, and Church Discipline in the Baptist South, 1785–1900*. New York: Oxford Univ. Press, 1996.

Wolever, Terry. *The Life of John Gano, 1727–1804: Pastor-Evangelist of the Philadelphia Association*. Springfield, MO: Particular Baptist Press, 2012.

Wolfe, Alan. *The Transformation of American Religion: How We Actually Live Our Faith*. New York: Free Press, 2003.

Wood, Gordon S. *The Creation of the American Republic, 1776–1787*. Chapel Hill: Univ. of North Carolina Press, 1969.

———. *Empire of Liberty: A History of the Early Republic, 1789–1815*. Oxford and New York: Oxford Univ. Press, 2009.

———. "Evangelical America and Early Mormonism." *New York History* 61 (October 1980): 358–86.

———. *Radicalism of the American Revolution*. New York: Vintage Books, 1993.

Wright, John D., Jr., and Eric Christianson. "Transylvania University." In *The Kentucky Encyclopedia*, edited by John E. Kleber, 894–96. Lexington: Univ. Press of Kentucky, 1992.

Wyatt-Brown, Bertram. *Southern Honor: Ethics and Behavior in the Old South.* Oxford and New York: Oxford Univ. Press, 1982.

———. *The Shaping of Southern Culture: Honor, Grace, and War, 1760s–1880s.* Chapel Hill and London: Univ. of North Carolina Press, 2001.

Dissertations

Deal, John Gordon. "The Forgotten Southerner: Middle-Class Associationalism in Antebellum Norfolk, Virginia." PhD diss., Univ. of Florida, 2003.

Feight, Andrew Lee. "The Good and the Just." PhD diss., Univ. of Kentucky, 2001.

Levens, Laura Rodgers. "Leaving Home and Finding Home: Theology and Practice of Ann Hasseltine Judson and the American Baptist Mission to Burma, 1812–1826." ThD diss., Duke Divinity School, 2015.

McCullom, David C. "A Study of Evangelicals and Revival Exercises from 1730–1805: Tracing the Development of Exercise Tradition through the First Great Awakening Period to the Southern Great Revival." PhD diss., Southeastern Baptist Theological Seminary, 2009.

Teute, Fredrika Johanna. "Land, Liberty and Labor in the Post-Revolutionary Era: Kentucky as the Promised Land. PhD diss., Johns Hopkins Univ., 1988.

Index